Excluded from the Record

KATHERINE STORR

Excluded from the Record

Women, Refugees and Relief 1914–1929

PETER LANG
Oxford · Bern · Berlin · Bruxelles · Frankfurt am Main · New York · Wien

Bibliographic information published by Die Deutsche Nationalbibliothek.
Die Deutsche Nationalbibliothek lists this publication in the Deutsche Nationalbibliografie; detailed bibliographic data is available on the Internet at http://dnb.d-nb.de.

A catalogue record for this book is available from The British Library.

Library of Congress Cataloging-in-Publication Data:

Storr, Katherine, 1934–
Excluded from the record : women, refugees, and relief, 1914–1929 / Katherine Storr.
p. cm.
Includes bibliographical references and index.
ISBN 978-3-03911-855-7 (alk. paper)
1. Women refugees--Europe--History--20th century.
2. Refugees--Europe--History--20th century. 3. Europe--Emigration and immigration--History--20th century. 4. Refugees--Services for--Europe.
5. Refugees--Legal status, laws, etc.--Europe. I. Title.

HV640.4.E8S77 2009
362.87082'094--dc22

2009038359

ISBN 978-3-03911-855-7

Cover image: Belgian girls doing raffia work in internment camp in Holland. Photograph courtesy of the Religious Society of Friends in Britain.

Hochfeldstrasse 32, CH-3012 Bern, Switzerland
info@peterlang.com, www.peterlang.com, www.peterlang.net

Contents

Plates, Figures and Tables

Acknowledgements

When studying at the University of Sussex in the 1990s my need for a subject to research for my MA was filled by a serendipitous finding of the collection of letters written to his politician father Augustine by Francis Birrell, who served with the Friends War Victims Relief mission in France during the Great War. My interest in the Great War had been raised by my mother, who remembered ladies giving white feathers to men not in uniform, and by a family friend, Percy Rowe, who fought at Ypres. I had no previous knowledge of the Friends but became fascinated. My research extended into further work for my DPhil and my thanks go to my supervisor, Professor Alun Howkins, for his patience in reading my many drafts and for his helpful advice, suggestions and support. In addition, my sincere thanks go to the ESRC whose non-ageist policy resulted in funding my research and the writing of the thesis which led to this book. Learning about the lives of women relief workers of many political and religious persuasions led me to marvel at their humanitarianism, indomitability and courage, characteristics combined with practical compassion and political acumen. The relationship of these with religious belief was particularly meaningful and uncovering their networks helped me realise the support these gave was a vital part of the foundation from which they operated.

My book is designed for students of women's history, gender studies, the social history of the Great War and the League of Nations. It will be of special interest to those doing research on suffragists and Quakers, offering fresh empirical research and new theoretical approaches to illuminate this significant, but unexplored subject. At the same time it helps our understanding of later twentieth-century events.

In the eleven years since I began researching this topic, so many people have helped me that I cannot name them individually; I hope they will forgive me. Members of the Women's History Network provided helpful observations at conferences, including Elizabeth Crawford, Anne

Wheeldon, and Professor Joyce Goodman, who planted the seed of the idea to develop the suffrage–Quaker connection. My thanks go to staff at the Holbeach Public Library who found themselves dealing with unusual requests from a refugee from Sussex! Thanks to all at the Imperial War Museum and especially to Mary Wilkinson, Head of Acquisitions at the Department of Printed Books and to members of the Department of Documents. My sincere thanks also go to the librarians at Friends House Library, especially Malcolm Thomas, Josef Keith and Joanna Clark who helped me with the photos, and Julia and Jennifer, all of whom have been extremely helpful and supportive during my many visits. They have indeed become my friends.

I owe thanks to many people at the University of Sussex; to Dorothy Sheridan at Mass Observation; Bet Inglis, Joy Eldridge and Fiona Courage at Special Collections. Thanks to Sibyl Oldfield, Pat Thane, and to Carol Dyhouse, who provided valuable suggestions for references on women's caring role and help on education; to my fellow-student Eugene-Panagiotis Michail for help with Seton-Watson. Special thanks to Dr Gerry Holloway who first taught me about women's history, inspiring my subsequent passion for it, and who has given advice and help throughout. She, with Professor Sally Alexander, gave helpful advice for turning the thesis into a book.

Thanks also to Mr Jack Lander for his permission to use the Birrell material held in the University of Sussex Special Collections; to the Society of Friends in Britain for the use of their photographs and other material; and to David and Jane Garnett, for introducing me to the late Frances Partridge, all of whom welcomed me to their homes and talked with me about Frankie Birrell. Thanks also to Nick Reynolds at Peter Lang Ltd, for coping by email with my many questions and quirky sense of humour.

Last, but not least, my thanks to my dogs for taking me for walks to clear my head and to my partner, David Budgen, for being my support during the whole period.

Abbreviations

ARA	Aliens Restrictions Act
CLWS	Catholic League for Women's Suffrage
COS	Charity Organization Society
CRB	Commission for Relief in Belgium
CWL	Catholic Women's League
FAU	Friends Ambulance Unit
FEC	Friends Emergency Committee to assist Germans, Austrians and Hungarians in Distress in the UK
FEWVRC	Friends Emergency War Victims Relief Committee
FLWS	Friends League for Women's Suffrage
FTFC	Fight the Famine Council
FWVRC	Friends War Victims Relief Committee
HO	Home Office
ILP	Independent Labour Party
IWM	Imperial War Museum (in references this relates to the Department of Printed Books, Women's Work Collection)
IWM. DD	Imperial War Museum, Department of Documents
IWRC	International Women's Relief Committee
IWSA	International Women's Suffrage Alliance
LGB	Local Government Board
LSWS	London Society for Women's Suffrage
NCWN	National Council of Women of the Netherlands
NFF	National Food Fund
NUWSS	National Union of Women's Suffrage Societies
NUSEC	National Union of Societies for Equal Citizenship
PRO	Public Records Office, London. Now the National Archives
RNRC	Royal National Relief Committee, The Netherlands
SCF	Save the Children Fund
SRF	Serbian Relief Fund

SSFD	Society of Friends of Foreigners in Distress
SOF	Society of Friends (Friends or Quakers, used interchangeably)
WEC	Women's Emergency Corps
WFL	Women's Freedom League
WIL	Women's International League
WILPF	Women's International League for Peace & Freedom
WL	Women's Library
WRC	War Refugees Committee
WSPU	Women's Social and Political Union

Introduction

If history is a political battleground as Jordan and Weedon say (1995: 125), then women's history is an amazon warrior on it. Hugo Gryn, an Auschwitz survivor, called the twentieth century 'the century of the refugee' yet historiography of the First World War, by focussing on men's heroism and sacrifice, has excluded from the record the history of families who were driven out of their homes, villages and countries by the fighting. Marrus (1985) has famously dubbed refugees 'the Unwanted' but gives those of the Great War very limited space in his book, implying irrelevance to his thesis. Investigation of this ignored history reveals that the majority of these refugees were women and children. Does their history support his theory?

Andrews (1997: 3) claims that history is a crucial tool in the maintenance of any hegemonic power bloc. It is therefore important to reveal voices which have hitherto been silenced, such as these refugees and the voluntary relief workers whose humanitarian activity alleviated the suffering consequent upon the orgy of destruction and killing. This hitherto excluded history questions the attitude, expectations and assumptions of society towards women, children and the elderly of their own and other nations because it highlights women's role and experience and therefore questions the way in which society values male endeavour and undervalues that of women. It raises questions about what happened to these non-combatants when the war was over, showing that the plight of erstwhile enemy civilians was especially desperate. Consequently, the narrative is extended into the later 1920s in order to discover what happened once the Peace Treaties were signed and whether women implicated the League of Nations, founded during the Armistice, in refugee aid; the 1930s (Hamilton 1944: 99) are a 'different chapter under a different sky' and are only briefly mentioned. The first purpose of this book is therefore to reveal this excluded history of aid to civilians; military relief is considered only where it overlaps with that for non-combatants.

In reclaiming this history, the non-heroic side of war is highlighted and certain myths are exploded. According to Roland Barthes, myth is a mode of signification, a type of speech chosen by history which hides nothing, but since its function is to distort it is therefore more dangerous. There is, as Samuel and Thompson say (1990: 17, 4), 'an undisclosed misogyny which runs as a current through the universe of myth', which includes that women are protected by war's prosecution. As many women of the time realized, this is untrue, particularly when a wider geographical view is taken. Myth blinds us of much of our power to understand and interpret the past. What is forgotten may be as important as what is remembered; for instance, that women broke food blockades as well as working in munitions. As Roy Porter stated (1992: 1–11): 'We live in a culture highly preoccupied with the past, but fascinated with it for all the wrong reasons; out of nostalgia, rather than the urge to understand the present and forge the future.' Military history feeds nostalgia by claiming that war is exclusively a male matter, that wartime death and suffering are gender-specific and quantifiable according to the wearing of a uniform, and that courage is an exclusively male attribute called on in combat. Most importantly, the history of civilians *appears* to detract from the bravery of soldiers. What it really does is call into question the justifications given for going to war and indicate the comparative lack of anxiety by governments for the greater proportion of people who remain on the Home Front when compared with political or military objectives. Paradoxically it shows the relevance of that Front to the successful conclusion of the war and to reconstruction afterwards.

This is clearly shown by the story of Belgian refugees in Britain, who have been ignored until recently by later writers; by focussing on military history, the ominous turn European history had taken was overlooked. In her theory of gender inequality Walby (1986) suggests the operation of patriarchy in cultural institutions of which this historiographical omission is a demonstration. Cahalan's 1982 *Belgian Refugee Relief in England During the Great War* opened the subject, but his patriarchal approach obscures the fact that most refugees were women, children and the old and that relief workers were also mostly women. In 1999 Kushner stated this neglect was unfortunate since it diminishes our understanding of the Great War. He then considered local responses and the significance of place in

Belgian refugees' welfare. Myers (2001) and Storr (2003) then examined the education of Belgian child refugees in Britain. Such history is not only 'social' and 'educational' but mainly 'women's history' that only in recent decades has begun to be published. Another example of cultural patriarchy relates to the theory of a publishing silence until the publication of battalion histories in 1927. In fact, there was no such publishing silence for women; many woman-authored books were published during and immediately after the War. Three of many possible examples are Mildred Aldred's *A Hilltop on the Marne* in 1915; Sarah Macnaughtan's *A Woman's Diary of the War*, also 1915 and Lady Frances Balfour's *Dr Elsie Inglis* in 1919. However, later women's biographers are guilty of reinforcing the silence about the war as though it is unworthy of examination. For example, Moberly Bell's *Flora Shaw* (1947) and Enid Huws Jones' *Margery Fry* (1966), skirt over it. Some biographies stop at 1914, like Vellacott's biography of Catherine Marshall; other work stops at The Hague Congress in 1915. Also relevant here is the claim of the sense of a gap in history that the war engendered. Did relief workers experience the war as a gap? Friends War Victims Committee (FWVRC) worker Francis Birrell used the metaphor in 1917 in a letter to his father, politician Augustine Birrell. But did women also experience the war this way? If so, which women and where? In *Hidden from History* Sheila Rowbotham (1975) linked the question of women's liberation with the way capitalism affected women's independence through the economic opportunities allowed to them. I want to suggest that women's ability to act as informed citizens is curtailed through a lack of knowledge of their history, their role in international politics and the way that war affects them, matters which are relevant to the current 'war on terror' and might have made more people suspicious of George Bush's claim that the Iraq war would emancipate women. The absence of this narrative therefore contributes to women's continuing subordination in society.

This brings me to the major theme of the book in which I stress the overwhelming importance of women and women's work as it had been perceived in the nineteenth century with its emphasis on caring for others. After 1750 a new humanitarian sensibility emerged, fanned by the rise of Evangelicalism. This led to a philanthropic and social reform movement in which women had a significant role in the development of humanitarian 'care'. Care is the technique through which Foucault's 'new pastoral power', a self-sacrificing but productive principle for others' good, is expressed. Oldfield's definition of 'humanitarianism' is also pertinent. It is an imprecise concept that 'embraces people who relieve life-threatening suffering wherever it occurs, or who attempt to prevent mass suffering, or who rescue helpless civilians in imminent danger' (2001: xi). Women realized that men abused other women, and therefore had to intervene on their behalf; this motivated them to identify reasons, why *women* should help *women*, thereby gradually transforming it into 'caring power', defined as a mode of power that operates through a commitment to the well-being of others.

Although it is argued that job segregation is central to men's control over women in all spheres of society, what women are allowed to do sometimes enables extension of their role. Van Drenthe and de Haan argue (1999: 18, 19) that caring power had in previous centuries extended the limits of what women's role was perceived to be. Caring for others of their own sex created a process of gendered self-formation which made available new public identities for recipient and giver of care which helped to constitute women as social subjects and promoted female agency. Since at least 1821, when Elizabeth Fry had founded her Ladies' Society to help female prisoners, women's public activities had been concerned with the well-being of other women and care had become a gendered activity. Van Drenthe and de Haan state that (1999: 14–19) 'Gender is a historically changing, constitutive element of personal identity and social organization, and thus inherently related to power.' Quakers, members of the Religious Society of Friends (SOF), were deeply implicated in the spread and process of caring power. It developed into a religiously founded, special responsibility of women for others of their own sex. The new social category of 'women' became involved in public activities in specifically female associations and also where women and men jointly participated, for example in charitable care of the poor through social work, including that of the Charity Organization Society. Such activism led to an increasing awareness of women's subordination and the rise of first wave feminism, leading to the women's suffrage movement, which in turn led to fighting for equal rights and for the ending of male domination and privilege and for many, attempts to prevent war. The International Women's Suffrage

Alliance (IWSA), formed in 1902, stressed the need for enfranchisement of women as a defence against war.

In the Great War women's responsibility for other women meant that support was given by a vast number of women to foreigners. Marrus (1985: 11) considers analysis of the variety of agencies that assisted refugees is vital. At the time of the Great War, women did not have the vote and lacked rights resulting from full citizenship; many women engaged in refugee care were suffragists and continuities with the pre-war suffrage campaign are considered. The suffragette members of militant groups, such as the Women's Social and Political Union (WSPU) led by the Pankhursts, were not generally involved in relief although some women, like the Quakers Alice and Hilda Clark, were simultaneously or at different times members of militant and constitutional societies. As Holton explains (1996: 167) the constitutional militancy which marked much of the WSPU's early work fitted well with the Quaker outlook on social protest. Militants' war-time work is only considered in relation to civilian relief. Nevertheless, the humanitarian instinct over-rode differences in belief about suffrage, imperialism, religion or justification for war. Some saw it as part of their gendered role as supporters of the British Empire, Quakers as part of their religious witness and suffragists as an indicator of the importance of women's role in society. Women involved in relief include committed imperialists such as Millicent Garrett Fawcett, President of the National Union of Women's Suffrage Societies (NUWSS), Victoria League members Dame Flora Lugard and Lady Edith Lyttelton, founders in 1914 of the War Refugees Committee (WRC), but also anti-imperialists such as Emily Hobhouse and the Quaker Dr Hilda Clark. Consequently, within this theme of women's key role, I examine members of the imperialist Victoria League, Quakers, and constitutional suffragist members of organizations such as the NUWSS.

Women were helping refugees arriving in Britain prior to the Government's invitation in September 1914, and although press propaganda constructed the Belgians as heroes and emphasized the 'debt' owed to Belgium and Serbia, while this affected expectations of Belgian behaviour, the prime motive for giving relief was humanitarian. However, the British Government's expectation that private philanthropy could cope with the approximately 260,000 Belgian refugees who fled to the UK was unrealistic, therefore the state and the philanthropic community found themselves working together in a manner that nineteenth-century social workers and theorists had argued for. Women had a key role in the European philanthropic phenomenon and subsequent humanitarian movement to help children and refugees that had its roots in conflicts such as the Boer War when they, or members of their families, had undertaken relief. Liberal ideology as expressed by these women resulted in the formation of the Save the Children Fund (SCF) and the expression of disquiet about women's place in world societies, topics which are now all incorporated in the United Nations agenda. 'Society', which had also been 'imperial', thus became international through women's caring role in charity and boundaries between the 'public' and 'private' were made more permeable. Relief work was familial, but it impinged on the male public sphere through provision of workshops and the teaching of skills that enabled refugees to earn their own livelihoods. It also involved women in negotiations with high-ranking politicians, statesmen and businessmen of other countries. Although the British of both sexes tended to patronize foreigners, relief arose from the belief in the equal worth of all human beings.

Amongst pacifist/suffragist women were those who, in the summer months of 1914, actively worked for mediation to avert, then stop the conflict. The Women's Co-operative Guild, the Women's Labour League and the IWSA, to which the NUWSS was affiliated, organized a peace rally at the Kingsway Hall on 4 August. Two thousand women called on governments to restore peace following the German invasion of Belgium, and the NUWSS passed a resolution to undertake relief work as a disguised and alternative campaign for enfranchisement. It was, as Mrs Fawcett wrote (Fawcett 1924: 218), 'as true a service to the country as that which men were rendering' and was genuinely humanitarian. Further, 'it would not arouse antagonism from Quaker members who formed an important element in many of our organizations'. Chapters 1 to 3 explain how suffragists began by assisting British women suffering from industrial and economic dislocation; helped foreigners who were now designated 'enemy aliens', and quickly extended this work to aid refugees. This provides a format for relief given in countries considered in Part Two including Belgium, Holland

and France, and the help given to Serbian refugees evacuated to Corsica and Corfu. Chapters 4 to 7 show how, for some women, especially those who worked with the Quakers, relief meant going abroad to help people in other countries.

Suffragist and Quaker groups were unique because between them they helped all types and nationalities of refugees and others needing assistance. Such social services and philanthropic activities were not new to these groups. Their concern with women's sufferings was formulated with reference to Elizabeth Fry's prison work and Josephine Butler's work with prostitutes. Women had received an education that did not dispute the cultural and patriarchal principle that care of others was 'naturally' women's responsibility but they did not accept the corollary that members of their sex were therefore congenitally unable to perform other tasks, or to perform them as well as men. Now, by cloaking their franchise campaign in 'caring power' suffragists had a chance to show that they were worthy of citizenship and that their 'natural' roles were vital even when excluded from society's main activity of fighting a war. At a NUWSS meeting at Kingsway Hall on 20 October, the Quaker Isabella Ford said that women could gain from war (Hannam 1989: 169). The Government was calling on them to serve the State by saving life. Her view was that women had a duty to relieve suffering and were likely to achieve suffrage though this contribution. What was the thinking behind this opinion?

The women's movement, particularly the suffrage campaign has been portrayed as political, but Helena Swanwick emphatically qualified this. She said, 'This movement was not primarily political: it was social, moral, psychological and profoundly religious.' This did not mean that it was linked to an established patriarchal church system since she described herself as 'not a Christian' but that the movement sprang from women's oppression as described by Mrs Emmeline Pankhurst, 'whose eloquence came from the deep heart of womanhood and put into burning words what millions of women must have inarticulately felt for centuries' (Swanwick 1935: 187). Women's duty to relieve suffering formed the spiritual aspect of the movement and fulfilment of that duty would lead to citizenship. It brought suffragists and Quakers together in the suffrage campaign and in relief. This critical link with the religious origins of 'caring power' provides a crucial intersection between suffragists and the SOF; it is an important part of women's history and is particularly significant. The quiet influence of Friends, together with the fact that they were 'always good fighters' (Fawcett 1924: 218), had a bearing on the suffrage campaign and inspired relief.

Corporately, Quakers were not always a force for social reform and followed society rather than leading it. Nonetheless, individual women, acting out of their personal concerns, were involved in political and social work and had been among the early suffragists; for example, the Bright-Priestman-Clark circle was in the vanguard of campaigning for women's rights and enfranchisement. In contrast, the Friends' suffrage society was not formed until 1911, taking the name the Friends League for Women's Suffrage (FLWS) in 1912 (Lunn 1997: 33–4). In 1914 there were approximately 1,020 members. Their indomitability is epitomized by their President, Gulielma Crosfield, now aged 63, who served on the FWVRC and travelled to Holland to help refugees. Quakers took part in the extensive movement to keep Britain out of the war in the first few days and were in the forefront of helping foreigners. They campaigned for an end to war and had a tradition of helping refugees. At the London Yearly Meeting in 1915, Friends examined the basis of their testimony against war to determine whether it was based on humanitarian and philanthropic arguments (Hirst 1923: 524) and decided they must have a positive, constructive message. Love towards God and love towards Man were intertwined so helping victims was a testimony against war.

New Committees were formed by both Quakers and suffragist societies as a result of the emergency. In August 1914, the IWSA formed an International Women's Relief Committee (IWRC) which cooperated with the Friends' Emergency Committee (FEC) to help repatriate stranded enemy aliens. Women Quakers' concerns were responsible for the formation of the FEC and the rebirth of the FWVRC to help refugees. Since their formation as a separate religious group with their own identity, Quakers had much experience of persecution and marginalization; it can be argued that this also applied to women. The issue of women's suffrage was a challenge to the system of *femme couvert* and chivalric ideals of British patriarchy which subordinated women. Quakers' pacifist witness presented a challenge to militaristic British society. Their focus on the victims of war rather than the fighting of it was a means of alleviating misery and at the same time protesting against militarism. Historians' emphasis on Quaker men's peace witness through conscientious objection to war, and the work of the Friends Ambulance Unit (FAU), mean that other Quaker activities, including women's work escorting female and child enemy aliens to the continent and FWVRC work in many countries, has been given little recent attention. Suffragists' connection and cooperation with Quakers in Great War refugee relief is revealed as a new and significant factor in women's history.

A second theme of the book is therefore the suffragist–Quaker connection in relief. Quakers were the predominant religious group to help refugees and the continuities with relief undertaken by them in previous centuries and with their spiritual witness during the 1920s are considered. Traditionally but not always pacifist, Friends claimed that men and women were equal because the spirit of Christ spoke to women as well as men. However, the SOF did not practise true equality. The FLWS was not an official SOF body and was late in forming because they were gulled by the belief that equality already existed in the Society and were woken to the needs of wider society by the militants. There was, therefore, a flow of Quakers into the suffrage movement. The outbreak of war meant that each used the others' organizations to undertake relief in the manner to which they felt called.

Women's involvement in relief necessitated the examination by society of disputed concepts which in some cases led to the passing of more appropriate laws to accommodate the new models; others remain unsettled. Citizenship and national identity are examples of the former; democracy and patriotism of the latter. People were told they were fighting for democracy, yet Britain was undemocratic in its exclusion of women and certain men from the franchise. One of the political actions relinquished by the NUWSS *pro tem* was the Election Fighting Fund policy formulated by Kathleen Courtney and Catherine Marshall which created three-cornered political fights and was an effective move towards democracy. However, 'democracy' is a vague concept which has several forms and definitions and carries a value judgement. As Vellacott says (1977: 414) what seemed clear was that a democratic government rested not on brute strength but on the consent of the governed, and represented a higher stage of civilization which many considered was indicated by women's position within individual nations. The Women's Freedom League (WFL) and NUWSS were both democratic institutions. The WSPU was not; some women resigned from it for this reason. Chapter 8 shows how relief workers witnessed the Russians' struggle to determine whether democracy would be installed after the first Revolution; the consequent terrible civil war exacerbated famine in the stricken areas they were trying to help. President Wilson of America had democracy as an aim when, at the Peace Conference, considered in Part Three, decisions were made about new national boundaries and the placement of some countries under the protection or 'mandate' of others; he hoped this would lead to new democracies such as the short-lived Armenian Democratic Republic considered in Chapter 9. Women were involved in making the emergent League of Nations more democratic. Caring power is shown to be the final part of the franchise campaign which successfully demanded that 'Citizenship' and 'Democracy' should be redefined to include women.

Patriotism was an important motive for relief work and is therefore a further theme. It did not necessarily obscure the feminist understanding of common womanhood, of humanity, that motivated suffragists to support each other in their fight for equality or in alleviating suffering that men's wars engendered. Nor were Quakers excluded from patriotic motivation or from seeing imperialism as a blessing. The discourse of war demanded that women show their patriotism by supporting the war and by 'go[ing] home and keep[ing] quiet', the command being given to the suffragist Dr Elsie Inglis by a War Office official following her offer of Scottish Women's Hospital Units (SWH) for medical and surgical military relief. Dr Inglis, Honorary Secretary of the Federation of Scottish Suffrage Societies, first offered her Units to the Scottish Red Cross in Glasgow where Sir George Bealson warned her that the War Office would have nothing to do with her, although by the end of the war their attitude might change. The first prediction was correct, the second not so. Although formed to help wounded military personnel, SWH assistance to French and Serbian civilians was significant and is therefore considered in Chapters 5 and 7. In fact, medical relief highlights the problematic boundary between military and civilian and shows how relief workers become prisoners, refugees, and are killed on active service by warfare or epidemic.

Part of what was required of patriots was an unquestioning acceptance of the war's righteousness, whatever the cost. The leaders of women's organizations understood that war was a time when everyone was expected to be patriotic. Having lived through other wars, they also knew that the brunt fell on non-combatants, especially women and children. Nonetheless, Millicent Garrett Fawcett was ardently patriotic, holding views different from the women identified by Margaret Llewelyn Davies as democratic suffragists, such as Kathleen Courtney and Helena Swanwick who were internationalists by conviction, and had different ideas about how to express their patriotism. Emily Hobhouse, a woman supported by Quakers, held an even more advanced and internationalist version. Vellacott (1993: 39) rightly says of democratic suffragists 'This was no body of women socialized to submissive gentleness, reacting with appropriate distress to the horrors of war, and anxious to fulfil the maternal role of applying band-aids to the wounds the boys had inflicted on each other.' Nonetheless, this is a limited and derogatory description of relief work, ignoring the suffering the 'boys' of both sides inflicted on women and children. It does not take into account relief to civilians in the war zone and therefore lacks appreciation of the characteristics and abilities required to ameliorate their condition, including an acceptance of personal danger.

The story of civilians exposes Man's inhumanity to non-combatants consequent upon the propensity for war, which manifests as a violent instinct to take possession, dominate and destroy other groups of humans. In war people form a collective response to killing which might be different from their individual views under different circumstances. Powerful institutions such as the church legitimized the slaughter, numbing consciences and exonerating the servicemen. The required version of patriotism involved showing a lack of humanitarianism towards the defeated enemy. As Joanna Bourke (1999: 192–3) has shown with Australian and American civilians, the response to civilian slaughter is denial or resignation – such things are 'bound to happen'. Apathy also exists towards suffering in foreign countries when non-combatants become refugees or when their suffering is caused by the actions of 'our' country's armed forces. Xenophobia takes many forms – 'our' women are expected to serve only 'our' men; those who care for people of other nations, even if Allies, are quickly forgotten. After the Armistice it was 'bad form' to talk about the war. Patriots were expected to approve the Peace Treaty, the exclusion of Germany from the League of Nations, the reparations, and to continue to hate former enemies; after 1917, enemies included Bolsheviks. They were expected to support the League, but put their own country first.

Nonetheless, for democratic suffragists and pacifist Quakers non-violence led in 1915 to the holding of the International Women's Conference at The Hague to discuss possible peace terms. Mrs Fawcett's strong disapproval resulted in ten NUWSS members resigning from the Executive including Helena Swanwick, Kathleen Courtney, the Quakers Alice Clark and Isabella Ford, and Maude Royden, who also resigned as editor of the suffrage journal *The Common Cause*. The foundations of the Women's International League for Peace and Freedom (WILPF), still in existence today, were laid at this congress. Those who wanted to work for peace as well as campaigning for equality became members. Its British section was the Women's International League (WIL), with Chairman Helena Swanwick. The following month the SOF convened a Representative Peace Conference at Devonshire House. Both conferences considered what was needed for an early cessation of hostilities, the ultimate settlement of the war, continuous mediation and reduction of armaments. It is noteworthy that the Quaker Conference was not quite unanimous that the word 'population' in certain proposals should be understood to include women equally with men. An Executive Committee was formed to make the resolutions passed as effective as possible and included Charles Roden Buxton, G. Lowes Dickinson, Marian E. Ellis, Isabella Ford, Joan Fry, Carl Heath, and Arthur Ponsonby, MP, people whose names recur in this book. After the war Friends and suffragists continued to work together through WILPF, the American Quaker Emily Greene Balch being the first International Secretary at their HQ. WILPF was based in Geneva in order that they could work closely with the League of Nations.

The second purpose of the book is therefore to discover whether there is any continuity between women's relief work among refugees and their work with the League of Nations. The contacts suffragists made during campaigning facilitated their work of aiding civilians and were central to subsequent work at the League. Various writers and websites credit the American President Woodrow Wilson with the idea of the League. However, the proposal had been previously discussed in many nations across many generations. In Britain there were groups of people planning the possible formation and constitution of an international arbitration body. This network included Friends and suffragists some of whom later had close involvement with the League. Relief workers who were members of this network will be identified. Since only a few women could have direct contact with the League, others worked through the League of Nations Union (LNU), a voluntary body which first promoted the formation of an international League and then built public support for it. Helena Swanwick and Kathleen Courtney were prominent in the Union. Together with the Quaker Philip Noel-Baker, Kathleen Courtney devoted herself to LNU for most of its history, becoming its Vice-Chair in 1939. In 1946, after the League was superseded by United Nations, she became the United Nations Association Vice-Chair and Vice-President of the World Federation of UNAs.

Part Three, which discusses the foundation of the League of Nations, primarily focuses on relief given to erstwhile enemy countries during the Armistice, and also to Russia and Armenia where Quakers worked before, during and after the Great War. Women's initial exclusion from the League resulted in a feminist 'backlash' which took the form of the holding of a conference to define strategies and the subsequently successful demands for women's international citizenship to be recognized in the League Covenant. Once having gained admission, they were placed on committees and commissions where concern for others could be demonstrated, such as those dealing with prostitution and the white slave trade. It was recognized that women had a rightful interest in minorities and mandates because of their womanhood, enabling them to be central in providing the most successful work within the League, including care of refugees. The Commission on Deported Women and Children in Asia Minor, described in Chapter 9, is an outstanding example of 'caring power' in action at different levels. Women's approved role of care resulted in the League acknowledging the rights of the child, the earliest printed draft of the Children's Charter having been produced by the International Council of Women (ICW) in 1922.

Individual women such as Emily Hobhouse, Grace Vulliamy, Hilda Clark, Ruth Fry, Kathleen Courtney and many others all play different parts in the story. For some, relief did not end when hostilities ceased. Others, such as Helena Swanwick and Edith Lyttelton, were among those who became League delegates, and, since this is an international story, women of other nations such as Karen Jeppe, and Anna Bugge Wicksell are rightfully included. The work of some women will be examined in a certain amount of detail, identifying some of the missing 'women worthies' and indicating the obscured presence of many more, but also offering a challenge to the traditional perspective of the Great War by giving insiders' views of aspects of civilian life in wartime, foregrounding gender. My focus is on coping with and changing the results of war, rather than the fighting of it.

In uncovering the work of refugee relief during the First World War, the most fruitful sources have proved to be published and unpublished primary records written by people concerned with refugee support, especially those of the FWVRC held in the Friends House Library in London and the Women's Work Collection in the Department of Printed Books of the Imperial War Museum. These consist of reports from local committees, whose purpose was to inform subscribers of work undertaken to maintain support. Together with newspaper articles or government reports they depict British attitudes to the situation. The voices of refugees are not heard except through mediation by British people, yet despite this, we gain some idea of, and can empathize with, refugee experience.

Examination of these issues is undertaken through a geographical and chronological approach; these allow a comparative perspective concerning differences and similarities in the methods adopted by relief workers, due not only to the political and military situation, but also the geography. They show why an international organization such as the League of Nations was the necessary and right place to try to solve the problem of refugees. The war is referred to throughout as the Great War, as it was at the time and place names are spelled as in the sources.

PART ONE

Relief in Great Britain

CHAPTER 1

The Dislocation of War. Aliens, Refugees and Volunteers: Women and National Identity

Relief is the new suffrage campaign

On Sunday 2 August 1914, Albert, King of the Belgians, refused Germany permission to enter his country in order to attack France. From this day, Belgium was referred to by the British press as 'Brave little Belgium' and the Belgian people were heroes, as though each had individually defied a German soldier. This rhetoric represented the war as meaningful and obscured other reasons for its declaration, such as to further imperialistic ambitions and fulfil secret agreements between Britain and France. Miss Mary Coules of Folkestone (IWM. DD. 97/25/1) wrote in her notebook diary that her schooling taught her to accept the inevitability of war which helps to explain the war fever, and why the feeling of 'At last' when it was declared. On Monday, German troops crossed the border and declared war on Belgium and France. In anticipation of this disaster, during July a few Belgians crossed the Channel. They were mostly middle-class people who came over to England on the normal ferries, and did not regard themselves as refugees because they were merely having an extra holiday until the trouble blew over. The term 'refugee' implied being absent from home under different social and financial circumstances, denoting unwelcome implications of class and morality they were not prepared to accept as applicable to them. From September, Belgian refugees were welcomed as 'guests' and provided with hospitality which, for those who needed it, meant all necessities were provided.

In Britain the first weekend of August was the summer Bank Holiday. The Hon. Edith Lyttelton, a supporter of the British Empire, executive member of the North of England Women's Suffrage Society, and widow of Alfred Lyttelton, Colonial Secretary during the Boer War, was at home in Kent. The Foreign Secretary, Sir Edward Grey, wrote to her (IWM. Belgium 2.2/14): 'I'm afraid we are going to turn a united back instead of a united front to the enemy.' Consequently, she spent most of the day 'on the end of the telephone wire' with Downing Street, where the Cabinet was deliberating far into the night. Cabinet met twice on Saturday and also on Sunday. Parliament was recalled from its summer recess and met on Monday 3 August.

Learning that Britain had sent an ultimatum to Germany, Edith Lyttelton immediately drove to the House of Commons, arriving at the Lobby just as the members streamed out after the 'fateful division'. She saw the 'final ceremonial' when 'His Majesty's Commons came to the bar [of the Lords] and reported'. As a member of the political *élite* it was important for her to see these events personally. The next day she went to the Victoria League headquarters, an imperialist organization of which she was founder and Honorary Secretary, to see if there was something useful to do. Two weeks later, her restless need for wartime occupation was further satisfied by assisting Lady Flora Lugard in the foundation of the WRC at the Aldwych, London, which the Government subsequently made responsible for all refugees who came to Britain. For Edith Lyttelton, this was an additional means of supporting the Empire and of aiding women and children.

Sir Edward Grey's remark shows he hoped Britain would stand up to Germany even if this meant warfare, but many people, including members of the NUWSS Executive Committee, believed until the last moment that he was endeavouring to maintain British neutrality (Swanwick 1935: 239). As Norman Angell, a writer and founder of the Neutrality League, and later an executive member of the League of Nations Union, wrote in his letter to *The Times* dated 31 July, Grey had 'solemnly declared' on several occasions that Britain was not bound by any agreement to support France in the event of a German invasion. Angell pointed out that the last war fought on the Continent was to prevent the growth of Russia; it was proposed to fight this one in order to promote that growth. Britain could best serve civilization by staying out of any conflict. As the nation was about to discover, Angell had correctly argued in *The Great Illusion* (1909) that a European war would be economically disadvantageous for victor as well as vanquished. Nevertheless, the German invasion of Belgium made dampening rising war fever impossible.

Among the few people sceptical over prospects for continuing peace was Helena Swanwick, Edith Lyttelton's suffragist colleague, the anti-militarist former editor of the suffrage journal *The Common Cause*, and member of the NUWSS Executive, now aged 50. She had been warned by C.P. Scott of the *Manchester Guardian* during the Agadir crisis of 1911 that Britain and Germany would eventually fight (Haslam 1999: 41). When she came out of Kingsway Hall at 11 p.m., she heard the expiry of the British ultimatum to Germany and felt engulfed by black despair, recognizing that a state of war existed. The NUWSS Executive had prepared for the eventuality of war and temporarily suspended 'ordinary political work' (Fawcett 1924: 217). Its definition was unclear, leaving branches to decide how to comply. Consequently, as Alberti says (Alberti 1989: 51), suffragists' lives were dislocated. Alice Clark said: 'What a horrible dark place full of emptiness, East Wind and bitterness we seem to have come to.' Her Quaker friend, Margery Fry, was in Capel Curig, Wales, with her artist brother Roger. She did not return (Jones 1966: 92).

Helena Swanwick's colleague, Mary Agnes 'Molly' Hamilton (1944: 66), who had a Quaker background, worked on *The Economist*, edited by F.W. Hirst, an ultra-pacifist member of the *Nation* group and one of Sir Edward Grey's harshest critics. She cancelled her visit to friends that weekend because she suspected their views would be different from hers. Instead, she went to the Neutrality Committee in Kensington; collected their leaflets and while distributing them had her hair pulled by a censorious member of the public. That day's news included fighting in Serbia, which despite bowing to Austria's ultimatum, had been invaded; mobilization in Russia, and in Paris the Socialist leader Jean Jaurès had been killed. On Sunday she joined the fringes of the vast crowd in Trafalgar Square. Margaret Bondfield, Mary Macarthur, Arthur Henderson, Cunninghame Graham and Keir Hardie were the speakers; they opposed the possibility of the Government supporting Russia in case this dragged Britain into war. On Monday the evening papers carried Grey's speech.

On 4 August, prior to the declaration of war, the Government set up a Committee to advise on measures necessary to prevent or deal with any distress resulting from it. Indicating that the Government recognized the distress caused to women could not be subsumed under men's problems, one of the sub-committees was for Women's Employment. Members included Mary Macarthur, Margaret Bondfield, Violet Markham, Dr Marion Phillips, Susan Lawrence and Edith Lyttelton, all activists in connection with women's working conditions, the latter two members of the National Federation of Women Workers, and all pro-women's suffrage, except for Violet Markham, who converted, and Susan Lawrence, who did not. Realising that women would be the first to suffer, suffragist Federations and Societies offered to assist local authorities in the alleviation of distress, a few of whom ignored or refused their offer, while others were surprised, not realising that women's help was desirable. The most immediately pressing work was care of soldiers' and sailors' families. The recognized channel of relief, the Soldiers' and Sailors' Families Association, was overwhelmed by the volume of work because the War Office delayed paying separation allowances in advance as men enlisted and reservists were called up. Many women did not know they were entitled to such money; many had used every penny they possessed. Some did not receive their allowance until several weeks had passed. Sylvia Pankhurst, who organized assistance for mothers and babies in London's East End, thought soldiers' dependants were shamefully treated (*Englishwoman* 1914: 47–51). Suffragists across the nation helped in sorting this out. The Government Committee report when issued reflected these matters, showing that unemployment and distress was more severely felt by women who were also more immediately thrown out of work than men.

Friends and suffragists therefore joined groups organized by the nation at large to work in hospitals, canteens, and among Belgian refugees (Hirst 1923: 494). When the first Belgian refugees arrived, members of NUWSS branches and other women's organizations met and helped the needy Belgian 'heroes', the majority of whom were women and children. Quakers such as Isabella Ford, whose mother, Hannah, had helped Russian refugees, became personally involved in their care as did suffragists such as Catherine Marshall and her parents, who described their family of refugees as 'delightful inmates' of their home. For Catherine, this probably did not compensate for being removed from the House of Commons arena by the cessation of NUWSS political work. Nonetheless, many people found an area of activity appropriate to some easing of their war-time disquiets. Kathleen Courtney, having helped to establish WILPF, travelled through Europe to help refugees of many nations, especially those from Serbia. Edith Lyttelton was responsible through the WRC for overall care of Belgian women and children, including raped women and their infants. Helena Swanwick first co-operated with the Richmond Suffrage Society in forming a Committee to assist women thrown out of work, but her heart was not in it. She considered that (1935: 315–16) relief required feminine capacities and had no permanent effect on policy which she wanted to help formulate. Continuing her pre-war political interests, she joined the newly-formed dissident Union of Democratic Control (UDC), formed by Ramsay MacDonald, Norman Angell, E.D. Morel, Arthur Ponsonby and others, which pressured for peace by negotiation and the establishment of a body to prevent further war through mediation. She said this was her 'consolation' but the war probably accelerated a change of emphasis that would have happened anyway. She could not have anticipated that ten years later she would be a delegate to the League of Nations, appointed by the first Labour administration, and part of her job was to deal with refugee problems. Molly Hamilton, then an MP, joined her there in 1929.

As a contributor to *The Common Cause* had written in September 1914, pre-empting second wave feminism's 'the personal is political' slogan, relief was 'none the less political because it is social' and as a subtle but powerful franchise campaign method its influence was significant, although it had dangers. It indicated women's continuing willingness 'to do work which men found disagreeable or for which they were ill-equipped' (Prochaska 1980: 222) and their ability to clear up the mess created by wars they found difficult to prevent because they were not full citizens could be construed as being in favour of war. Some suffragists thought emphasis on the practical expressions of sympathy by providing food, clothing and maternity care, typical domestic activities, would prejudice their integrity in their fight against discrimination. That this was possible was indicated at Bishop Aukland where a Special Relief Committee was formed entirely of women because the men denigrated them and the tasks under discussion as 'women's work' and left them to it (*Common Cause*: 28.8.1914). But Fawcett's suggestion to undertake relief was not without merit. She subscribed to the view of fitness for citizenship through service and 'caring power' fitted the social-service model of citizenship. Liberal discourse had shifted from the view of citizens' rights to citizens' duties as a check to untutored democracy and underpinned Fawcett's concept that relief was a means to citizenship because it indicated patriotism. Taken to its logical extent, any woman who undertook relief was unwittingly contributing to the citizenship campaign. However, democratic suffragists like Alice Clark thought it was the duty of the women to educate themselves about the causes of war; they promoted education and the eschewing of violence as citizenship qualifications. This model found expression in organizations such as the UDC, and emerged as a demand that the League of Nations Covenant recognize women's international citizenship. The models combined in the humanitarian social work of the League's Fifth Committee.

Not all suffrage societies abandoned campaigning; some incorporated relief work into their political agitation. The radical WFL, a group that broke away from the WSPU over its lack of democracy, was in North Wales in the middle of a successful campaign which was continued until the middle of September. Nevertheless, on 6 August they formed the Women's Emergency Corps (WEC) to organize and prevent the overlapping of volunteer aid and to assist refugees of the 'better classes'. Members of the Actresses' Franchise League and the Tax Resisters' League co-operated in the formation of the Corps which reflected many conflicting views. Mrs McKenna, wife of the Home Secretary, and a noted concert pianist, was a member, but the Executive included prominent suffragists, including Mrs Pethick-Lawrence and Lena Ashwell. Suffragist members included Eva Moore, actress and charity worker; Mary Macarthur, the Independent Labour Party (ILP) activist, and Caroline Spurgeon, Professor of English Literature at Bedford College. Miss Maud Bell, an Executive member of the Church League for Women's Suffrage (CLWS), worked with WEC from its inception. It is not known whether Maud Bell was related to the Miss Bell, aged 19, who was reported in *Jus Suffragii* of 1 January 1915, as having both legs shot away by a shell while tending the wounded at Mons. Although not affiliated to the NUWSS, the CLWS followed its lead regarding relief. Organizers in Birmingham, Manchester and Swansea gave their time to relief work under municipal authorities in their towns; Bromley and Dublin branches opened workrooms for women and girls unemployed because of the war.

In its first Annual Report, WEC listed nearly 30 societies taking part in its work, of which half were directly related to the fight for women's equality and others, such as National Society of Day Nurseries, were concerned with women's welfare and work. One of WEC's first tasks was meeting and homing the earliest Belgian refugees. Miss Grace Vulliamy helped to form their Interpreting Department prior to any such Department being started by the British Government; working with the Local Government Board (LGB) she helped weed out undesirable refugees at Gravesend where one 'benevolent-looking old gentleman' was seized by police as a bank robber. On 25 October the *Mid Sussex Times* reported that although only a few weeks old, the WEC 'was already a beacon of light for many'. It originated the National Food Fund (NFF), which supplied the four great Belgian refugee hostels in London set up by WRC for whom they were official distributing agents. Coffee stalls were started in various districts. With the co-operation of leading men at Smithfield, Covent Garden and Billingsgate markets, Miss Carey organized a Food Depot utilising surplus stores as a result of which much preventable waste was discovered. This idea of waste prevention was adopted by the government. The National Food Fund also came to the rescue of professional classes, regardless of sex, age or politics. WEC helped about 5,000 refugees, officially closing on 13 April 1916, although its Hostel remained open till 10 January 1917.

Identity in war

As Michel Foucault shows (Rabinow 1984: 8), dividing practices where people are given a social and personal identity create a process of self-understanding that facilitates control by others. By identifying different groups, discourses were constructed that stigmatized certain categories of refugees as 'unwanted' and even dangerous, including people already living in or visiting Britain, who found that they needed to leave quickly. This was particularly so for enemy aliens; 'alien' was the legal term for foreigners.

The categorization arose from a new Aliens Restriction Act (ARA) passed by the Government on 5 August due to fear of spies. It enabled control of foreigners' entry into Britain, deportation or internment of those already here and limitation of the areas where friendly foreigners could live. Nationality was now key. National, ethnic and gender identities took on important new meanings and became discriminatory. This preoccupation with spies, together with anti-semitism, created a situation where national identity and the term 'refugee' became fractured by ethnicity, religion and above all by class. These intersected with further categorization into 'allies', 'aliens' and 'enemy aliens' which opened the way to greater control, including discrimination against British-born women married to foreigners, exposing an important reason for enfranchisement. Throughout the nineteenth century, women's legal situation, especially that of married women, was increasingly perceived in terms of slavery. The legal situation of *femme couvert*, where a married woman's interests were presumed to be identical with, or covered by her husband, was fundamental in this; consequently the women's movement focussed on liberating married women. Unlike men, women's nationality was not permanently fixed by place of birth or father's nationality. If an English woman married a foreigner she lost her British nationality and took on her husband's, becoming an 'alien'. Enemy aliens immediately faced intolerance in various forms, including job loss and physical attack. British women married to Germans were now classified as enemy aliens and treated accordingly, but they sometimes fared no better in Germany. An English wife of a German was sent to her husband's parents in Bavaria because she was now legally German. The neighbours were disagreeable, saying she should return to England. A month later the husband contacted the London Quakers. His wife had been going between Folkestone and Flushing (Vlissingen), not allowed to land. There were children born from such marriages who could speak no German; despite in one instance being 'obvious little cockneys' (*Friend*: 2.10.14), they were nonetheless 'repatriated'.

German-born women married to Englishmen were in a similar situation. Thea Mertelmeyer, of Die Frauenbewegung sent a report to *Jus Suffragii* of 1 September 1916 about the families of men interned at camps such as Ruhleben, near Berlin.

> Whoever comes into frequent contact with German wives of aliens interned at Ruhleben will have been able to judge of the tragedy of their fates. Many had never been out of Germany, had lived there with husband and children, never dreaming until the outbreak of war but that they were Germans. Suddenly their eyes were opened and they were stamped as aliens, enemies. The physical, but still more the mental suffering of such women, not only here but in every belligerent country, is beyond description.

Men's laws dictated women's national and personal identity and made them vulnerable. A suffragist deputation had waited upon Cabinet Minister Lewis Vernon Harcourt on 27 July regarding British wives with foreign husbands. They were apprehensive about the status of women in the British Nationality Bill before Parliament. Mr Harcourt's remarks were private, but 'the wrong done to women as a sex is likely to be disregarded, and in the opinion of the Government it is of far more consequence that British law should be in conformity with international law than that it should afford protection to women'. As Mary Sheepshanks noted in *Jus Suffragii* of 1 August, this was 'One more disability incurred by women through marriage'. The British Dominions Woman Suffrage Union, which worked continuously with the chief British Societies, observed in its *Report of Work 1917–18* that 'Sir W.H. Dickinson's attempts in the House of Commons to secure that a British woman married to an alien should preserve her own nationality, as in English law before 1870, have again been unsuccessful.' The erosion of women's rights as a result of their having no vote is very clear from this statement. Unless their husbands became naturalized, British-born wives had to register as aliens, but they would have a separate card. A widow needed to apply for naturalisation so that she did not need to register with the police. The rules were so intricate the police even asked the Friends for assistance (Thomas 1933: 24).

A sexual double standard operated towards British women who had married foreigners. Their patriotism was rendered highly questionable and they were particularly distrusted by officials. British-born wives with alien husbands were confined to a five-mile radius of their homes; British-born men with foreign wives were not similarly restricted. A letter in the correspondence columns of *Common Cause* stressed the monstrous injustice by which women married to foreigners were treated as aliens. This meant that there were many wives of aliens needing help. In November *Jus Suffragii* reported that the IWSA had dealt with about 1,200 cases, 450 being helped 'back' to Germany. The question of women's nationality was one that women's international organizations raised with the League of Nations and their own Governments during the 1920s, resulting in changes to some countries' laws.

'Repatriating' enemy aliens

The Friends' Emergency Committee to assist Germans, Austrians and Hungarians in Distress in the UK (FEC) was established in August. Travelling home to Birmingham from campaigning in London for the Neutrality League, Sophia Sturge wrote to the Quaker Stephen Hobhouse asking him to help stranded Germans and Austrians and suggesting a committee. Aged 65, a Home Rule supporter with a Quaker background, she devoted herself to helping interned aliens in Birmingham and on the Isle of Man. After the War, she frequently spoke on the League of Nations at public meetings and in secondary schools, educating adults and children for peace and internationalism rather than nationalism and conflict. The aliens who concerned Sturge were people like the elderly nuns whose lives had been spent nursing in a Ramsgate sanatorium, now suspect because their nationality was perceived as a threat and who faced having to return to Germany. Sturge's request bore fruit. Following an expression of concern by Hobhouse, the Meeting for Sufferings, the Executive Committee of the London Yearly Meeting, appointed a small Emergency Committee. The Quaker journal *The Friend* announced on 14 August that a special office had been opened at 58 City Road, London, to provide assistance for those whose Embassy or Consulate was no longer open. There were branch committees and representatives in the provinces, almost entirely staffed by volunteers, many not Friends. For example, the committed suffragist, social worker and labour activist, Eva Gore-Booth, younger sister of the Countess Markiewicz, and Eva's friend Esther Roper worked for the FEC (Mitchell 1966: 344). Esther Roper was then secretary of the North of England Society for Women's Suffrage, of which Edith Lyttelton was a member. According to Leigh Tucker (1972: 47), half the Executive of the FEC was outside the Society and it had non-Quaker support throughout its existence. The Archbishop of Canterbury and other influential non-Quakers supported it. A great part of the funds came from outside sources (Hirst 1923: 494, 497). In December, Committee member Lady Kate Courtney of Penwith, sister of Beatrice Webb and an attender at Quaker meetings, assisted Mrs Franklin to gain membership as representative of the National Union of Women Workers. Lady Kate Courtney was born in 1847 and was therefore aged 67 in 1914. Although this period is acknowledged as being that of the decline of liberalism, the women who led relief were highly individual and few fit neatly into established categories. Nonetheless some broad generalizations can be made. As indicated, most were mature, middle-class and childless; many were single; this made relief possible. In addition to her membership of FEC, Lady Courtney was an intermediary channelling funds from the Anglo-German Society into the hands of the American Ambassador, Walter Page, to be used for Germans in England. She also enabled funds from the Anglo-German Friendship Committee to be directed *via* the American Consul, Mr Lowry, and used in part for the 'repatriation' of German women some of whom were British born.

On 10 August, in the House of Commons, the Quaker MP T. Edmund Harvey voiced his anxiety for stranded Germans, mostly women and children. The Quakers' press report was attacked by two evening papers because it was unpatriotically sympathetic to the plight of enemy aliens. Nonetheless, their appeal had raised £230 by 25 August and Caroline Playne, the Quaker writer, reported that about 50 cases of distressed foreigners had been sent to them, some of whom had been advised to apply for Poor Law relief. FEC was the only committee to deal with the enemy alien problem in its entirety in that it sought admission to Prisoner of War Concentration Camps and dealt with men, which the IWRC did not do. Quakers hoped that the 'moral effect of Englishmen' would be beneficial, an indication that humanitarianism was combined with patriotism as well as a way of carrying out the Biblical command to 'love your enemies' which did not stop at the coast of Britain. In 1916, when the War Charities Act became law, the Emergency Committee was registered by the London County Council as a War Charity and by 1920, when it amalgamated with the

FWVRC, it had 240 workers in London, besides those in the provinces (Hirst 1923: 497) and had expended about £100,000 in work in England. This was a considerable sum, since, according to the National Archives, London, in 1915 £1 was worth £43.06 of 2009's money, although by 1920 this had fallen to £21.21.

Oldfield's definition of 'humanitarian' as not dependent on religious belief, but implying awareness of the sacredness of life which can be expressed through a variety of activities, can be applied to the atheist editor of the international suffrage journal *Jus Suffragii*, Mary Sheepshanks, Helena Swanwick's second cousin. A friend of Bertrand Russell, and a 'trenchant, no-nonsense, highly articulate' woman (Moorehead 1992: 43), Sheepshanks was Honorary Secretary of the IWRC. The normal IWSA work was suspended and the office turned into a relief centre for women of all nationalities trapped in Britain without money. Quaker connection with the IWRC is particularly noteworthy, emphasizing the importance of care in the philosophy of both groups.

During August the IWRC received over 250 applications for help. The IWRC and FEC both appealed in the press for hospitality for aliens, Germans being dealt with separately from Belgians and the French. As Bertrand Russell discovered (Moorehead 1992: 217), there were people with 'a core of decency' around the country, who, knowing that Germans had been hounded out of their jobs and were unable to pay, took them in without charge until they were interned. Quakers found that people's motives included practical Christianity and the reciprocation of kindness given and received in previous wars. However, although there was a good response for women, it was difficult to find accommodation for families, single men, and women and children left destitute by the arrest of the husband/father. Anna Braithwaite Thomas, FEC's Honorary Secretary, reported that among the enemy aliens helped was an elderly German and his wife who had lived in Britain for 40 years doing translations but were now in dire financial distress because their customers had deserted them. By 29 September FEC had helped 331 people, with seven cases refused for unexplained reasons. This number excluded 'travelling cases and those outside London'.

Quakers and suffragists were jointly involved in relief work by November when Dr Hilda Clark and Caroline Playne were supervising the applications for relief received by the IWRC, whose volunteers had met trains, packed clothes for refugees and provided outfits. It had received 200 offers of hospitality for Germans. Suffragists at St Hilda's Hall, Oxford, had been among those providing hospitality. By April 1915 the IWRC had helped 868 cases, of which 660 were Germans and Austrians. A 'case' might be a mother and children, and therefore does not express the total number of individuals. Some enemy alien women were cared for in the homes of English families, or sent on to another Society with which the Committee worked, one being the by now authoritative WRC which had Lord Gladstone as its Honorary Treasurer. However, of the 660 cases, only 132 were found situations or hospitality, indicating the powerful anti-alien feelings evoked by war, and possibly the fear that if help were given it would rebound on the helper. A Bohemian suffragist who came to Britain to study the suffrage movement, suddenly found herself cut off and destitute; she was finally helped by women university students at University College, Bangor. Also helped were Russians, French and Hungarians, including a journalist, a teacher, the wife of a teacher, governesses, a laundress and mother's helps. The IWRC referred cases in the provinces to the local secretaries of the NUWSS, who visited, gave whatever aid or advice they could, and in some instances referred the needy person to the appropriate charity, including Poor Relief. This type of work was extended to British wives of interned German husbands, who did not immediately receive maintenance allowances from the British Government. However, the IWRC's Report (IWM. Suffrage & Politics II) recorded that:

> English people have not as a rule been helped, as other funds and societies are open to them. Exception has occasionally been made for fugitives from France and Germany … temporary help and hospitality have been given to English teachers obliged to leave Berlin and other German towns.

The FEC authorized three forms of relief: changing foreign money, paying board and repatriation. In repatriation they closely co-operated with the IWRC, and, after its formation in 1915, the Women's International League.

Anna Thomas's daughter, Dr Henrietta Thomas, an American-born Quaker and therefore a neutral, and other German or American ladies such as Miss Dickson and Miss Stickney, escorted parties of children, young servants, old and helpless women and mothers with children back behind German lines. Miss Stickney, later Dame Adelaide Livingstone, was an American Quaker who made trips to Holland, coming into contact with Edith Cavell. On her marriage to a British officer she was no longer a neutral and had to discontinue these rescue activities. A woman's nationality change resulting from marriage was therefore shown to have far-reaching effects beyond the purely personal. Nevertheless, because she had reported to Lord Robert Cecil he later enlisted her aid in the Prisoners of War Department under Lord Newton, whom she accompanied to The Hague to confer with German Generals on the treatment of prisoners. Grace Vulliamy was also involved in this work. There were potential dangers for the escorts of enemy aliens: one was persuaded not to go beyond the Dutch border and in March 1915, the IWRC sent parties of German girls only as far as that point. It is not always clear for which society workers were operating in repatriation work, or whether both at once. For example, Dr Thomas escorted girls back to Germany for the IWRC, but was reported in *The Friend* of October 1914 as having escorted some refugees. She was 'now escorting a party to the German frontier and hopes to go to Berlin to bring back British girls and women, via Cracow and Prague to Vienna, collecting *en route*'. Dr Thomas made at least six journeys behind enemy lines escorting German girls, once going to Vienna to rescue English music students. On another occasion she took 14 orphans, including many tiny babies, and was helped by several German ladies going as far as Flushing where they were met by German fathers. On yet another journey she took 80 refugees, and, proving that war does nothing for women's human rights, among them was a girl with appendicitis who had been discharged from hospital and told to go to Germany for her operation. It is thought possible that the strain of such journeys contributed to Dr Thomas's later breakdown. She died on 4 August 1919.

These refugees and their escorts used the Zeeland shipping line between Flushing or Dieppe and Folkestone, which constantly had a two-way traffic. Arrangements were made with steamer and railway companies but journeys had to be discontinued for a fortnight when the issue of permits was stopped. Up to then weekly parties of girls had been returned to Germany. By 4 September the IWRC had already dealt with 230 cases. Readers of *The Friend* were warned not to speak German in Folkestone because there were so many Belgians in the streets. Port officials could be intrusive, reading the girls' letters and confiscating books and newspapers. A medical student who had invested all her money in medical books but been refused her degree because of her nationality, wanted to go to Switzerland for her degree. She got through. However, in late February a party of 40 was delayed in the searching rooms because a woman had been discovered the previous evening with £58 in gold concealed in the padding of her hair.

Cooperation between Committees led to awareness of duplication of effort. As early as 20 August Stephen Hobhouse convened a Meeting of the FEC because it was realized that the IWRC was dealing with the same type of people the Friends were trying to aid. The IWRC wanted the Quakers to appeal for money to share with them as they did not expect to make an appeal, although it is not clear why. Both groups were strict about the source of their funds, and how they were spent, and although the Friends were willing to co-operate, appeals went out in their name only. The Fund to cover this work was to be called the Aliens Relief Fund.

The IWRC worked for relief of foreigners in conjunction with many organizations including the Belgian Refugee Committee organized by Belgian diplomats in London. One of the IWRC members, the *Union Internationales Amies de la Jeune Fille*, had been formed in 1877 to prevent young girls from being drawn into prostitution by meeting them at railway stations and providing accommodation in order to ensure their safety. The Emergency Committee also co-operated with other relief agencies including German, Austrian, Hungarian and Polish Societies and the English Society of Friends of Foreigners in Distress (SFFD). Founders of SFFD, started over 100 years previously, included Friends. The overlap and differences in the amount of monetary relief given meant that co-operation was vital and Stephen Hobhouse provided a key link. A pacifist Quaker (contrary to popular belief, not all Quakers were pacifist), and in his case an absolutist, Stephen was sentenced first to hard labour and then to jail in 1916 for refusing to enlist, sacrificing his health in the process. On Tuesday

25 August he attended a meeting of the SFFD who wanted to co-operate with the Quakers. He reported to the Friends Committee on the following day and they were glad to co-operate, but not to link funds or merge. This policy was attacked by the SFFD at an acrimonious meeting between the two Societies, but later the SFFD softened its attitude and asked again to cooperate. The problem of finding accommodation for foreign men necessitated another link between Committees. British people who provided hospitality risked being penalized should the 'guest' be found to be a spy. But at an interview with the Aliens' Committee at the Home Office later that month a scheme whereby hosts would not be punished was considered. To further the co-operation a Central Council was formed with the SFFD. Their Miss Woodward, 'as representing the Committee on the Executive of the IWRC' and present by invitation, was appointed Hospitality Secretary, indicating further between-Committees links. Such co-operation was vital when resources were limited and the need great. Although a somewhat exclusive sect, Friends are notable for the way in which they liaised with many other non-Quaker relief committees from the outbreak of war. Nevertheless, such breakdowns of exclusivity may have contributed to the post-war desire to focus on their spiritual message by creating Quaker Embassies, the new Council for International Service (CIS) continuing with relief.

The American Embassy, as the neutral in charge of German and Austro-Hungarian subjects in Britain, entrusted some of its work to FEC and provided funds. The Home Office referred women's enquiries to the IWRC and had to ask the Friends for assistance because the need was so widespread. Quick to stir up prejudice, newspapers abused the Quakers over this work. Nonetheless, the IWRC 1915 Report stated it was useful to the Foreign Office, Home Office, American Embassy, and Scotland Yard who made full use of the IWRC and gave it every assistance. The work was also useful to the German authorities. In return for the repatriation of German girls, the German Government enabled British women, children, and men of non-military age to be collected in Belgium by the American ladies and by July 1915 about 200 were brought out, including many from the war zone. Representatives of the IWRC went to Arlon in Luxembourg, to Ghent in East Flanders and to Menin, close to the firing line, and gathered from remote parts of Belgium young girls who could not travel alone. Some had parents in Canada, others in India. Parents in England had no news of their daughters most of whom were in Convent schools in outlying districts. The escorts took them to Brussels and from there, having procured their passports from the German authorities, conducted them through Holland to England. They were met at the station by Committee members and handed over to their parents and guardians.

On 20 April the Emergency Committee decided to ask Dr Henrietta Thomas to speak on their behalf to Dr Elizabeth Rotten at The Hague Women's Conference being called by democratic-pacifist suffragists. Dr Rotten was a Jewish Swiss woman who formerly taught at Newnham College, Cambridge. She had close connections with both the suffrage and the Quaker movements and undertook work on the Continent on behalf of suffragist and Quaker Committees. She was not an enemy alien, being Swiss born, but was a German scholar, and her movements across the Channel probably did not meet with the British Government's approval. Consequently she was expelled. An Emergency Committee Minute dated 28 July 1915, stated that 'Dr Rotten left England last night, by order of the Government'. She became Secretary of the Berlin Committee for the Relief of Foreigners which cared for British prisoners, foreigners and enemy aliens, doing similar work to FEC and IWRC. Dr Rotten has been described as the 'Florence Nightingale' of the Internment Camps for Allied nationals in Germany such as Ruhleben and deserves to be more widely recognized. On 23 November 1915 the Friends Committee reported receiving a letter from her in which she described her journey to fetch French and Belgian children out of occupied areas and repatriate them. She was a friend of Philip Noel-Baker, the Nobel Prize-winner whose book *The Arms Race, a Programme for World Disarmament*, she translated.

Anti-alienism was inflamed when, on 7 May the luxury Cunard liner *Lusitania* was torpedoed and over 1,000 lives were lost. The feminist Margaret Haig, later Lady Rhondda, founder of the Six Point Group, was one of the survivors. She wrote (Haig 1933: 240): 'The war formed for most of my generation the bridge that separated us from our youth. The *Lusitania* disaster was the apex of my bridge.' The sinking resulted in anti-German riots in ten London districts. A woman went into premature labour in a china shop wrecked by rioters. In the House of Commons an MP said that these riots 'expressed the righteous indignation of the nation' giving almost official endorsement, and obscuring the suspicion that there were probably weapons hidden aboard, making *Lusitania* a legitimate target. As a result of the riots the Quaker offices were crowded with refugees and police permission was given for the North London Meeting house to be used for refuge; 70 people were there for a month. Worry about aliens led Stephen Hobhouse, Miss Braithwaite and Mr Baker to obtain an interview on 19 May with John Pedder and Haldane Porter of the Aliens Department at the Home Office. They were told that the Government was unlikely to set aside 'any quarters to which aliens in danger might flee for shelter and safety in the event of further riots. The ordinary workhouses are supposed to be available for them.' This meant all aliens were to be treated as the lowest possible social class. The Friends requested a Government grant for the maintenance of refugee families in Holloway Meeting House, and mentioned a possible increase for the wives of interned aliens. Repatriation was discussed and they were assured this was entirely on a *voluntary* basis. Most, especially Germans and Austrians, paid their own fare, or were helped by the American Embassy. Compulsory repatriation would follow but it was unlikely that British-born wives would be forced to leave although some were being given permits at their own risk. The Department representatives acknowledged that the Emergency Committee could give considerable assistance by helping the travellers in various ways and the Home Office promised to provide necessary support. According to Cesarani and Kushner (1993: 35), in the next two years, numbers interned rose to 32,000 and 10,000 were forcibly deported, despite Home Office assurances.

The IWRC's repatriation work closed when 80 refugees, 56 of them British, arrived in London from Belgium with Miss Dickson on 13 August 1915. Twelve of these refugees were French, there were ten nuns from Tournai, and four Belgian children. In the opposite direction the last party of 28 German girls were conducted to the German frontier by Mrs Llewelling (sic). During this year of war, the IWRC escorted over 1,000 German girls to the German frontier and over 260 British women and children were conducted from Belgium. The German Governor of Belgium wrote that he wished to express his appreciation of the work of the IWRC.

Belgian refugees' journey and arrival at ports

While 'enemy aliens' were being escorted across the Channel in both directions, Belgian refugees were crossing from east to west. Whereas only internationalist humanitarians such as the SOF and suffragists assisted people with enemy alien status, people willingly helped the Belgian heroes who, following the Government's offer of hospitality on 8 September, were given hospitality as guests of the nation. On 6 September six steamers arrived in Folkestone with nearly 3,000 Belgian refugees, mostly, as *The Times* wailed on 7 September, 'terribly poor', so 'how are they to exist in Britain?' Some were in despair, wondering what they had to look forward to but a ruined Belgium. Welcome leaflets were distributed as refugees arrived.

Initially few people recognized the scale of the refugee problem, or the need to provide accommodation and other material assistance. On 4 September a letter from Harold Marsh was published in *The Friend*, suggesting the establishment of a Belgian Relief Committee to support refugees when they landed in Folkestone in the 'next few days'. The next week Marsh told readers that French and Belgian refugees were coming over in their thousands. There was, however, no Friends' committee and a central one was not formed, Quakers who wanted to help being able to do so though other organizations or forming their own committees locally, such as at Hampstead, where Mrs J. Rowntree Gillett and Mrs Crosfield were Committee members. On 4 September *The Friend* reported that four Friends in Croydon had joined a Central Committee set up by the Mayor but on being informed that part of its duty was to urge enlistment, Quaker members resigned.

Most Belgians were Roman Catholic and, emphasizing that care of the needy was women's responsibility, Cardinal Bourne charged the Catholic Women's League (CWL) with refugee provision, although this proved impossible in view of the numbers. The CWL primarily dealt with the middle and upper classes, but created hostels for the working-class and handled 10,000 refugees. They had a home at Deal, probably for unmarried mothers, and helped Catholics' marriage and funeral expenses.

During the first week of August the London Society for Women's Suffrage (LSWS) established the Women's Service Bureau, a clearing house for voluntary workers, supported by Lady Gladstone and Lady Lyttelton and with Maude Royden as an executive member. Over 1,200 workers enrolled and 283 were involved in work with Belgian refugees. Already 'refugee' was a relative term that needed qualifying by nationality. Some refugees were British, like the 56 mentioned above. WEC was one of several groups to report distress among English refugees. Miss Burke described several cases of English men and women in business in Europe who had lost everything, were out of touch with England, having no friends or relatives here. WEC provided for them as far as possible in hostels, but the problem became an increasingly difficult one. While there was no difficulty in getting help for the Belgian refugees, the same assistance was not available for English refugees because the need was unrecognized. On 3 March the *Morning Post* advertised for helpers to investigate cases of distress and hospitality for English refugees, but such a request did not compare with the amount of information about the 'brave Belgians'.

Refugees left from Flushing, Boulogne, Calais, Dieppe, Antwerp and the Hook of Holland. The ordinary cross-Channel services between Dover and Calais or Ostend were suspended immediately war was declared, but some boats were chartered especially for refugees. A number of uncomfortably crowded smaller boats brought peasants who then had to be transferred to rowing boats to come ashore. Refugee boats were directed to Folkestone, but some arrived at Chatham, Dover, Gravesend, Tilbury and Hull where they were allowed to discharge their human cargo at special quays; some also arrived at West Country ports and even at Liverpool. In one instance where boats were sent from Dover to Folkestone, a one-day-old baby was in one boat and a two-day-old in another; both born at sea. The authorities then realized that women were needed at ports to undertake pre- and post-natal care. Few boats arrived at Harwich because the approaches were mined. Among the few who arrived at Lowestoft were an old Flemish couple, Jan and Elizabeth Van der Wielen, driven by fire out of their farm at Pulte, near Malines. This was the start of a complicated journey to safety which took them first to Antwerp, then Bruges, Ostend, Lowestoft, Alexandra Palace (London), Port Sunlight, Cheshire, and finally to a farm near Manchester where some 'kind ladies' had a cottage for them. This kind of experience was not unusual and must have added considerably to the strain of being refugees.

Refugee relief committees

Some Belgians who arrived at Folkestone unexpectedly early in August on the night ferry were the first to be recognized there as refugees because of the numbers and the fact that no arrangements had been made. Women members of the Baptist Church rushed down to the harbour to help, hastily provided sandwiches and canvassed for free homes for the night. Mrs Knight and Miss Willis began to organize a strong contingent of ladies to meet the boats, producing sandwiches and obtaining accommodation averaging from 150 to 200 beds for each night's arrivals. These first refugees could speak only Flemish, so volunteer translators were quickly convened who sought to turn Flemish to French and then into English. Some refugees who had money preferred to remain in Folkestone because of proximity to their own country and the Press had predicted the war would be over by Christmas.

Everything affecting refugees was organized initially on an *ad hoc* basis. The Folkestone committee was appointed about the same time that the WRC in London was established, with Mrs Fitzgerald a leading spirit from the start and Miss Weston as its Chair. Mrs Carlile, the wife of the Baptist minister, was in charge of clothing, which refugees needed urgently on arrival, and later Mrs Drummond-Hay took control. A large hall was lent for reception and the Corporation gave a house for bedrooms. Miss Parsons supervised medical care and also assisted the police and Intelligence Departments. About 150 men and women volunteers worked under Basil Williams, who was appointed LGB representative on offering his services. The majority of the workers were women who continued to provide meals for embarking and disembarking travellers until repatriation was completed after the Armistice.

In Hull, the Refugee Relief Committee was formed on 7 September following the arrival of the first Belgian refugees on the two previous days. Accommodation was found, fund-raising, food and clothes organized. In Grimsby the death of the Mayoress, Mrs Tate, on 31 October delayed the formation of an official committee, but 154 Belgian refugees were already being cared for in and near the town. A working committee was formed on 6 November with Mr Tom Wintringham, JP, as Chair. Eleanor Rathbone (Rathbone in Strachey 1936: 32) said Wintringham's wife Margaret was not part of the women's movement, by which she presumably meant the suffrage movement. However, she may have confused Margaret with her sister-in-law, Mrs W.H. Wintringham, since Margaret was involved in many social and political organizations, including the National Union of Women Workers. This was established in 1874 under the trusteeship of Millicent Fawcett partly to monitor legislation affecting female employment. It changed from anti- to pro-suffrage and later became the National Council of Women. Margaret Wintringham became a member of the NUWSS's successor, the National Society for Equal Citizenship (NUSEC) and, when she stood for Parliament after the death of her husband in 1921, was denigrated by the Lincolnshire press and public for her support for the League of Nations. During the War she helped administer the Prince of Wales Fund for the relief of industrial distress of British workers and lodged some Belgian refugees in her home at Tealby, east of Market Rasen.

In Tilbury Mrs Henry was horrified by the condition of the first refugees she saw so the next day, and for nine months thereafter at her own expense, she distributed scones to the hungry arrivals who were 'of all classes'. Daily numbers at Tilbury varied from 131 to 880 and up to December 1914, 6,590 refugees were dealt with, of which 1,598 were men, 2,138 women and 2,854 children, a typical proportion; there were also wounded soldiers. Anyone sick was landed in a carrying chair, taken to a First Class train compartment reserved for the sick, the very old and feeble. All were given refreshments, milk and water being provided for babies. Mrs Henry arranged for voluntary helpers from London, including a nurse and an interpreter. In October Francesca Wilson (1944: 1), an author and later a relief worker with the SOF, went to Tilbury where she found the first refugees she had ever seen. 'Few of them knew on what shores they had arrived.' Because she could speak French she went each day until a 'young man wearing an armlet told me I was a nuisance and that refugees were the concern of officials', indicating the early professionalization and masculinization of refugee relief. Sarah MacNaughtan (1915: 81–2), whose fourth war this was, put it succinctly:

> the Voice of Authority abrogates command to itself … initiative which had the courage to launch schemes becomes hidebound and even penalized. Workers are dismissed, or put in their proper place.

This happened at the WRC after Lord Gladstone took control.

During August the WRC approached the Belgian Minister, M. Edmond Pollet to transfer the Belgian Legation Refugee work to the WRC headquarters at the Aldwych from Finsbury Square, where two of the workers were the Misses Lea and Myriam Rothschild. From 26 August an ever-increasing stream of refugees arrived following the fall of 'invincible' Namur on 22 August. All thought a few pounds would last till the end of the war which they anticipated would be before the autumn. Miss Rothschild stopped predicting two years' duration because of the tears such unthinkable ideas provoked. They worked at the Legation for nearly three weeks, leaving at 7 p.m. to meet the boat trains, but found it difficult to collect the Belgians on the platforms and although the South Eastern Railway gave them a small room for registration inevitably some people were unregistered. The Legation moved on 6 September to an enormous hall on the first floor at the Aldwych to join the WRC and remained for two months, M. Pollet placing the Misses Rothschild in charge. They regarded this as a great honour and display of trust in their ability to cope.

Cheap accommodation was sought in London, but in contrast with the later enthusiasm with which the British offered homes, few people were anxious to take in refugees at first. Most refugees were shopkeepers, shop assistants, clerks, artisans and labourers, the vast majority undoubtedly decent, honest, and wanting to work for their keep. As at Folkestone, so elsewhere: better-off refugees at first took furnished houses at their own expense, or were arranged for through friends, church or suffrage affiliation. Committees were established to care for refugees who, as private hospitality or the refugees' money ran out, were sometimes housed in hostels run by organizations such as WEC.

The Germans were approaching the coast and this caused a stampede at ports but nonetheless some British people went to Belgium to support the allies. *Jus Suffragii* announced on 1 October that a party of six women doctors, among whom were some well-known suffragists, plus 12 nurses, seven orderlies, three cooks and an interpreter, all women, had gone out to Antwerp. Among them was Dr Helen Hanson, an Executive member of the CLWS.

The suspension of the Folkestone steamer service meant a reduction in refugee numbers, but still about 1,000 to 2,000 a day arrived from France and Holland. Destitute people were subjected to medical examination through a Board of Trade Committee run by Nicholas Reyntiens before being allowed to cross the Channel. Reyntiens was of Belgian extraction on loan to the LGB in Ostend organising refugee registration with Dr Farrar, the Board's medical inspector. Reyntiens was also responsible for the Double White Cross Committee, whose aim was to assist non-combatants, paying fares for both Belgian and English passengers. Its clothing department was superintended by an Englishwoman, Mrs Coster. Reyntiens and Farrer were helped by the Quaker Percy Alden, Liberal M.P. for Tottenham, the Warden of the Canning Town University Settlement, who was later involved with refugee relief in Holland, and by Grace Vulliamy. Initially, the policy was to admit only women and children and the severely wounded, but soon the crush at French and Belgian ports made it impossible to adhere to this. The influx of refugees was reputed in September to amount to 20,000 in one week alone and there were similar numbers around 13 October during the military 'race for the sea', when Farrar and Reyntiens explained that they were unable to inspect all the refugees, and again in January 1915. Young men of military age were, however, removed and not allowed to board.

Antwerp surrendered on 9 October, the month that brought most refugees to Britain. Between 20 September and 24 October 35,000 refugees landed in Folkestone and on one October day 13 passenger boats arrived. Civic guards acted as special constables to help control harbour traffic; Scotland Yard and customs officers examined passengers, their passports and baggage and a nucleus of VAD's helped the wounded at Folkestone and Shorncliffe. On 15 October the passenger steamer from Ostend to Folkestone was suspended when it was seen that the German Army would reach the Belgian coast. On that day small tugs, pilot cutters, a steam yacht belonging to the Royal Belgian Yacht Club and fishing smacks all brought refugees into Folkestone; a Dutch hoy with 43 passengers took 20 hours over the crossing. About noon the final ship to leave Ostend, a blue-funnelled coal-transporting tramp steamer, the *Kenilworth*, brought its cargo of refugees into Folkestone, the captain having taken off every man, woman and child he could find, even packing them into the hold. He thought he had about 1,500 passengers, but when counted there were 2,263 – a number which made the ship top-heavy and risked sinking.

Escape routes from Belgium were cut off and people struggled to board the last ferries. From Ostend, LGB officials Nicholas Reyntiens and Dr Farrar reported 'In the general struggle to get on the boats several people fell into the water ... and were rescued with some difficulty'; Sir Francis Villiers, British ambassador to Belgium, reported fatal accidents from Le Havre. The captain of the Belgian State Railway steamer *Leopold II* from Antwerp tried to return to Ostend for more refugees, but had to stand off at Dunkirk, and learned that many people had made their way to France in rowing boats. The other Belgian State Railway steamer, the *Princess Henriette*, picked up passengers from boats, logs and rafts in the river, landed soldiers in France and then took the remaining 2,000 refugees to England.

After the fall of Antwerp further problems arose which highlight contemporary attitudes. Many 'respectable' people had escaped with no papers, prisoners were mixed with the refugees because the Germans had opened jails and, indicating serious anti-semitism, there was difficulty of housing thousands of Russian Jews who were mostly second or third generation settlers who had taken refuge in Antwerp following earlier pogroms. They were often highly skilled, such as diamond-cutters, or well-to-do but the Jewish community's separate shelters were intended for working-class Jews. This increased the problem of separating Jew from Gentile, the 'better' from the working classes and also, as the British now realized, Fleming from Walloon among the Belgians, partly because of different language and ethnic antagonism, but mostly because of class.

By 2 March 30,000 refugees had passed through the Misses Rothschilds' hands. They were awarded the *Medaille de la Reine Elisabeth*, the medal specially instituted by the Belgian King to honour those who helped civilians, but they refused to accept it, perhaps, like other women who also refused the honour, considering that they should not benefit from the suffering of others. However, even during the early weeks the numbers were so vast that Miss Rothschild realized that the Government would shortly have to take up the question of the Belgian Refugees and make arrangements for them in England in a bigger way than the philanthropic community was able to manage. This was facilitated through the Local Government Board and Lady Lugard's War Refugees Committee.

CHAPTER 2

Preparing to Welcome the Heroes: Women, Imperialism and Government Restrictions

The Victoria League and the War Refugees Committee

On the declaration of war a friend of Edith Lyttelton, Lady Flora Louise (Shaw) Lugard, colonial editor of *The Times*, began to make arrangements for Belgian refugees to be homed in Britain. These plans resulted in the foundation of the WRC. Flora Lugard had married Sir Frederick Lugard in 1902 and spent some time in Nigeria where he was Governor-General. She was a friend of the pacifist journalist W.T. Stead, and was convinced that colonization through British imperialism would alleviate poverty and be a beneficial means of spreading the gospel of imperialism world-wide. Her devotion to Empire led her to oppose Home Rule for Ireland where her family lived. An independent woman, who crossed the gender boundary in regard to her journalism which she regarded as active politics, she nonetheless displayed double consciousness in being against women's enfranchisement. These philosophies were at the root of the WRC and were connected with Lord Milner, who was on its General Committee.

In 1914 Milner was part of the movement that raised funds to support Sir Edward Carson's proposed provisional Government and was believed to be head of an underground Unionist movement, attempting to stop the passage of the Home Rule Bill. Trying to awaken public opinion to the dangers of civil war, according to her biographer E. Moberly Bell (Bell 1947: 275), who was later on the WRC's General Committee, Flora Lugard 'threw herself wholeheartedly into the Ulster camp' co-operating in the Ulster Council's preparations to bring to England the female and infant population from areas likely to be fought over. The evacuation scheme was a very elaborate one whereby the wives and families of the Ulster Volunteer

Special Force, and women and children in exposed districts, were to be evacuated to England and Scotland.

> The names of the people concerned had been entered into huge ledgers at Headquarters, refugee officers appointed, and transport arranged, while on the English side rest stations at Eaton Hall and elsewhere were being got ready to receive them. (Stewart 1967: 231–2)

Eaton Hall, near Chester, is the home of the Duke of Westminster's family, the Grosvenors, to whom Edith Lyttelton was related; for a time she had been on the Ulster organization's English Committee. However, the Austrian ultimatum to Serbia postponed the thought of civil war and Flora Lugard turned her attention not, as David Mitchell says (1966: 86), 'set[ting] herself to sort the sheep from the goats among the Belgian refugees', but to the relief of Belgian refugees of all classes.

Cahalan (1982: 34) says that 'What is most striking about the early nucleus of the Committee, however, is less that it was born of woman than that it drew its strength from no clear political group', failing to realize that this was so precisely because it was born of middle-class ideological hegemony and of women devoted to Empire and therefore crossed party political boundaries. Lugard made it a condition that the WRC should have 'no politics and no religious distinctions'. It reflected the fact that Flora Lugard was an Irish Protestant, although 'not a Christian' (Trollope 1988: 135) and was similar to the Victoria League of which Lugard was a founder member.

As Riedi says (2002: 572), the Victoria League was an imperialist propaganda organization, creating links with 'Greater Britain' in ways that could be seen as legitimate extensions to women's 'approved domestic sphere'. Edith Lyttelton (1917: 280) explained that its aim was 'to promote a greater understanding between the people of Great Britain and the Colonies'. Members organized hospitality for visiting colonials and reception of emigrants abroad; during the Boer War they evinced patriotic humanitarianism by organizing charity for victims, including relief for loyalist refugees, and tending war graves. However, the League presented itself in deliberately unassertive terms – to do otherwise would have challenged the man's world of Empire. Like other women's imperialist emigration organizations to which most members of the League's executive belonged, (such as the Girls' Friendly Society whose first love was the Empire), the League was based on upper and middle-class women's friendship networks, forming part of their politics and, as Bush shows (2001a: 5), signifying 'realization and use of existing power structures as one of the means through which they could gain agency'. Such structures involved caring power. However, the actions and commitments of individual members were not identical to those of the Victoria League as an institution; for example, they belonged to women's organizations of different political parties and there were individual differences over imperial controversies. They were located in a complex historical situation, therefore 'Western women who took part in the British colonial enterprises [were] both resistant to and complicitous with men's policies and activities', individually and collectively (Callaway in Chaudhuri & Strobel 1992: 79–80). This extended to acceptance of, or resistance to, some of the expectations of gender and the issue of women's suffrage. For anti-suffragists like Lady Jersey, Britain's imperial role was the key reason for not having the vote; Mrs Humphrey Ward, who was one of those responsible for organizing opposition, considered voting inappropriate to woman's divinely ordained separate role; voting would 'destroy the family and endanger the progress of the race' (Burton 1991: 56–7). Nonetheless, anti-suffragists dealt with women's issues: both Violet Markham and Mary Ward had undertaken 'scientific charity' and campaigned against sweated trades.

Fletcher (2000: xviii–xix) realized part of what Swanwick had pointed out, that suffrage was a social movement and a political discourse. Transnational forms of suffragism bore the marks of hierarchy as well as prefiguring what is now known as 'internationalism' and this presents 'intriguing links between Victorian discourses of religious humanitarianism and interwar internationalism'. Antoinette Burton (1991: 48, 56–7) has shown that imperialism and feminism were not mutually exclusive. However, although imperialism advanced during the nineteenth and twentieth centuries, so did resistance. This surfaced among Quakers, such as in the strongly anti-imperialist Bright-Priestman-Clark family; it pleased Helen Bright Clark at a lunch for Campbell Bannerman in 1901 that the one imperialist speaker was received very coolly (Holton 2007: 203).

Nevertheless, imperial identification allowed British suffragists to link the preservation of British imperial rule to arguments for female emancipation and to propose an imperialism based on feminine values and oriented toward peace. As Julia Bush (2001a: 4) argues, since approximately half the leading women imperialists were suffragists, this demonstrates compatibility in this period between the Victoria League's practical imperialism and the suffragism of some of its members, despite the obvious tension between them concerning hierarchy. Only a few contemporary women associated imperial domination abroad with gender and class inequalities at home. Founder members like Meriel Talbot and Millicent Garrett Fawcett were two examples of Victoria League suffragist imperialists. Fawcett endorsed empire as a paternal responsibility within which women could show their fitness for citizenship by supporting it in its wars, yet remain within the socially acceptable feminine role of social reform, which for suffragists like her, necessitated gaining the vote. Victoria League members also accepted the method of using social means to political ends in the manner of the great nineteenth-century hostesses but across the 'imagined community' of Empire. Using the gendered language of 'home' helped to legitimize the Victoria League women's imperial activism: extending the traditional role of hostess became a route into the masculine domain of empire politics. Providing hospitality was part of their gender role; organizing this for Belgian refugees extended it vertically into a different class and out of the Empire towards internationalism.

Edith Lyttelton was a member of the intellectual 'advanced' group known as the 'Souls'. Oliver Lyttelton (Chandos 1968: 59) wrote that his mother's life was restricted to social events up to his father's death in 1913. This is evidently incorrect. She was President of the National Union of Women Workers, an opponent of sweated labour and founding member of the Personal Service Association. What Bush (2001b) calls her 'disguised autobiography' in the form of her husband's biography, indicates worry about prostitution and the white slave trade as well as Home Rule. She wrote plays on these subjects. Suffrage work spread to a wide range of philanthropic, educational and other social causes and these surfaced in

Edith's work at the League of Nations in the interwar period. If Chandos perceived his mother's life as primarily social, it merely confirms that for women of the social elite, social and political were intertwined; in fact, Edith frequently needed to go away alone to recuperate from exhaustion, an indication of the tension between the role of a political 'new' woman, and her identity of wife and mother.

Through family and friendship these women were connected to the highest levels of government and Cabinet. Therefore they were positioned *within* this powerful arena, not excluded or disempowered. Politicians' wives needed to be politically well-informed and Edith Lyttelton's frequent presence in the House of Commons gallery was only part of her participation in her husband's political life. When he was ill she did his constituency rounds, speaking on public platforms on his behalf. Alfred Lyttelton was strongly influenced by Edith over women's suffrage. In May 1910 (WL. 9/01/0824) she wrote to the NUWSS, asking for copies of Fawcett's speeches and any other useful literature as material for Alfred whom she hoped 'may speak in debate next week'; adding, 'he is a tepid supporter but still a supporter'. With Lord Lytton and Lords Robert and Hugh Cecil, he supported the cause in Parliament until his death. Edith and Alfred were both supporters of Lord Milner and the Boer War and Edith was inspired by South African loyalist Dorothea Fairbridge to found the Victoria League on their return from South Africa.

The Victoria League's first meeting was on 21 May 1901 at 10 Downing Street at the invitation of Alice Balfour, the Prime Minister's sister. There were 25 women present including Lady Jersey, Lady Hilda Brodrick (wife of the Under Secretary at the Foreign Office) and Maud Selborne, a suffragist who thought that differences of opinion on suffrage should not prevent civilized friendship. Many of these first members had South African connections and other relief work experience significant to the foundation of the WRC. Violet Markham, who joined in 1904, had experience of social work through running a Settlement in Chesterfield, was influenced by the Quaker Hilda Cashmore and was to be involved in Save the Children work. In 1899 she visited South Africa where she met Milner and Rhodes. During the Boer War the class conscious and near-atheist Violet Cecil had devoted some part of every day to receiving refugees at the railway station and worked for the Cape Town refugees committee. These Victoria League women were about to become involved in Great War relief.

Quakers and the Boer War

In the same way that the WRC's refugee work was related to the Boer War *via* the Victoria League, so the Great War FWVRC was rooted in previous relief. Quakers had contributed to famine relief in Ireland in the 1840s and 1850s (Brayshaw 1921: 330).They worked in France from 1870 to 1875, during and after the Franco-Prussian War, when they built up ruined villages and towns and set farmers and others in a position to resume their businesses. This was carried out to an even greater extent in the Boer War for which relief in the Crimea and the Bulgarian insurrection against the Turks in April 1876 provided experience. In November 1899 Albert Prust of Launceston, Cornwall, suggested a relief fund for Afrikaner non-combatants of the Boer War and a proposal was made of creating a South African War Victims Fund. There were worries that fund-raising methods too often appealed to martial instincts, whether helping everyone regardless of nationality would aid combatants, and anxieties about what effects this would have if Quakers were thought to be materially aiding the nation's enemies. Additional qualms were that Friends had no experience of such service when Britain was one of the belligerents and where all parties in the field would have furnished fighters, voluntarily or under pressure.

Quakers tried to find out about conditions in South Africa through Joshua and Isabella Rowntree's visit in December 1900 and sent out Frances Taylor and Anna Hogg with Helen B. Harris on 4 May 1901. However, Emily Hobhouse, an Anglican with many Quaker friends, who was supported by the Quaker Sir Edward Fry and the Clark family at Street, had moved more quickly, having already set up her South African Women's and Children's Distress Fund, and left on the same ship to begin work. While in the Cape Emily met Jan Smuts and stayed with him in Pretoria (Brian Roberts 1991: 266), remaining in contact with him for most of her life. Hewison says (1989: 237, 189) their friendship accelerated his career as leader of his people. However, this was in the future, and now Dorothea

Fairbridge, the spokesperson for the Guild of Loyal Women of South Africa, reported Emily Hobhouse to the Governor for stirring up discontent among 'otherwise contented and grateful Boer women' in the camps. Following her revelations about the conditions, Emily was hounded by the British authorities and refused entry to South Africa. However:

> in claiming the right to define her role as a British humanitarian abroad, she indirectly advanced the position of women within government by prompting the Commission of Inquiry into the camps ... Her involvement illustrates how a role could be carved out for women *as* women, within war and international politics. (Brown 2003: 171)

Despite anxieties, the Friends' South African War Victims Fund was formed in November 1901. They considered the Boer War the inevitable culmination of misplaced national values although this did not mean an abandonment of imperialism (Rempel 1975: 76). Nonetheless, the Boer War moved some Quakers towards social Liberalism and the Labour movement. However, there was little unity among so-called pro-Boers because they opposed the war from different bases, including anti-semitism, but they became aware that engaging in well-publicized relief work, and by attacking the policies of farm burning and concentration camps, they were criticising the Government. Helping non-combatants was understood as forming part of their peace testimony. In a turnabout of national values, many pro-Boers held high office after the war, including Lloyd George, George Burns and Ramsay MacDonald. Such reversal of fortune was to be repeated after the Great War.

In July, two months after the Victoria League's foundation, Mrs Fawcett was commissioned by the War Office to head a Ladies' Commission to inspect the Boer camps in an attempt to discredit Emily Hobhouse's scathing attack on conditions; more adult Boers had died in camps than in battle and over four times as many children. It is significant that a *Ladies'* Commission was sent, and that a suffragist was chosen to lead it; Millicent Fawcett had been a member of suffrage societies since 1867 but was an establishment figure, well known as a social worker (Brown 2008: 77). This drew women into the male sphere of foreign politics in a role than emphasized women's responsibility for other women. It was a tactical choice by the Government. The Ladies' Commission could not criticize too fiercely because this would be disloyal.

Mrs Fawcett was a friend of Lord and Lady Courtney, Emily Hobhouse's uncle and aunt and closest friends, but disagreed with them over the Boer War (Hewison 1989: 189). Lady Kate Courtney was a founder of the South African Conciliation Committee, founded by Quakers and other Liberals, to educate the British public about the facts of the Boer War. In June 1901, the death rate at Bloemfontein was reported in *The Friend* as 383 per 1,000, but Flora Lugard accepted the excuse that this was due to heat, ignoring, or unaware that such a mortality rate did not apply when the refugees were living in their own homes in the same temperatures. The Ladies' Commission left Britain in August and their ambiguous report, reflecting differences of opinion among members, was published in November, citing causes for the mortality rate as lack of water and no sanitation, poor administration and misdemeanours by the Boer women, the latter indicating views of upper-class women that poverty and disease were linked with bad morals. Despite Mrs Fawcett's connection with Emily Hobhouse, the Ladies declined to meet Emily who thought their report superficial. When their reports were first issued Emily Hobhouse and Joshua Rowntree were both denounced as unpatriotic. As Brown states (2003: 170, 176):

> It was presented as not only an imperial problem, but also an international one, because of the Afrikaners' close ties with the Netherlands. Both Hobhouse and Fawcett were therefore drawn directly into the masculine sphere of foreign politics.

Nonetheless, Joshua Rowntree's description of conditions in the camps confirmed Emily's report and was effectively quoted in Parliament on 17 June 1901. Friends and others were then allowed to distribute clothing, food and medicine in the camps (Hirst 1923: 485). Black refugees were excluded from help in the Boer camps because it was feared bringing them into the scheme would prejudice the chances of obtaining help for the others, and relief workers' racial prejudices are clear from the records.

In the early months of 1902, Flora Lugard, who deplored the Boer War but did not believe the ugly stories of concentration camp brutality, spent an 'interesting morning' visiting an 'admirably organized' and 'much abused' camp containing 7,000 refugees outside Bloemfontein.

Devotion to Empire blinded some to realities but the Government had publicly acknowledged women's responsibility for refugees and for interned women and children. Emily Hobhouse wound up her Fund in November 1904 at the same time launching the Boer Home Industries scheme in the home of her aunt, then Mrs Leonard Courtney. It included people later linked with Great War relief. For example, Margaret Clark, John Bright's grand-daughter, helped her open her first spinning and weaving school at Philippolis in March 1903 and in 1907 Ruth, Emily's friend and the youngest daughter of Lady Mariabella and Sir Edward Fry, was appointed Treasurer of her Boer Industries scheme. Margaret and Emily travelled home with General Smuts in November 1905; Smuts became a welcome friend to the Clark family. Hewison says (1989: 237) they had long connections with South Africa, and helped to provide boots and shoes for children in the camps. Emily Hobhouse's friendship networks are evidently of considerable significance.

Underlying these events was a contest between two definitions of patriotism, Millicent Fawcett's approximating to the discourse of 'my country, right or wrong'. In contrast, Emily Hobhouse was expressing a newer form, where 'my country' should take a moral stand on humanitarian internationalism (Hamilton 1944: 74) and where 'Patriotism is the power to be ashamed of your country'. Although it appears Fawcett's form 'won', there was, however, a flood of Victoria League initiatives linked to South Africa and funds were set up to aid British refugees and Dutch women and children in the camps. This was due largely to Emily Hobhouse's attempts to publicize conditions. Having seen St John Brodrick, one of the Lyttelton circle, on 4 June and sending him her recommendations for improvements in conditions, he subsequently gave permission for a Victoria League appeal. Hobhouse was eventually vindicated and her ashes are buried at the foot of the National Memorial at Bloemfontein. She is valued in South Africa, but comparatively unknown in Britain.

Foundation and work of the War Refugees Committee

In addition to heading the Ladies' Commission, Millicent Fawcett was much involved with Great War relief of various types, but was not directly involved with the WRC, but other Victoria League members were. These included its President, Lady Jersey, who was on the WRC's General Committee; Violet Cecil, who had lobbied on the humanitarian needs of refugees and wounded soldiers in the Boer War and would marry Lord Milner in 1921; Lady Emmott was on the WRC's Executive; Meriel Talbot, Alfred Lyttelton's sister, former Honorary Secretary of the Lambeth Charity Organization Society (COS), was Secretary of the Victoria League, and had visited Milner; during the Great War she became Chief Women Inspector at the Ministry of Agriculture, where Edith Lyttelton joined her as Deputy Director in May 1917. During that year Edith Lyttelton was made a DBE and in 1929 a GBE in recognition of her many public services. She was also awarded the *Medaille de la Reine Elisabeth* for her work for Belgian refugees.

The Victoria League's ethos regarding class, devotion to the Empire and humanitarian instinct united its members, especially where the needs of women and children were affected and these became part of the founding principle of the WRC. It is not surprising, therefore, that the WRC organization bears striking resemblance to that of the Victoria League. The fact that women of different religious and political persuasions used their Boer War experience to help Belgian refugees cannot be ignored. The influence of women's politics and experience of Boer War relief, however contradictory, was central to Belgian refugee relief. Helping Boer women and children in the camps had stigmatized women as pro-Boer and unpatriotic, but aiding Belgian refugees was patriotic, publicly approved of on an international stage, and involved unprecedented numbers of refugees and of rescuers.

The WRC inevitably reflected the gender, political and cultural divisions and constructions in British society both in its constitution and in the manner in which refugees were helped, with class being the prime determinant. The acceptance of Dorothy Gladstone's offer of her husband's help on the WRC reflects not only the League's realization that exclusion of men was 'tactically unwise' but also the significance of this family network. Lord Herbert Gladstone provided another South African connection: he had been Governor-General of the Union of South Africa. However, for some of the WRC workers, Gladstone's presence was a mixed blessing. When he became Treasurer it was the cue for men to take charge. The WRC therefore started as an inspirational idea by the imperialist Lady Lugard, being both political and humanitarian in its concept as her involvement in and use of the Ulster Volunteer Force refugee administration shows. Those devoted to the British Empire assisted Belgian refugees out of a mixture of patriotism, humanitarianism and the need to show the benefits of the British Empire within the hierarchy of Empires, with Britannia coming to the rescue of a smaller imperial nation in trouble.

Flora Lugard was a woman with initiative, working to get a powerful organization started about two weeks prior to the actual Committee beginning work on 24 August, but she was eased out of the work and then almost written out of its record by Gladstone. Nevertheless, as McLaren says (1917: 135) she was responsible for a 'truly great service ... She stands out amongst the throng of splendid volunteers in the service of Belgium.' Her first arrangements for the care of Belgian refugees began on 17 August when, recognizing the value of transferring the Ulster organization for the use of Belgian refugees, she telegraphed Captain Craig, Ulster Unionist leader and organizer of Ulster Relief, asking him if he would let her use the hospitality lists and administrative set-up, including registration forms, transport and accommodation arrangements. In 24 hours she had preliminary arrangements to evacuate and then re-home Belgian refugees. Since they were predominantly Roman Catholic she approached Cardinal Bourne to ascertain how many secure homes could be placed at the refugees' disposal. Monsignor Bidwell received her and agreed that if the Government viewed her scheme favourably, the Catholic authorities would help. This was the first step towards official recognition by the Government of the WRC as central responsible authority for refugee care. On Saturday, 22 August, prior to the formation of the Committee, she was informed by Mr Reyntiens and Mr Wintour of the Board of Trade that the Admiralty had promised transport to bring over refugees on the following Monday. This implies early government involvement and already quite large numbers of refugees arriving in Britain, probably by the normal ferries. When questioned as to numbers, Reyntiens said anything from 100 to 1,000 and told her it was up to her to deal with their reception. That evening, Edith Lyttelton and Flora Lugard summoned Miss Ada Streeter of the CWL to an information conference and she then became responsible for the central organization of the CWL's work for Belgian refugees as London Organizer, working from offices in Victoria Street. She also served on the WRC Allocation Committee. Mrs James Hope, the CWL President, was on the WRC Executive, indicating the close co-operation it sought with the Catholic community through its women.

According to Edith Lyttelton's account of these events (IWM. Belgium 2/2.14), 'that first weekend, about a Thursday', Flora Lugard attended the meeting held in Lady Emmott's house for Lady Gladstone's working party. After the meeting Flora Lugard asked her if she knew that Reyntiens had 'permission to take a ship over to Belgium and bring off the women and children who are flying before the Germans'. Lugard said she proposed to put the Ulster Refugee organization at the disposal of the Belgian Minister the Comte de Lalaing, and Sir Edward Grey whom she had already seen.

The LGB signified their approval and the Foreign Office arranged an interview for Lugard with the Comte de Lalaing, to request him to approach the Belgian Government to accept the proposal. Edith Lyttelton recorded that he was 'frightened by our vehemence'. Cahalan (1982: 197) scathingly refers to such women as being 'self-willed' failing to recognize that assertiveness was necessary to get men to act or make decisions. The authorities agreed to make the scheme known and to direct refugees to Ostend. They also called on Sir James Dunlop Smith at the India Office, another Victoria League member, who helped to obtain 49 St George's Road, the first house offered for refugees. Between Saturday 22 and Monday 24 August a committee was formed. Flora Lugard credited Edith Lyttelton for this, and for getting Lord Hugh Cecil as Chairman and Lord Gladstone as Treasurer.

To get Catholics well represented they secured Monsignor Bidwell, Lalaing and the Duke of Norfolk, who then withdrew to run his own Committee. Mr F. Norie-Miller, the General Manager of the General Accident Fire and Life Assurance Corporation Ltd, who was one of those employers who actively encouraged staff to join up, offered three small offices free of charge and after meeting there on Sunday, the Headquarters of the WRC was established at General Buildings, Aldwych, with a male secretary and a typist. The Victoria League women had left publicity in the hands of male members and for this reason they contacted Mr (later Sir) Herbert Morgan. He sketched the diagram of an organization and dictated an appeal to the Press to the typist he brought with him. A name for the Committee was chosen and the appeal sent to the papers on Sunday night, 23 August; on the Monday their letter appeared.

As a result they received offers of hospitality for 100,000 refugees during the first two weeks, not all of it appropriate. Gladstone unfairly blamed this on Flora Lugard's inefficiency. He later criticized her for being too generous with government funds and keeping the better class refugees in idleness, refusing to assume responsibility for her expenditure so that the LGB took it on instead. He also criticized Lady Emmott's contract for £7,000 for boots made by a swindler. The Clothing Department was therefore taken over by the LGB which caught the swindler but spent a further £1,000 on prosecuting him. Work began on Monday morning, 24 August although the Committee did not meet until the following day. The offices were almost entirely without furniture, and as the electric light was not working, they operated by candlelight.

In the first five days the WRC received 15,000 letters and on the fifth day 1,200 callers offered help. To start with, the WRC had far more helpers than refugees, as did other Committees. On 31 August Miss Wolsely (WL. LSWS 371/1 VV/71) wrote to the LSWS:

> I found my services were not required. In fact it seems to me that there are millions of women longing to do something and there is nothing for them to do. It is a pity there are so many women.

About 100 refugees arrived on the first day and were temporarily housed in St George's Road, where the front room was set aside for registration. The printed forms for the Ulster organization were arranged on one long table, and voluntary clerks took down the names. Miss A.M. Mercer (IWM. Belgium 2.4/4), a member of LSWS, was approached by Mrs Gilbert Samuel on behalf of Mrs Lyttelton and helped the WRC from that weekend. She went first to St George's Road, where Mrs Lyttelton, Lady Gladstone and Miss Bidwell were at work, with registration being done by Miss Strachey, Miss Boyd and other members of the London Society. One Sunday in August Miss Mercer was sent to Oxford House, Bethnal Green, which had offered to take in 50 refugees temporarily, but who had instead received 50 from St George's Road and 50 direct from the Aldwych. Such refuges were only intended to be used for the first three to five days until alternative accommodation was found, but this was impossible when numbers became too vast. Camberwell Council gave them the use of Dulwich Baths which had been prepared as a hospital for wounded soldiers, and Battersea followed their example. These, plus private offers in the first few days meant they had about 200 beds available. However, although about 250 refugees arrived between Monday and Wednesday, Reyntiens' shipload did not materialize.

On Wednesday 26 August at 7.30 p.m., just as they were leaving, they received a telegram announcing that 1,000 refugees were arriving in Folkestone and 500 would need help in London; this was the Reyntiens shipload. The Army and Navy Stores' empty shirt factory was available and Mrs Walter Cave stayed up all night, directing the conversion of the premises into a hostel for 250 people. Reyntiens had spoken of women and children but no-one had considered the likelihood of pregnant women arriving. They were also unprepared for men. Edith Lyttelton (IWM. Belgium 2.2/14) wrote:

> What we should have done without the ready made VAD organization I cannot imagine. The very first Company we had was officered by Mrs (now Dame) Katherine Furze, and Mrs (now Dame) Rachel Crowdy who at that time were desperately struggling to get their organization used.

The VADs, whose services had been refused by the War Office, 'arrived disciplined, silent, efficient'. They met refugees at stations and took over the staffing of 49 St George's Road and other hostels. Miss Mercer then took over St Giles, Endell Street, a former workhouse where the main difficulty was to avoid friction between WRC workers and the Metropolitan

Asylums Board staff who were not used to having outsiders in their premises. St Giles accommodated 500 to 700 comfortably, and frequently in those early days 1,000 would sleep there. One day 200 fishermen's wives arrived. Their menfolk had dropped them at the nearest point while they took their boats to Cardiff and Swansea because they knew those ports, and Miss Mercer was responsible for accommodating the women and children for a night or so and then arranging to get them all to Cardiff. They also had refugees who were not strictly Belgians and were therefore difficult to accommodate elsewhere as hospitality was only offered to the Belgians. She remembered a young Turk whom no-one would help. This was largely due to fear as Turks were considered exemplars of barbarism, ogres used to frighten children at night. Their fierceness was legendary and people were uncertain about giving hospitality to someone of that nationality. In another instance fear was linked with colour prejudice. Miss Mercer described a tragic little family, a Belgian mother, a little daughter and the father a 'full blooded West Indian negro' who was a British subject. Directly people saw the husband, despite his respectability, they 'jibbed' and would have nothing to do with them, black skins being equated with savagery and a lower position on the evolutionary scale. Finally the Moravian community took them on. There were also 18 Swiss gipsies from Ticino who lived at St George's for over six weeks. The men had musical instruments and collected money by playing in the streets with placards on their backs 'We are Belgian Refugees', to the horror of the other refugees who thereby displayed their class and race prejudices. Eventually they got rooms and proposed to support themselves. St Giles closed in November and was then used as a military hospital, run by Dr Louise Garrett Anderson.

Government invitation to Belgian refugees

News of the formation of the WRC travelled quickly across the Channel and on 28 August Sir Francis Villiers, British ambassador to Belgium, sent telegrams to the Home Office from Antwerp trying to make contact and, in view of the ARA, to find out which ports could be used for landing about 2,000 refugees. Home Secretary McKenna's reply was evasive (PRO. HO

45/10737/1). Although they should be 'shown friendliness', he doubted whether it was really to their advantage to come to England, because large numbers could be an embarrassment to the host country. The Government regarded refugees as a potential danger and possible financial burden. It is doubtful this attitude really changed even when, after the British retreat from Mons, the President of the LGB, Herbert Samuel, announced on 9 September in Parliament that the Government had formally invited the Belgians to come to the UK to receive the hospitality of the nation. Despite this, the Government did not intend to take responsibility. The use of the terms 'hospitality' and 'guests of the nation' was intended to rally philanthropy and instigate a manifestation of patriotism, whereas 'relief' would have totally different connotations of class and provision, harking back to the COS's judgmental stance in the last decades of the previous century (Prochaska 1980: 8). This, together with the concept of the Belgians as 'heroes', put the refugees and the British philanthropic community in a false position. Further, it indicates that the invitation was a political move towards the Belgians, not a primarily humanitarian one. The Government undertook to make provision for temporary reception on landing, and food and shelter until the refugee was allocated hospitality. It would also pay for transport but no further expense was to be incurred. The contrast between the official welcome and the limitations imposed by the ARA shows that Governmental obsession with spies over-rode any worry about the effects of the Act on hospitality and public attitudes, in fact underlining ambivalent feelings towards refugees.

Cahalan (1982: 77) says that in making the announcement Herbert Samuel wrongly implied that the LGB had been co-operating with the WRC from the start. However, the LGB was involved with refugees very early in August, prior to the formation of the WRC. Mrs Henry at Tilbury witnessed LGB workers taking refugees off the boats that month. Furthermore, at the NUWSS Executive Committee meeting of 6 August, Kathleen Courtney expressed unease that the LGB was training young men to meet refugees although they had trained nurses, certificated mid-wives or sanitary inspectors on their staff. This was unsatisfactory since the majority of refugees were women and it was decided that Miss Courtney should write to Lord Lytton, a suffrage supporter, to make representations to the

LGB. This confirms that during the first week of August more refugees were arriving than most sources reveal while the communications between Lugard and Reyntiens indicate co-operation between the WRC and the LGB at the earliest time possible.

Apparently, the Prime Minister's decision that the LGB should be responsible for refugees puzzled its President, the Rt Hon. Herbert Samuel, and reasons remain obscure. Nonetheless, historically the LGB was the logical choice. On its formation in 1871 it had been involved with the COS in a joint crusade to eliminate extravagant outdoor relief. This involved thoroughly investigating and categorizing applicants as deserving or undeserving, and attempting to make them the responsibility of other family members or neighbours. Although COS influence was waning by the Great War, there are striking similarities between its ideology and practice and that of the LGB's refugee support. Despite the loosening of the COS/LGB link by Chamberlain it was a department with experience of what became recognized as 'cold charity' based on classical economic doctrines and could be relied on not to get involved in profligate relief of the refugees (Humphreys 1995: 160) at a time when financing the war was the priority. The decision to involve the LGB was also linked to public health, for which it had responsibility. Between 9 September and 9 October 200,000 refugees entered Britain.

Now, women's traditional caring duties were emphasized; indeed, the Government officially encouraged women to provide succour and called on their organizations to help. The feminized 'social' that had arisen from the nineteenth-century tradition of 'womanized' philanthropic care expanded to include refugees within Britain; the boundaries of women's gender role within the separate spheres ideology therefore became blurred and permeable. Upper- and middle-class women were traditionally the dispensers of charity that had by this time become a status symbol for both giver and recipient, but women did not count as citizens, being unenfranchised. Legally, they were not part of 'the nation' giving hospitality.

By September the WRC was changing into a vast organization operating with a number of departments, offers of hospitality being received in such numbers that professional indexers were called in. Lady Gladstone, Edith Lyttelton and Mrs Gilbert Samuel initially supervised Department

Alpha 2, Allocation to Hospitality. Lyttelton (IWM. Belgium 2.2/14) supervised the interviewing of refugees on arrival and getting hospitality from private homes. Despite this, she said she had little contact with refugees, and regretted it. However, she made a friend of one young woman, Marte Verbist, who had been raped. Undecided whether to have an abortion or have the baby taken away at birth, the Belgian doctor told her she was no true patriot if she kept it. When the baby, a boy named Albert, became seriously ill, Lyttelton helped care for it in its dying hours. In 1919 she went to Brussels and visited Marte whose father had died and whose fiancé, traumatized by his war experiences, had deserted her. This young woman's life was one of thousands devastated by war.

Edith Lyttelton's WRC office opened out of the refugee centre at the Rink, a huge disused corrugated iron hall, built on a piece of waste land, almost next door to General Buildings. However, allocation was being done at two offices and people had different ideas how it should be dealt with; also hostels were springing up in the suburbs and allocators had to visit them. Edith Lyttelton, who was in charge of hostels and flats, thought standardisation was essential and drew up a paper for Lord Gladstone which resulted in her method being adopted. She was alarmed by the waste of food at the Rink and suggested the refugees pay for it. Gladstone, who soon styled himself Director of the WRC, did not see the waste and was reluctant, but nevertheless her suggestion resulted in immediate savings. Other successes included a scheme to assist refugees with rents and getting the nearest Labour Exchange to set up a Table in the Rink where men willing to work could register. Gladstone disapproved because she did not seek his permission which she judged probably would not have been given. Edith Lyttelton was an able administrator but Gladstone wanted to be in total control. He liked women, but in their subordinate place. For example, on 31 March 1916 he declined to attend an interview with Walter Long and Lady Lugard who thought the WRC had violated an agreement made with her in October. She thought refugees were not properly treated by the Aldwych Committee and said there had been scandals in connection with their treatment. Gladstone wrote (PRO. MH 8/6) 'To tell the truth I think I was best away from the Conference because I feel so strongly and indignantly against the lady that I might have exploded, and to no good purpose.' Furthermore, according to Dobbie (1979: 35) he was not beyond striking a woman. At a suffragette demonstration at Lympne on 5 September 1909 he had given Jessie Kenney 'a nasty blow on the chest'. It was Gladstone who ordered suffragists to be force-fed when in 1909 they began hunger strikes on a significant scale. He wrote to Emily Hobhouse on 9 November 1909:

> My duty is unpleasant & distasteful enough, but that is no reason why I shd. [sic] shirk it ... forcible feeding is not punishment. To let women starve wd not only be inhuman but in the event of death wd expose all concerned to a charge of manslaughter. (Matthew. Gladstone: DNB)

Obviously indifferent to this form of physical violence, when told in Parliament no civilized country treated political prisoners as he was doing, he said other countries should follow Britain. Born in 1854, his attitudes towards women, the Empire and racial hierarchy were typical of his generation and class but were partly responsible for the decline of Liberalism. Although he reputedly became a women's suffrage supporter, he rightly believed that their enfranchisement would only be settled by a coalition government. From 1918, with the Belgians returning to their homeland and the closing of the WRC, Gladstone, needing new outlets, gave his support to the LNU.

The WRC therefore grew from an extension of women's Empire-orientated domestic sphere into a 'miniature Government of a miniature state with all the functions well defined'. In January 1915, when the Government began making grants to refugees, the WRC had a General Committee of 108 men and women, the Chairman was Princess Christian of Schleswig-Holstein; Patrons were Paul Cambon, French ambassador; Count Beckendorff, Russian ambassador and Paul Hymans of Belgium. The Executive Committee of 27 was chaired by Lord Hugh Cecil with a further Managing Committee of nine. In mid-1916 there were still 400 staff at Aldwych. Such a vast organization required huge amounts of money as many of the workers could no longer exist without pay. In November 1915, the Government took over paying the WRC workers, and inevitably volunteer numbers gradually fell. Yet despite this, in July 1916 (IWM.

Belgium 1 8/4) Gladstone told Walter Long, President of the LGB, that 'to this day the House of Commons is in complete ignorance of the work of the War Refugees Committee and its relations with the Government'. This puts into perspective the motion of gratitude passed to Belgium on 27 August by the House of Commons and the fulsome parliamentary speeches extolling 'the heroic resistance' of the 'gallant' Belgians, and the 'sympathy' and 'admiration' felt for them.

The WRC incorporated the hierarchy of empire, including that of gender. After the War Lady Lyttelton termed Gladstone its 'dictator'. She said that Aldwych was difficult:

> a place ... where inefficiency was patent at once, and in the struggle for supremacy in direction, nothing but real ability could survive. I do not think any record was kept of the people who in one way or another were eliminated. Lord Gladstone formally constituted himself head of the whole organization, and directed it with great ability. (IWM. Belgium 2.2/14)

He was known in his family for his irritability and some personality clashes appear gender-specific. Cahalan says Lady Lugard 'abandoned' the WRC to found her Hospitality Committee for better class refugees (1982 197). However, it is clear she was pushed out. Lord Lytton and Lady Lyttelton also left, although the latter remained on the Executive Committee till its dissolution.

Aliens Restriction Act, spies and prohibited areas

Despite the Government's invitation, when refugees arrived in the UK a legal barrier in the form of the ARA had been erected against them. It was promulgated by Reginald McKenna of 'Cat and Mouse' fame but had been prepared in 1910 by a sub-committee on espionage chaired by Winston Churchill under the Committee for Imperial Defence. In rushing it through all its stages and publishing it as an Order-in-Council (which did not require Parliamentary debate), McKenna announced that 21 spies had been arrested during the previous 24 hours, thereby emphasizing the Government's alarm and susceptibility to panic. The treatment of Great War aliens was firmly based on fears of espionage, xenophobia and misogyny. The Security Service thought women spies were 'numerous' especially if Swiss, Dutch, Scandinavian or Belgian. Their perfume was thought to conceal invisible ink, and clothing seams presumed to hide messages; Belgian refugees were particularly suspected. In fact, though there may have been more, and women were implicated, only eleven men were shot as spies. The Act required all foreign nationals to register with police and allowed for their deportation.

The 1914 Act had been preceeded by the Aliens Act of 1905, which had been designed to restrict entry of immigrant Jews who were presumed responsible for increases in unemployment, sweating and racial decline; Jews were not seen as refugees, therefore people had to prove their case before being given asylum. This Act, which had been passed despite the Liberals' attempts to prevent it since Akers-Douglas had introduced his 1904 Aliens Bill, confirmed that 'aliens were problematic' and resulted in an increase in anti-alienism. The Liberal Government, with Herbert Gladstone as Home Secretary, refused to endorse it but nonetheless the work of its administrator, John Pedder, led to a fall in the number of Jews entering Britain; between 1906 and 1910 over 5,000 aliens were refused permission to land at the 14 approved ports. The Act established means whereby steerage passengers, but not the better off, could be inspected and thereby confirmed discrimination against poverty and Jews. Deconstruction of the term 'refugee' was therefore undertaken for economic and racial reasons and began the process of creating later categories such as 'asylum seeker' or 'economic migrant'. Lloyd George extended the ARA through Orders-in-Council and there were 27 war-time amendments, some specifically directed at Belgian refugees. The Belgian 'guests' once accepted were expected to stay for a very limited period, and then return to their own country. The authorities recognized that, even if initially welcomed, they may become burdensome as the war increased the economic difficulties of the host nation, thereby also increasing the psychological strain for hosts and guests and hampering the war effort. As the ARA demonstrated, refugees were still aliens; their labour was at first forbidden and then controlled; they needed to be registered and counted; they were all, especially Jews, thought to be a security risk.

Although Cahalan (1982: 95) argues that the links between the two Acts are tenuous, the 1914 Act strengthened the 1905 Act, controlling entry of refugees by facilitating 'sifting' at Calais and elsewhere. Sifting was acceptance or rejection by class, religion and ethnicity. As Foucault theorizes, dividing practices enabled the identification of different categories such as social classes and facilitated the exclusion of Jews. This process enabled authorities to categorize people as 'deserving' because they were from devastated areas or had private means, which was taken to imply the necessary good character and class.

Significantly, the ARA meant that aliens could be required 'to reside and remain within certain places or districts'; they could also be prohibited from 'residing or remaining in any areas specified in the Order' (Aliens Restriction Act, 1914, section 1 [d] and [e]). This severely limited the areas in which Belgians could be given accommodation, making about a third of Britain prohibited to aliens, whether allies or enemies. Prohibited areas became almost as militarily sensitive as ports. The restricted areas were settled after full discussion between all the Authorities concerned, naval, military, Home Office and Police, and in the first instance they were confined mainly to those parts of the East Coast where it was thought necessary to take immediate precautions. The authorities had thought of having any place within 10 miles of the coast made into a prohibited area but the War Office subsequently agreed it was better to specify precise locations. This gave them licence, as on 21 October, to prohibit whole counties such as Sussex, Essex and Norfolk and, as the writer of a post-card to the LSWS informed them, 'roughly 20 miles round the coast from Northumberland to the Devonshire-Dorset borders' (WL. LSWS 371.2).

There was disagreement at high level about implementation of the ARAs. On 18 October Sir William Graham Greene, Secretary to the Admiralty, told the Home Office to get refugees out of prohibited areas as soon as possible, but a letter from the Home Office to Sir H.C. Monro, Secretary of the LGB, said that 'established refugees need not be disturbed', but that some areas should be thinned out, with the Chief Constable deciding 'grey areas'. Inevitably, interpretation of the law became an individual matter and the Chief Constable at Bodmin was among those who sought clarification. However, the Government could not be unmindful that they had invited the nation's guests and some amendments to the ARA were intended partially to ease the problem of accommodation by reducing the size of the prohibited areas.

Numbers – registration

By 28 September the Belgians, who like the British kept no official register, estimated that between 7,500 and 8,000 refugees had left for Britain, but these figures did not tally with British estimates. By 13 October over 100,000 Belgians were in Great Britain. Seven days later, Folkestone had about 15,000 refugees who were likely to remain there all winter, so the women members of the Folkestone War Refugee Committee with whom rested the main responsibility of caring for these people, therefore appealed in *The Times* for funds.

Nevertheless, numbers could not be known unless the refugees were registered. Numbers were not merely a subject of academic interest. There was the question of what would happen if the philanthropic community failed to cope because they could no longer afford to raise money or provide accommodation. In such circumstances the Government would have to become further involved. The Police wanted to know how many refugees there were in each area to make the work of surveillance easier. There was also the matter of eventual repatriation and the logistics of getting them home. Furthermore, the Belgian authorities wanted to know how many of their people had accepted the British invitation and Lalaing prompted closer control by requesting Sir Edward Grey for official registration. The LGB then sent a circular to Local Committees, asking for forms to be completed, including by those who had gone into private hospitality, with the revealing phrase 'if they can be traced'. But most refugees had already registered three or four times. On 23 October de Jastrzebski, the official put in charge of registration by Bernard Mallet, the Registrar-General, began work, meaning that several weeks had already elapsed, with chaos exacerbated by the fall of Antwerp. Bernard Mallett acknowledged his figures (IWM. Belgium 1/20. Cd 7763) dated 14 December 1914 were inaccurate, but nonetheless showed a prurient interest in women's marital status. Of the women over 16 years old, 30 per cent were unmarried, 65 per cent married, and 5 per cent widows. Men's status was not so categorized. As the comment about the 15- to 25-year-olds in Table 1 admits, the statistics dated November 1915 cannot be taken as accurate, but show that women and children are in the majority.

Table 1. Refugee numbers, November 1915

	Males	*Females*	*Children*
Infants under 5, both sexes			18,500
Children age 5 to 15			23,500
15 to 25, inexact as many have enlisted and not told the Central Registrar	19,000	20,000	
25 to 65	52,500	51,000	
Over 65	2,000	3,500	
Total	73,500	74,500	42,000

Taken from T.T. de Jastrzebski, 'The Register of Belgian Refugees', *Journal of the Royal Statistical Society*, March 1916.

Even when the numbers subsided, figures changed constantly due to both arrivals and departures between Belgium, Holland, England and France, many refugees returning to Belgium voluntarily, such as eleven nuns recalled to Antwerp by their Order in December 1914 and March 1915. Some returned because they could not stand the strain of being refugees and disliked being beholden to their hosts, therefore tactfully telling the Committee they had been recalled by their employers. In Henley-on-Thames, the first family to stay with Mrs Noble arrived on 8 September, but returned to Antwerp after a few days because the three daughters declared they could not put up with the dullness of a country winter; when Antwerp fell they fled to Holland. Not knowing who would win the war, others returned because of the German blackmail in February 1915 when all absentee property owners became subject to a levy ten times the normal tax. Some came to England with unrealistic expectations, and returned because no arrangements had been made or because they were not given everything they wanted. Others went to France for work. However, by the end of 1914, although still not a precise figure, 156,000 civilians and 36,000 soldiers had come to England, but between then and February they had been arriving at the rate of about 300 to 500 per day. Of this number 10,000 refugees in London had not been allocated to hospitality. Refugees were also shipped from Holland to England to ease the Dutch burden, but this was economic as much as humanitarian and stopped in 1915 because of submarines. Women moved backwards and forwards following their men, in search of work, or, like Godeliva Persyn, aged 20, in January 1916, to get married. A number of women were deported. Undesirables of either sex could not be kept in detention by the police, so might be kept in workhouses; but if men remained troublesome, they could be deported to Holland or France, and some escaped during transfers; others were conscripted. This refugee movement included *réformés*, Belgian soldiers invalided out of the Army, and the 'Invisible Army' – men who were spirited out of Holland and occupied Belgium to serve in France or clandestinely recruited for work in Britain. It was uncertain whether *réformés* and 'invisibles' should be counted as refugees. Gradually, as warfare stagnated into the trenches, the flow of refugees, at its height up to the end of March 1915, reversed so that by the end of that year the outward flow was in excess of inward. It was estimated according to Home Office statistics that at least 250,000 refugees came to Britain, although Gladstone thought 260,000; nevertheless, the maximum number at any one time was about 210,000 and by the end of 1916 it had fallen to 160,000.

Belgians and work

Other regulations, notably about whether and where refugees could work, were further barriers to the Belgians. Employment was at first strictly forbidden: competition was feared and it was recognized that there was a danger of exploiting refugees as unpaid servants. An unexpected complication found by the Misses Rothschilds, working at the WRC, was that 'the first ones all wanted work, NONE wanted hospitality'. The Government did not resolve this until 30 September but when permission to work was granted it was stipulated that Trades Union wages must be paid. In October 1914 a Committee was appointed under Sir Ernest Hatch to consider and report on questions arising in connection with the reception and employment of Belgian refugees into Britain. Among members were Arthur Henderson, Susan Lawrence, and Edith Lyttelton. It was particularly concerned with what action could be taken which would allow refugees to work without competing with the employment of available British labour and Susan Lawrence reminded the Committee of the serious unemployment among English women workers. The Committee's recommendations were not put into effect.

By 17 February 1915 there were Labour Exchanges at each of the three main reception centres of Alexandra Palace, Earl's Court and the Aldwych, and Belgians elsewhere in the country were being urged to register at local exchanges; in addition, there was co-operation with the Belgian military. Wealthy Belgian men secured advances from Belgian banks, established successful businesses and contributed to WRC funds. Some set up factories and employed other Belgians; Belgian munition factory owners gave work to poorer Belgians. They formed their own communities with laundries and shops. From February 1916 aliens were only allowed into prohibited areas if they had an identity book. The Committee at Hull found that this simplified movement as refugees daily came to and fro for work.

In Belgium and Britain women were constructed by contemporary patriarchal discourse as wives and mothers, so it was considered essential that married women stayed at home to care for their families. Nonetheless, many Belgian women did work for their living, sometimes combining it with domestic duties. Suffragists were often at the forefront of providing the means whereby this was possible. For example, WEC set up workshops for lace-makers, and at Bedford College, Belgian women made toys as substitutes for those that were now not being imported from Germany. In April 1915, the NUWSS claimed that it had the satisfaction of seeing work which it originated, such as opening workrooms, adopted and extended by other organizations. Workshops had a social as well as an economic benefit, providing a place where women could meet compatriots. Belgian women also worked in munitions.

The Chelsea Committee for Belgian Refugees organized work for women in London and other parts of England. Edith Lyttelton was Chair of this Committee and among its 21 Patrons were Lord and Lady Courtney of Penwith and Mrs Francis (Eleanor) Acland, Honorary Secretary of the Liberal Women's Suffrage Union. Housed with their families in flats or hostels, Belgian women did a certain amount of housework, looked after their children and were sent materials and instructions; made up items were returned and forwarded to Belgium. In July 1915 over 820 women worked on materials provided by English Relief Societies, but wool and money were also sent from America as a result of contacts with Mrs Fiske Warren of Harvard, Massachusetts, and Mrs Erskine Childers. This type of industry was much adopted in connection with refugees. By today's standards it was probably exploitative, as was Queen Mary's Needlework Fund, but it enabled refugees to help those living under German occupation while they were being supported by the Chelsea people. Chelsea also organized an industry for wounded Belgian soldiers, about 45 at a time, who made wool socks on hand machines. The socks were sold in a shop on the Kings Road, lent by the WSPU Secretary, Miss Florence Haig. The men received a share of the proceeds and the remainder was invested in new machines. It was felt this was good preparation for repatriation, a matter of vital importance. The over-riding factor was to provide the means of self-support and empower people by giving them back self-respect.

Like those of the British middle classes whose financial position was made difficult by the war, those of the Belgian middle classes found it difficult to find work. Penniless Belgian doctors gave their services free as did shoemakers at Folkestone. Women took jobs below their social status, becoming domestic servants: the wage at that time for maids was about £18–£20 per year. A professor, Mr P.J. Tysmans, aged 74, remained under the care of Grimsby with his crippled son, aged 42 and daughter aged 34. He was given £1 10s. 0d. per week and his house rent free, with the local Committee paying for water and clothing. However, his other daughter, Clothilda, a teacher, was employed in London at £60 per annum. Angelina Tysmans, another teacher, (the surname may be a coincidence) earned

£100 at the Municipal College, Cleethorpes. Some got jobs as machinists and tailoresses. Emile Van der Heydon, a clerk aged 48, was employed as a groom at 15s. per week, but two young women, possibly related to Emile, were also employed as grooms at £1 per week each, an unusual example of women being paid more than a man for the same work. Cahalan's (1982: 293) patriarchal approach is revealed by his opinion that British women should not have taken vacancies the Belgians could have filled. He refers to unemployed British women as rivals for clerical work that:

> could have been filled by Belgians, but by the time an agency existed to seek work for them, English women had filled the vacancies and demonstrated their capabilities. Women also *deprived* Belgian men of their chance at many light jobs in munitions [my italics].

This implies British women did not need the work, which is incorrect. Holloway indicates (2005: 141, 134) the number of employed women rose from approximately 4,900,000 in 1914 to about 6,200,000 in 1918, an increase of roughly 24 per cent. Since the Factory Acts were suspended, women, Belgian and British, had to cope with twelve-hour shifts and the double burden of paid employment, plus domestic duties and childcare. This implies economic necessity rather than working for luxuries. Lyttelton served on a Government sub-committee which concluded that since infant mortality had declined under these circumstances, women could manage better when they had control of family money. This laid the foundation for Eleanor Rathbone's Family Endowment campaign in Britain and at the League of Nations. There were, however, many middle- and upper-class women whose financial position enabled the free time that was central to supporting the refugees who fled to Britain.

CHAPTER 3

Supporting the Refugees: Refugee Relief in Britain

Care of refugees in London

Most refugees were sent from the ports direct to London where they were met at railway stations by volunteer relief workers, who sorted out Belgians from French, Russians, Americans 'and even Armenians' (IWM. DD. 86/48/1), so lists of volunteers who could speak Flemish, French, German, Dutch, Italian or Spanish were sent to the WRC. Working with the WRC the Women's Service Bureau agreed to undertake official registration and provided French- and Flemish-speaking interpreters who were needed to welcome and register refugees at the ports and in London. Volunteers had to be task-matched according to the languages they could speak and their particular preferences: one preferred not to sleep away from home; some were willing to visit hospitals, to write letters, or go to Folkestone. Volunteers also transported refugees, interviewed other volunteers, dealt with the many enquiries for Belgian servants, or desire to adopt children.

As the numbers of refugees increased, the responsibility became heavier. Registrations at the various London centres took place daily from 8.30 a.m. to midnight and 187 interpreters were enrolled, 150 of whom were actually employed. Each voluntary society registered the refugees they assisted so that families could be reunited. These records were sent to the WRC at Aldwych and refugees were guided there when searching for family members. The Red Cross provided meals for registrars, interpreters, and for varying numbers of refugees at short notice. The situation provided many middle-class women with opportunities otherwise denied them and for which they had received no training. Their resourcefulness is typified by Miss Carey of WEC. On 28 August the *Morning Post* reported that she had been requisitioned to supply food for 100 Belgian refugees but although this increased to 300 the necessary amount was provided as a result of efforts she had made throughout the night.

Once the need was recognized, offers of accommodation flooded into the offices of relief societies. Women of all political and religious persuasions gave aid, including food and clothing, and used existing social, political and cultural networks to provide longer-term assistance and wider geographical support. The LSWS made lists of names of people offering hospitality and over 200 offers of private hospitality were furnished through the Central Office. Philippa Strachey, sister of Lytton Strachey and Hon. Secretary of the LSWS, was one of the volunteers notified of refugees' arrival. On 4 September she wrote in *Common Cause*: 'Mrs Streeter, one of our organizers who has been for ten days engaged on care committee work at Fulham, is now in the Office, arranging hospitality. Offers are coming in well, but more are wanted.' LSWS branches ran London hostels at Northwood, Blackheath, Highgate, South Kensington and New Malden.

Miss Alice Selby of the LSWS wrote from the Lady Margaret Hall Settlement: 'I took this house in Fulham for Belgian refugees – I have ten and am in direct communication with the Committee at Aldwych.' Lady Margaret Hall was where the suffragist Henrietta Jex-Blake was Principal, and where Kathleen Courtney had studied in the late 1890s. In April 1915, the NUWSS reported that Societies in the Union had undertaken the support of entire families, and provided gifts of clothes, funds, and furniture; houses were lent and hostels opened. Reports received by LSWS, such as that Rugby was filling with refugees, indicate suffrage involvement nation-wide. In Lincoln, the Women's Suffrage Society provided a house. In areas where no foreigner was allowed to settle, money was collected to support Belgians in other neighbourhoods. As *Jus Suffragii* reported in February 1915, the:

> first active steps for the organisation of war relief work among women were those taken by the Suffrage Societies … Before any Government Department had approved official schemes … before authoritative effort had secured the registration of Belgian refugees, the women of Great Britain, and notably the Suffragist women, came forward unrecruited and uninvited, ready to work with organized skill at new and essential national tasks … NUWSS … has provided interpreters for hospitals and for refugee depots; it has organized and provided numerous hostels for Belgian guests.

Alice Essington-Nelson (IWM. DD. 86/48/1) of the CWL explained they knew when to set off to meet refugees at London termini because:

> The Authorities would telephone to Miss Streeter directly they knew a refugee train was expected and we hurried to the Station wearing our White Sashes with 'Ligue des Femmes Catholique' written in black letters across them.

These sashes gave them entrance to all the places closed to the public. However, trains expected at Charing Cross might instead be sent to Victoria necessitating, as with the boats, long and sometimes fruitless periods spent waiting. The refugees also spent considerable amounts of time waiting about as this photograph shows. Plate 1 shows middle-class refugees waiting outside the warehouse of Hudson's Removals Ltd at Victoria to be taken to their next destination.

Plate 1. Belgian refugees outside the warehouse of Hudson's Ltd, Victoria, London, 1915.* (Photograph courtesy of the Imperial War Museum, London. Q 53305)

* This firm was owned by the author's grandmother's family, but the connection with Belgian refugees was not known until the photograph was discovered.

In addition to coping with these practicalities, there were other worries. Gerodetti and Bieri (2006 (7): 69–85) argue that geography and space are always gendered and that train stations represent a border point or gateway for different dimensions of sexuality. Foreign sexualities were represented as dangerous, even corrupt; women on the move also represented a sexual danger, but they were also vulnerable. Margaret Damer Dawson, a suffragette and Head of the Transport Committee formed by the Chelsea Refugee Committee, had been involved in an incident when some refugees had been spirited away by white slavers, as a result of which she founded the Women's Police. Similar events had taken place at railway stations in the 1880s and people were reminded of the Belgians' previous connection with the white slave trade. A worried contributor to *Common Cause* of 18 September 1914 wrote about:

> the serious condition of things existing at our railway stations on the arrival of the Belgian refugees. Well-dressed ladies select the young women they want and take them for the White Slave trade.

W.T. Stead's article entitled 'Maiden Tribute', published in the *Pall Mall Gazette* and confirmed by a Mansion House Committee (Coote 1910: 4), had revealed how apparently respectable ladies were able to abduct young women, especially at railway stations, and later dispatch them to France and Belgium, particularly Brussels and Antwerp, as white slaves. In 1885, in response, William Alex Coote had founded the National Vigilance Association (NVA), with some prominent suffragists involved (Holton 1994: 1126). The NVA was now asked to supervise the stations.

Mr Coote responded:

> We have about 100 ladies on duty at the different railway stations … We have had the advantage of the help of ladies from the Women's Emergency Corps, the Women's Freedom League, St John's Ambulance, the Women's Service, the Catholic Women's League, the Girls' Life Brigade (who distribute water and milk to the refugees) the Red Cross (Camberwell Branch), and … the Boy Scouts.

Four of these organizations were suffragist or had suffragist links. Mr Coote surely knew this when he wrote to WEC on 17 September 1914 expressing his gratitude for their work at the stations: 'I could not help feeling that such women ... would ... become a great social, moral and religious factor in the regeneration of our beloved country.' Nonetheless, this vigilance did not stop the trade and later the Belgian Refugee Food Fund was suspected of being involved. The white slave traffic and its link with prostitution was of particular and current concern to suffragists. *Jus Suffragii* of 1 August 1915 reported that in Boston a white slaver had recently revealed that a big sum of money had been raised in order to defeat women's suffrage. 'Every unfortunate girl who is exploited by the traders in vice is being taxed an extra sum from her earnings, to be used in fighting equal suffrage.'

There was a further moral panic over the likelihood of an increase in VD through prostitution as troops arrived from the Empire. There were calls for reintroduction of the Contagious Diseases Act and representations were made by the Dominion Governments. A secretive Order-in-Council of the British Government approved Regulation 40D of the Defence of the Realm Act (DORA) on 22 February 1918. In all wars the rights of the individual come under threat and are reduced. This is particularly the case for women, for militarism is misogynistic. This Act was part of the Government's war against dissent. Under it the authorities could inspect and punish 'infected women' who had sexual intercourse with any member of His Majesty's troops. Across the Atlantic some people considered Britain a sink of vice of prostitution and theft and feared for their troops' vulnerability. As explained elsewhere (Storr 2002: 16–19), extension of Regulation 40D was proposed because the USA had asked to have it applied for the benefit of their forces.

The ideology of hierarchy in relation to gender, race and class was entrenched. What is now called ageism was also deeply ingrained. As Lerner says (Humm 1992: 325, 327), women are 'indoctrinated in a male-defined system and conduct their lives accordingly'. The old suffered worst in the allocation of scarce resources, their value in terms of experience being disregarded according to patriarchal standards which are still evident in the twenty-first century. People were judged by class and a reiterated phrase of surprise was that the refugees were of all classes. Up to this period, poverty and need were believed to be due to bad morals; Quakers disowned members who became bankrupt, for example. That the 'better classes' could become refugees was a shock, and people consequently felt that they suffered more than their lower-class compatriots and were compensated accordingly. Middle-class Britons were now giving hospitality to the mainly working-class Belgian refugees – an arrangement which put them into closer touch than was normal and may have contributed to some of the subsequent class changes in British society. Winter (1986: 19–20) says that 'Many middle-class assumptions about the poor were among the casualties of the Great War.' Nevertheless, as Orwell wrote (1959: 158): 'We all rail against class-distinctions, but very few people seriously want to abolish them.' Much trouble was taken over determining the refugees' class because class hierarchy was important in Belgian society. The Misses Rothschild, who had lived in Brussels for eight years, were aware that it was complicated by language and ethnicity. As Brand Whitlock, the American Ambassador, explained (Whitlock, Vol. 1, 1919: 14), the Walloons and Flemings met in Brussels where Flemish and French were spoken, as well as various forms of patois. Miss Rothschild (IWM. Belgium 9 1/2) wrote:

> We knew that the Wallons [sic] were very different from the Flemings. They are of different origin ... it would be fatal to house families of these mixed races under one roof ... the Belgians of the different classes of society do not associate at all and could not be mixed or disagreement would follow. Our first effort was therefore to differentiate between the classes.

During September the WRC began to give the refugees at ports either a pink card denoting middle-class, or blue for working-class. These were welcomed by the workers and still in use in November 1915, as the influx was beginning to subside. Mistakes in assessing class inevitably occurred, causing bad feelings when middle-classes were treated as peasants, leaving the voluntary workers with the task of mollifying wounded feelings, and deflating the unrealistic expectations of wrongly-categorized working-classes. This system guided the refugee at Victoria; pink cards advised the London representatives to give the refugee details about train services and accommodation lists to help them avoid hotel touts. Those who were unable to pay their train fare were given free transport and the blue card, which gave temporary lodgings in Government refugee camps such as Alexandra Palace and Earl's Court. London workers hoped that local relief committees or the local Authorities would sort out allocation errors by transferring refugees from one house to another. Later, red cards were used for better class refugees who were to be cared for by Flora Lugard's Hospitality Committee founded after Gladstone's take-over of the WRC.

As we saw earlier, the first refuge was at St George's Road, but it was soon evident that the numbers arriving had to be temporarily housed in buildings large enough to hold hundreds of people. On 8 September, the day on which the Government invited the Belgians to come to Britain, Alexandra Palace was taken to house 4,000 refugees, opening ten days later. That day, daily boats bringing 1,000 refugees from Antwerp were started. Hackney Wick took 80 poorer class people and there was another depot at Edmonton that housed the 'undesirables'. Military refugees, distinguishable as such in the records by their destination, were taken to St Giles at Endell Street which held 1,300. Earl's Court, which had a capacity of 4,000, was opened on 15 October taking 1,400 refugees that evening. When the influx was too great for London to cope, refugees were sent direct from Dover to Manchester, Glasgow and Liverpool where, on 15 October, 425 arrived at 4 p.m. on a special train. The next day the LGB sent a circular requiring Town Halls' assistance in finding accommodation; Mayors established Committees to comply but the appeal was not as successful as the Government hoped. During the following months members of the NUWSS Fulham branch (IWM. Suffrage 1/8) 'regularly entertained' Earl's Court refugees, although it is uncertain precisely what was meant by this. In addition, ladies were asked to supervise here and at Alexandra Palace. As van Drenthe says (1999: 18): 'Ladies embodied feminine character and behaviour' which would help 'to bring about a personal transformation in the women under their care'. It also confirmed that women should help other women and, as Thane says (1996: 73), this had been the LGB's usual approach in dealing with women and children. Often refugees had no idea where they were. There were rumours that England did not want them and if they were entrained on a Wednesday this meant being sent to Canada, while Saturday meant India. Some therefore refused to get on trains; others refused to get off.

From 18 September responsibility for registration was taken over by the LGB; the system which the LSWS had evolved was approved and used by them although the questionnaire was simplified. Mrs Lyttelton said 'what we had done for registration the Government was now doing "not half so well"'. About 20 October 1914, Aldwych became responsible for the meeting of trains and housing refugees for the first few nights. This meant that volunteers already doing the jobs, such as Miss Boyd of the LSWS, now did them for the WRC. Miss Boyd had responsibility for registration and allocating accommodation at Alexandra Palace, at Wilton Road, Battersea, and the Dulwich depot. An appeal in *Common Cause* of 4 September pointed out that 'Every Committee that can make itself responsible for a home will enable Miss Boyd to allocate even more worthily.' Suffrage campaigners were therefore involved in registration, allocation and other forms of relief at government refuges.

Among the large proportion of women and children who arrived in the first batch, three women were expecting confinement. Lord Gladstone acknowledged: 'We need the help of women workers to make proper arrangements.' These included the provision of baby clothes and the Balham and Epsom NUWSS Branches were among the groups who specialized in providing them. In addition, Mrs Webbe ran a Maternity Home for the WRC and the Salvation Army had 'plenty' of Institutions which catered for the birth of babies born to those who were referred to as the 'rougher girls'. The LGB Conference held on 11 January 1915 skirted round the issue of women needing maternity care, perhaps because it was not appropriate for men publicly to discuss such matters. Nonetheless, Metropolitan Asylums Board practitioners helped in this work at a dispensary and hospital set up in London, assisted by Belgian doctors and French-speaking English nurses. Medical care was needed for a wide variety of health problems including skin diseases, and dentistry; infections needing hospital care, and venereal diseases were sent to the Board's infectious hospitals. Patients also needed artificial limbs, and there were many ophthalmic cases; eyesight troubles arising from their ordeal were prevalent, especially among children, and refugees needed artificial eyes and spectacles.

Aspects of hospitality

On arrival in towns and villages refugees were given an enthusiastic welcome befitting their heroic status. They were met by civic dignitaries, accompanied through towns by cheering crowds, given fruit and flags; young children received an especially warm reception. This situation was unprecedented. Michael Amara (2004) attributes the response of France and Great Britain to the refugees as arising from the 'enormous respect and prestige enjoyed by Belgium in these two countries'. However, as Gann and Duignan (1979: 148, 132) point out, Belgium was not popular until the Great War when its ugly reputation was transformed. Belgium's connection with the white slave trade and violent cruelty in the Congo had made it 'the object of international odium' and 'infamous in Europe as a land where abuses were commonplace'. The transformation of this ugly reputation was achieved by making the Germans into even more terrible monsters by emphasizing German atrocities. In London refugees' stories were recorded, collated and, having been examined by a committee under Viscount Bryce, formerly British Ambassador to Washington, were published in May 1915 in 30 languages. As Playne (1931: 87) wrote, 'Hatred of the foe was counterbalanced by almost extravagant sympathy with Germany's victim, Belgium' by focussing on the people's heroic sufferings. However, until Belgium demonstrated it was resisting the German invasion, Britain could not act in Belgium's defence, so early on 4 August Sir Francis Villiers, British Minister at Brussels, informed M. Davignon, Belgian Minister for Foreign Affairs, that Belgium was expected to resist any territorial incursion. Constant reiteration of the argument that this left Britain in moral debt to Belgium since it delayed a possible invasion here, ensured people's monetary and practical aid for the refugees. An irony was that Germans felt they owed a similar debt to Belgium and also to Russian Poland. *Jus Suffragii* of 1 April 1915 reported:

> The Frauenbewegung publishes an appeal from Frau von Bernhardt for aid for the starving inhabitants of Russian Poland, whose country is divested by war. In her appeal Frau von Bernhardt says that help is being organized for suffering Belgium. Europe indeed owes a heavy debt to these two wrecked and ruined countries, and it is good to hear that German suffragists are trying to bring aid to the sufferers outside of their own borders.

According to the WRC there were 2,500 dedicated Belgian Refugee Committees and in 1917 Agnes Conway circularized them from the Imperial War Museum for records of their work. She had been at Newnham with Mary Agnes Hamilton (1944: 131) and had previously worked with Lady Lyttelton at the WRC. She and her American aunt, Mrs Marble, ran a hostel for Belgian wounded in Buckingham Palace Road, London.

The response to Agnes Conway's questionnaire was disappointing; only 256 people replied. Some people were by then tired of the Belgians, others were no longer helping them; some do not reply to circulars; others promised to do so and never got round to it. However, the responses indicate that many Committees had men and women serving on them, though often with women doing the work of collecting funds, daily care of refugees, teaching them English and even showing local people round the refugee home, as in Burgess Hill and Brighton. Men usually took the Chair and often the role of Honorary Treasurer; they might be in the majority on Executive Committees but a woman was almost always the Honorary Secretary, often indicating she was responsible for its inception. Porton, Wiltshire, had five men and four women on the Committee, but also 20 voluntary workers, of which 12 were women. Together they 'entertained' 17 Belgians. Refugee care, like all domestic work, was labour intensive and time consuming. At Burton-on-Trent there were 50 voluntary workers, 10 men and 40 women. Clothing Committees and House Committees usually consisted only of women. This gender pattern followed that of pre-war charity work with care of the unfortunate regarded as women's work. Sir John Barran, MP, was appointed by the Hatch committee (IWM. Belgium 1/21, Cd 7779: 5034) to visit various refugee centres and reported that:

> a very large proportion of those actively working on these committees are women. Indeed, the house committees, which in many cases look after each individual house, and often make themselves responsible for the finance of each house, are almost entirely women's committees, and that is natural.

Catholic women were expected to help their co-religionists. Miss Ada Streeter circularized all CWL branches throughout England and sent over 4,000 refugees to Catholic Centres including Liverpool. There the

Committee's Hon. Secretary was Miss Edith Rose, who in 1918, with Mr Sheppard of the Manchester Committee, became responsible for the repatriation of refugees from the whole of Lancashire. However, in Glasgow Mary Boyle wrote that in her experience the Roman Catholic Church was the Institution least anxious to help the refugees. The Sisters in a nearby Convent had refused to teach the children although they knew this meant sending them back to London.

One of those who did reply to Agnes Conway was the Rector of Portishead, Bristol, Revd H.W. Jukes, Chairman of the Portishead Committee which owed its formation to the initiative of the Quaker Lady Fry of Failand. In October she approached the Anglican Rector and Catholic Father Vincent and together they formed a Committee of six ladies and two men who decided to support 12 refugees. Lady Fry proposed to maintain eight refugees herself. This comparatively small, rural area typifies the different types of accommodation provided elsewhere, and the trouble taken for the well-being of the 'brave Belgians'. Her refugees arrived in October and were placed in the Temperance Hotel which was provided rent free; the Committee's first six guests followed, but later that month the Hotel was requisitioned by the military so new accommodation had to be found. On 5 November two further families were accepted at the 'earnest request of the Bristol Committee'. This implies lack of accommodation in Bristol, unsuitable accommodation due to social class, or families sharing accommodation being separated. In December 1914 several professional refugees arrived and were homed at Sea Bank, Nore Road, lent rent free by Miss Webb of Clifton. Another professional family of three arrived on 14 December and were put in furnished rooms. The house at Nore Road is by no means the only one to be lent rent free by a woman. One was offered in Holbeach, Lincolnshire, but could not be taken because Holbeach was declared prohibited.

The ARAs put a heavy strain on the amount of accommodation available. On 17 October, when the flood of refugees was at its height, the NUWSS Secretary of the Hunstanton branch, Norfolk, wrote (LSWS 371.2) offering to take refugees at her guest house in York Avenue. The writer continued: 'Quite a number of Belgian refugees have arrived in Hunstanton, some taking furnished houses at their own expense, others being arranged for.' However, on 21 October, several counties, including Norfolk, were made into prohibited areas and a suffragists' Refugee Relief Committee in Norwich wrote to the LSWS asking for help in sorting out the problem of a family from Dixmude who had been sent there. It is not known what became of them.

Committees had to house not only new arrivals, but re-home those who had to be moved out of areas where they had settled. By 24 July 1916, 133,689 refugees had to be reallocated to new hospitality including many in Hull, whose guests were looked after in places as far away as Canterbury. Nevertheless, the authorities were aware that their rules could result in further suffering for people who had already suffered more than enough, and created exceptions. An information letter sent out from the Home Office dated 21 September stated:

> On grounds of mere humanity, invalids, lone women with nowhere else to go, boys and girls at school or otherwise under British or friendly guardianship, may be exemptions; so too may dependants, governesses or domestic servants, provided the circumstances of the family do not present opportunities of hearing private conversation upon matters of possible importance.

This makes it clear that all Belgian refugees and foreign staff were to be treated as potential spies. However, the reference to boys and girls at school explains why in Aldeburgh, Suffolk, Mrs Fisher's School for Refugee Children, caring mainly for girls, was allowed to stay open although it was on the coast. Mrs Fisher was another recipient of the *Medaille de la Reine Elisabeth*. This recognition provided the recipient with a new public identity obviously related to their work of caring for refugees and their children.

Mrs Palmer, of Christ's Hospital, Horsham, a NUWSS member, formed a committee and provided a home, but when she applied for suitable refugees she was told that the whole of Sussex was prohibited. She tussled with the authorities and a Belgian family was eventually allowed to take up residence. In Cuckfield a Committee of seven ladies, possibly including members of the Central Sussex Women's Suffrage Society, were already caring for refugees and offered more houses, including one in Broad Street. They then learned more refugees were prohibited although those already there were allowed to remain. This decision was repeated elsewhere.

Airmen created a shortage of accommodation in Chingford, Essex, where the Committee found it impossible to obtain further rent-free accommodation and some houses were taken back by their owners. Chingford was declared a proscribed area on 8 November and Police notified all the Belgians that they must leave at once. There was consternation and many Chingford inhabitants were indignant. 'As the result of strong representations, however, the Powers-that-be relented somewhat' and allowed the existing guests to stay (IWM. Belgium 6.5 5/7).

Those offering hospitality were asked to specify on an Allocation card the type of accommodation offered, the number of men, women and children they were willing to take, and also the social class so that guests, accommodation and host could be matched. Even so, matching was not straightforward. Allocating a single refugee to hospitality was also problematic. Mary Sheepshanks travelled from Flushing with Mme Vanderbelle Genotte who later sought her help because she was being asked to do menial tasks and there was no-one with whom she could speak French. Help in the house was often part of the agreement between guest and host, but Mme Genotte was being treated as a servant and was lonely. Mrs Percy Wood, Southsea, who had filled in forms early in September for a Belgian servant, wrote ten days later 'Kindly let me know how long I must wait.' It had to be pointed out that the Belgians were in Britain as guests. From October, when the Government allowed refugees to work, such requests were referred to the SFFD which co-operated with the IWRC at the Labour Exchange, Great Marlborough Street, London. There was also a huge demand for children. Dr Helen Webb, a Quaker at Rotherfield, wanted two. However, it is unlikely she got them. *Common Cause* reported that the NUWSS could not supply Belgian babies, partly because the Government decided they were only being sent to Catholic homes.

In October, the Ealing and Acton branch of the LSWS combined with the Church League at the Haven Green Church to create a hostel for Belgian peasant women. Mr William Owen also offered The Elms, Castlebar Road on the condition that the Suffrage Committee managed everything. A few hours later about 60 Belgian guests began arriving, including one family of 16. There was also a Belgian refugee cat, and parrot in its Belgian cage. Readers of *Common Cause* queried how furniture had been obtained for the hostel. It was explained that the Branch appealed 'and it came in'. The Ealing hostel was one of many places that obtained food through the NFF. The LSWS appealed to Lady Julia Charlotte Chance (née Strachey), the Fund's Organising Secretary, on 22 January 1916 for help in retaining the food grant which had been cancelled by the woman inspector due to a misunderstanding over the men's financial contribution. A subsequent Report stated that having applied to WRC they obtained £10 per week so the hostel, subsequently registered as a War Charity, survived the crisis.

Female relief workers helped refugees settle after their ordeal. In Cheshire, Port Sunlight's Ladies' Committee supplied every woman refugee with a well equipped workbag to help solve the problem of lack of occupation and home sickness. They found, as did most committees that women were more easily satisfied than men, because they had the domestic work of kitchen, dormitories, hall and table service and children to look after.

Although wherever possible agencies organized refugee accommodation on class lines, religious affiliation attached to Fleming and Walloon ethnicity caused complications. The South Kensington Branch of the LSWS equipped a house lent by Mr Freemantle, KC, as a hostel for middle-class Belgians. It was to be opened on 10 November and the Branch appealed for a variety of household furniture, linen, utensils, coal, food and money, the latter in the form of donations or weekly or monthly contributions. When, on 23 November a correspondent from the Hostel wrote to Miss Gosse at the LSWS, she hinted at awareness of possible future difficulties between the guests. They were 'thankful to find themselves in a safe shelter and we think they bid fair to settle down together comfortably'. However, she added, 'This is not altogether easy of accomplishment for three strange families in close proximity, and after all their experiences they are still rather bewildered and nervous. What they most need is peace' (WL. 371/1).

By November better class hospitality offers were reduced and the stock of available accommodation was filled. The military wanted houses to use as barracks or as temporary hospitals for wounded British and Belgian servicemen. Hosts began to find the monetary and emotional strain too much and gave notice to their Belgian guests. Belgians who came over with money spent it all and needed hospitality. Convalescent homes, which normally took children discharged from hospitals, were requisitioned as hospitals, and these recuperating children needed hospitality. Homes were required for refugees of other nationalities as well as Belgians. However, the WRC's inadequacies meant that some offers were not taken up. According to the NUWSS Provincial Council Meeting at Wallasey on 12 November 1914 single offers of hospitality were being refused because the WRC wanted only to deal with large numbers. Portslade offered accommodation but after several weeks had received no acknowledgement and transferred their offer to the Brighton and Hove Committee. Offers from Mayoral Relief Funds were more likely to be accepted because they dealt with larger numbers whereas voluntary groups were better able to cope with individual cases of need and offers of help. In January 1915, the LSWS Women's Service Hospitality for Belgian Refugees Report stated that 'Some time ago there was more hospitality than refugees to fill it; but that has now been reversed and it is becoming the hardest thing to find hospitality.' Portishead agreed, but gave another reason for the difficulty (IWM. Belgium 6.192/5). Many guests had been provided with hostel-type or shared housing, but by the beginning of 1915, relief workers realized it was advisable to house each family separately.

Fund-raising and money matters

Although the Government eventually took some of the financial burden from the WRC, much relief work remained voluntary and therefore involved continuous fund raising. Networks were tapped to raise money, to provide food, clothing and hospitality. Protestant and Catholic churches, suffrage groups and groups of friends within a particular locality all came to refugees' aid. A considerable number of Quakers worked among the Belgian refugees giving money and other help. As Jane Lewis confirms (1991: 31), the ideology of duty was gendered; women were responsible for 'caring', yet also raised the funds that men then controlled. This division of labour applied to refugee relief.

Committees used national newspapers such as *The Times* as a means of gaining the practical expression of public sympathy in help, money and gifts. On 2 October Edith Lyttelton and Flora Lugard at WRC appealed for offers of money and hospitality. Suffrage journals carried similar advertisements. The Free Church Suffrage League appealed in *Common Cause* for books for refugees and PoWs. In December Helena Swanwick stated that through the 'energetic' work of the NUWSS, £5,500 had already been subscribed towards the 'Scottish Federation Hospitals ... which are staffed by women, in helping Belgian refugees, and in a thousand other social activities'. This combination of causes was typical. The IWRC had several funds. Their Belgian Refugees in Holland Fund raised £3,493 2s. 3d. up to 31 October 1914, and the General Relief Fund contained £473 9s. 4d. In November *Jus Suffragii* carried a list of donors to an IWRC appeal showing the Friends' Emergency Committee had contributed to it.

Most local groups also supported a variety of relief activities. For example, Maidstone NUWSS members engaged in Red Cross work, but also went on working parties for Belgian refugees making over 100 layettes, some of which were sent to the WRC at Aldwych, and some direct to Belgium. Individual members also sent offers of hospitality. Women made clothes and collected used ones to send to local refugee centres, the children's home at Aldeburgh or the Aldwych in London. Carlisle NUWSS offered to make garments. Locally, women compiled lists of donors and made regular house-to-house collections. Chingford was mapped out into 42 districts, and 50 ladies raised £1,244 11s. 10d. In contrast, the Hampstead Society of Friends inaugurated a Committee specifically to supply puddings one day a week for a local refugee hostel and also provided social afternoons and evenings, daily morning school for Belgian children, and English and sewing classes for the adults. Portishead received a special donation of £15 19s. 6d. towards nursing home expenses incurred by a refugee lady who underwent a serious operation. £6 contributed by one of the refugee families was returned to them when they left Portishead.

Another traditional fund-raising method was by organizing social events. A concert and entertainment was given at the Coliseum with Irene Vanbrugh and Maggie Teyte among the performers. Artists organized exhibitions for Belgian relief; ladies gave 'At Homes;' there were lectures, auctions, whist drives and dances. However, new ideas were needed. In Glasgow, Mrs Arthur Morrison of Merchiston, Scotstounhill, pioneered the Flag Day movement by selling tiny silk flags, cashing in on martial and philanthropic motives for giving. The first ever flag day was held on 5 September in Glasgow in aid of the Soldiers and Sailors Families Association raising about £4,000. Next Mrs Morrison held a nationwide Belgian Day on 3 October that raised £6,000, needing 5,000 voluntary sellers in London alone. By 18 August 1915 over £70,000 had been collected, mainly the work of women. At the end of the war the movement had collected £300,000. But it caused problems; there were too many flag-days and sellers were accused of pestering passers-by.

Some schemes also improved the income of British women impoverished by the war. The NUWSS in Newcastle ordered clothes for refugees from dressmakers and small firms that might otherwise be without work. The New Constitutional Society for Women's Suffrage set up a workshop in mid-August to provide stop-gap employment for girls made unemployed by the war and in September advertised for donations and orders for Belgian refugees to enable the opening of a second workshop, for which a studio had been offered. A vast army of young women workers in shops, restaurants, factories, and offices, who had been thrown out of employment because of the War, were assisted by WEC at two addresses in the City. It was an unresolved anomaly that young women who had experience but were now unemployed, were subordinate to the volunteers, whose social class was higher.

Businesses and professions established their own funds and, where women were still struggling for recognition, set up all male Committees such as the Belgian Doctors and Pharmacists Relief Fund. Its appeals through medical journals raised £9,000 by February 1915; it also helped Belgian professionals into work by organising their registration on UK professional rolls through the General Medical Council. Sometimes goods were the focus of attention. The Smithfield Market's Belgian Relief Fund established on 24 November 1914 was all-male. It distributed 377,272 lbs. of meat, including Argentine beef, and raised money totalling £527 19s. 4d. Auctions were held where an item such as a pear was repeatedly 'sold', raising huge sums. Farmers provided regular gifts of fruit and vegetables in season. However, the Darlington Belgian Market received and distributed food under the management of the Women's Suffrage Society.

Most Committees, like Darlington, whose experience of the refugees was disappointing and depressing, were nonetheless anxious that refugees should not go home empty handed. Once refugees began to earn money, arrangements were often made for saving part of their earnings while the local Committee continued to support them. Many Committees made arrangements after careful discussion with the refugees but sometimes this affected the relationship between British and Belgian, keeping the refugee in a dependant position. Darlington decided to extend their self support scheme and ask for nominal rent from all Belgians in work. Most responded well, though two or three boasted they were thwarting the intentions of the Committee. At Portishead it was decided that refugees earning must maintain themselves. Other Committees made arrangements for the refugees to take goods home with them. Indicating the expectations of a quick return to peace, on 17 September 1914, Cricklewood began its Home Box Scheme where each of the 30 families was given a lock-up box and material for household linen to make up and keep until their repatriation.

However, fund-raising also opened the possibility of fraud and the Government had to act. WRC Certification was tried and when this failed, the 1916 War Charities Act was passed, requiring fund-raising Committees to register through local councils giving details of five Committee members. Funds were required to have their accounts properly audited, but the Commission did not require copies. It is therefore impossible to assess amounts collected. By the time the Act was passed some funds had been closed because Belgians had left England, or were supporting themselves. Records show that although the major concern was, understandably, with comforts and medical aid for the troops, there was, nonetheless, a wider humanitarian impulse at work evident in the continuing care of Belgian refugees and especially of their children.

Education

As Myers (2001) and Storr (2003) describe, the younger refugee children were given education in local schools and some Belgian schools were also established. However, in addition, Belgian professors and students were offered help by British Universities. Cambridge offered its facilities to Louvain University; the University of London offered hospitality to about 70 members of French and Belgian Universities and help to students; the University of Oxford offered a home for the winter to the young children of Belgian professors at Louvain. In appealing for further help, Dr Charles Sarolea, a Belgian Consul, reminded readers of *The Times* (22.9.1914) that Belgium was fighting the battles of Great Britain, moral blackmail softened by his over-optimistic anticipation that the war would be over in a few weeks.

In Oxford Miss Helge Gill organized a Committee that included both suffragists and anti-suffragists. In September, 450 refugees arrived, 100 of whom were connected with Belgian Universities. The Oxford Women's Suffrage Society lent its office to Belgian women where they took daily English lessons until February 1915. Elinor Rokeby Price was full-time Secretary of the Belgian Refugee Relief Committee from December 1914 to May 1919, and was awarded the *Medaille* for her services. Some girls attended the Oxford Girls' High School and boys were taken at Magdalen and St Edward's Schools at specially reduced rates. The rest attended a special Catholic school organized at St John's College. By January 1915, when Miss Gill was in France with NUWSS Scottish Women's Hospitals, Oxford suffragists such as Cecily Jane Eden Lewis were helping refugees. Lewis also worked for the FWVRC at the Refugee Camp at Ede, Holland, from May to October 1916 and cared for Serbian refugees in France. Undergraduate suffragists organized fund-raising; the students at St Hilda's contributed clothes and put on a play. The Old Students Suffrage Society prepared the Belgians for repatriation, and trained volunteers to assist in reconstruction work. Eleanor Lodge, who also taught English to Belgian refugees, formed a Belgian Repatriation Committee which trained workers in camp cookery and camp construction, evidently anticipating refugees' return to conditions of devastation. During the War, Ruskin College was closed but approximately ten children and 18 adult refugees were placed there on 23 September. The Tutor H. Sanderson Furniss, a pacifist suffrage supporter, was appointed principal without pay in 1916 and remained in that post until 1925. On 17 February 1917 he signed the Oxford Memorial in favour of women's suffrage and when the college reopened in 1919 women were admitted as students.

As at Oxford, Cambridge Committees also included women suffragists. Margaret Heitland, who was fluent in French and German, was assistant secretary of the Cambridge Women's Suffrage Association, which her mother founded with Millicent Garrett Fawcett in 1884. Shortly after the outbreak of War, over 250 refugees from Belgium arrived. Margaret Keynes, sister of Maynard, the economist, was interested in suffrage, and helped settle some refugees (Wilson 1967: 148). However, as Chair of the Borough of Cambridge Committee, Heitland was ultimately responsible for their accommodation, support, and employment. Cambridge Town Committee's Report from 1914 to December 1915 expressed pride in the education they had been able to offer:

> However distressing their exile must have proved to most of our Belgian guests, their stay will, we believe, have proved advantageous to the younger people from an educational point of view. The fact of learning another language, and of being subjected to new – if possibly not to better – educational methods than those which they had known, must have had a stimulating effect. (IWM. Belgium 6 39/6)

As refugees approached school leaving age, Margaret Heitland began to help them train for future careers in Belgium. Several of the youngsters, on completing their secondary education, were helped to obtain technical training. One girl was sent to London to learn millinery. Another, who possessed previous trade experience, was employed as a shop assistant and one or two quite young girls were able to earn small fees by giving French conversation lessons to children. Such preparations continued into the final war months when arrangements were made for a refugee to attend design classes at the County School of Arts and Crafts. One girl became a fully qualified shorthand typist and another completed a course of needlework training. A third was at Wordsworth Grove Hospital training in massage, a technique used in the care of soldiers suffering from shell-shock which implies an extension in women's nursing role.

A women's network operated in the different Cambridge Committees, liaison between them avoiding the duplication which occurred in refugee relief. Cambridge Town's Hospitality Committee was able to take advantage of University facilities and horticulture training took place on ground lent by Girton College, the first residential college for women (IWM. Belgium

6 39/6, 39/8, 39/9). Town Committee's Honorary Secretary, Mrs Eaden, was active in arranging the educational and general welfare of the Belgians. She, with others, provided English lessons, and enabled Belgians who could teach French, Flemish and (in one case) Russian to earn a little by giving lessons. Her work was probably not limited to Town Committee, for on 1 June 1920, she belatedly replied on behalf of the Cambridgeshire County Committee to Agnes Conway's query about Cambridgeshire's work with the Belgian refugees. It is very probable that Mrs Eaden knew Margaret Heitland who was closely connected with Newnham College which created its own Refugee Relief Committee and subscribed for a house occupied by five Belgians, maintained partly by the Committee. The Newnham Students' Committee disbanded during 1917 probably because a now reduced workload could be undertaken by others.

Belgian Repatriation Fund

As indicated, from the beginning British hosts and Belgian guests planned for repatriation. The Belgian Repatriation Fund, of which Eleanor Acland, the Liberal democratic suffragist, was Hon. Secretary, was established in September 1914 by Madame Vandervelde, the English wife of the pacifist Emile Vandervelde, a member of the Belgian Cabinet and Belgian Socialist leader, whose influence, according to the *Englishwoman* (July–September 1915: 124), 'was one of the great factors inspiring Belgium's resistance'. Some British people considered him a malign influence due to fear of socialism; there was official British irritation with the socialist body, the *Union des Comités*, and Vandervelde as its President. However, the Conservative President Raymond Poincaré (Arthur 1929: 3) reported that: 'M. de Brocqueville told me yesterday that M. Vandervelde is at the moment of invaluable help, not only to his own Government but to the Allied Powers'. Vandervelde was very supportive of relief efforts throughout the war and Mme Vandervelde's speaking tour in England, the USA and Canada to prepare for the task of 'restoring prosperity to the free and glorious Belgium that is to be', raised about $300,000. The Belgian Repatriation Fund Committee formed after her speech in London, although 'representative of all classes and religious creeds in England and Belgium' typically had as patrons high-ranking men, such as the Belgian Prime Minister, the Baron de Broqueville, and the Belgian Minister in London, M. Paul Hymans.

The term 'Repatriation' was misleading, implying only post-war aid. Lord Gladstone thought funds should not be diverted from helping refugees' present distress and disapproved of the Fund, seeing it as useless. He reprimanded Hugh Cecil for allowing his name to be entered for the Executive, and Cecil admitted it was a 'foolish body', nonetheless continuing to co-operate. Gladstone was disgruntled because he suspected, correctly, that the Belgian Legation's Relief Fund received money intended for the WRC, money which therefore did not help the refugees in Britain for whom he was responsible.

Despite Gladstone's views, the WRC participated in a Joint Committee with the Repatriation Committee, the Royal Society of Agriculture, the Belgian Town-Planning Committee, and the FWVRC to share information and ensure integrated action when the time arrived. Eleanor Acland, who was awarded the *Medaille* for her work, organized fund- and goods-raising, and visited Holland to see Repatriation Fund schemes for housing Belgian refugees in internment camps. She explained in *The Englishwoman* (July–September 1915: 124), that 'Repatriation' included everything connected with reconstructing homes and industries in Belgium, so far as private enterprise could cope with it, including the provision of temporary huts. It incorporated the type of reconstructive work undertaken by Quakers in France after the Franco-Prussian war and in South Africa after the Boer War and included conferences with architects, visits to garden cities to study town planning and co-operative work with the Royal Society of Agriculture. She concluded: 'It would seem particularly fitting that English suffragists should concern themselves with this work' by contributing funds. Despite having Lady Selborne as its Chairman and Monseigneur Carton de Wiart on the Committee, it seems a comparatively small endeavour and funds were much needed as this inaccurate draft of receipts and payments shows. During this period the Fund acted primarily as a channel for Mme Vandervelde's efforts, receiving £10,941 she raised and making grants for work associated with Belgian refugees in Holland.

Table 2. Belgian Repatriation Fund.
Receipts and Payments 5 September 1914 to 30 November 1915
(FWVRC Box 9.3.5)

Receipts		*Expenses*	
Donations to Fund from Mme Vandervelde	£10,941	Performers at Tunbridge Wells Concert	£9 9s.
Donations from other persons	£4,297	Salaries & Insurance	£186
Funds transferred from Belgian Organisation Society	£14	Printing & Stationery	£49
Concert at Tunbridge Wells	£62	Postage, telegrams	£43
Collection in York	£5	Rent and cleaning	£51
Bank Interest	£37	Travelling	£7
		Advertising	£3
		Office Furniture	£21
		Miscellaneous	£9
		Grants	
		Mme Vandervelde for Huts in Holland	£1,000
		For Reconstruction des Foyer Belges	£200
		For Huts Eton & Linthwaite	£69
		Wages for making clothes	£5
		Money held	
		Investment £10,000 Treasury Bills due 4 December 1915. £9834 3s. 3d.	£9,834
		Cash on deposit	£3,700
		Cash on current account	£167
		Cash in hand	1s. 10d.
Total	£15,358	*Total*	£15,358

Public attitudes change

Underlying these efforts and hospitality was the hope that the Belgian guests would soon return to their own country. The discourse of hospitality together with the fact that the Belgians were at first not allowed to work, meant that there had been a tendency for the British to wait on the first refugees, especially in the south of the country, and Belgians' letters home had raised unrealistic expectations in the minds of later refugees. As the Aliens Act showed, anti-alienism had been a social, cultural and political discourse in the years leading up to the war confirming stereotypical images of foreigners as disease-carrying and untrustworthy. The Government's ambivalence towards refugees, together with newspaper publication of reprehensible actions by some, inflamed underlying prejudice, resulting in a gradual erosion of public sympathy to which some Belgian heroes contributed as their human failings became evident. The British realized that even heroic refugees could do certain tasks for themselves and began to question why the Belgians did not help themselves. British women found themselves working to keep their Belgian families in idleness, and while married Belgian women, especially those with children were not encouraged to find work, unmarried women were sometimes slow to support themselves. A writer to *The Common Cause* suggested the housing of Belgian refugees was on wrong lines. In hostels Englishwomen were doing the work while the Belgians were idle. They needed occupation and should cook and serve their own meals and do housework. Belgian men did very little to help themselves or their families until they were allowed to take jobs but some refused to work even when jobs were found. One explained this was because he was the King of England's guest.

WEC's impression of the Belgians was that they were 'slow to adapt', and 'exigeant', but agreed that:

> Very great mistakes were made in handling the Belgians, owing to the people put to interview them being ignorant of Belgian life and customs, so that much discontent was aroused and many unfair situations created altogether unnecessarily. Many families were spoiled in consequence and this created a difficult atmosphere later for both helpers and helped. (IWM. Belgium 5/7)

In May 1916 E. Hutchinson, Chairman, and Ronald Hodgkin, Secretary at Darlington (IWM. Belgium 6.71), wrote: 'Looking back we can see how some of the greatest difficulties have been due to this lavish hospitality.' Miss M. Coules of Folkestone and a group of 20 girls formed a choir to raise money and her mother organized a house.

> But the Belgians are not grateful. They won't do a stroke of work, and grumble at everything, and their morals ... It may be true enough that Belgium saved Europe, but ... save us from the Belgians. (IWM. DD. 97/25/1)

The reference to morals is not explained but there is evidence that the Belgian women's behaviour, described as 'loose', was disturbing. Accommodation was less frequently offered, fund-raising became more difficult. It was politic not to emphasize problems, such as those exposed by Mary Boyle. She wrote (IWM. Belgium 6.100. 28) of refugees' petty grievances; of the efforts needed 'to take thousands and thousands, house, feed and make them self supporting, give them back self-respect, and yet day by day suffer the abuse and the reproaches and very, very seldom, experience the gratitude of the people for whom they toiled'. Another problem was typified in Darlington. Throughout the whole stay of the Belgians there the Committee had to devote much time and energy to dealing with quarrels and disputes, consequent rearrangements and removals, finding suitable employment, arranging for insurance, and obtaining pensions.

While many British people continued their support of refugees for the whole war, public attitudes, as depicted by Horatio Bottomley of *John Bull*, gradually changed. Undoubtedly the most significant factor in changing attitudes was that Belgian men were perceived as cowards. When British conscription was introduced in 1916, it caused enormous resentment towards the Government, a fact often ignored in military historiography. This resentment rubbed off onto the Belgians and was exacerbated by differences in British and Belgian conscription rules. British men, including married, were conscripted at younger ages than Belgians whose recruitment was somewhat limited financially and logistically due to the invasion of their country. According to de Schaepdrijver (2002: 108), fewer than 20 per cent of Belgians of military age were mobilized, against 54 per cent of

British. The British perceived the Belgians as one nation, but as de Schaepdrijver points out (2002: 97), Walloons were unlikely to be willing to fight for, and die on, Flemish soil.

The role of the Press was central to the perception of Belgians first as brutal slave owners in the Congo and as white slavers in the late nineteenth century, and then as tragic heroes during the Great War. However, Belgium lost this image due to the low death toll (de Schaepdrijver 2002: 108). By the end of the war Belgian losses were approximately 11 per cent, against British losses of 13 per cent. The Press campaign against Jews, particularly Russians who did not want to fight for the Tsar, extended to attacking Belgians. However, a letter to Walter Long from a group headed by Lord Norfolk (PRO. MH8.7), warned that the Press should be told of political consequences arising from 'ill timed and injudicious references to Belgian refugees' and instead draw attention to their sacrifices, their exile, and the sufferings of those in Belgium.

When Belgians of military age were called up, many refugee women and children were left destitute and needed support from British hosts, but allowances to soldiers' wives were another cause of friction, since Belgian refugees could obtain higher rates than their British counterparts. There is no evidence that Governmental financial support for the refugees directly or indirectly reduced allowances paid to the British; this money formed part of the Belgian War Debt and was expected to be repaid.

On two days in May 1916 there were riots in Fulham. These were both socio-economic and xenophobic, the rioters being under the impression that refugees were being given preferential housing treatment and financial support. As Humphreys indicates (1995: 10), the investigation and categorization of applicants, crucial to COS philosophy, was continued by the WRC which nonetheless gave special grants from its Private Relief Fund, although in retrospect Gladstone considered some had not needed this positive discrimination. The COS had been investigating the circumstances of needy Belgian families in Fulham, reporting to the WRC and administering the grants. In October 1916, Basil Peto, MP, who was on the Managing Committee acting as unpaid Chief Commissioner for Belgian Refugee affairs under Walter Long, visited the slum area of Heckfield Place, where the refugees were housed, and it was decided that they should be provided with better accommodation, beds and furniture, and that there should be a closer supervision of the work. Consequently a WRC office was opened in Fulham under Miss Newton. She probably had social work experience for she offered prizes for the houses and flats kept in the best order and on Whit Monday these were presented at a ceremonial gathering. Like the COS, the WRC was aware of the danger of subsidising low wages and was anxious to detect fraud by both refugee and landlord or landlady, who sometimes also needed help having exhausted their resources.

Nevertheless, even scurrilous journalists like Bottomley could not totally quell the international, humanitarian spirit. Individual relationships frequently remained totally cordial. Many hosts and guests stayed good friends; some married into local families. For example, Rachel de Breffe in Grimsby married a local lad, and the family was helped by Committee members, especially the Wintringhams.

Repatriation

By October 1918, it was evident that the War would soon be over. In mid-December Basil Peto was appointed Commissioner to supervise refugees' repatriation, which included the offer of a free passage to Belgium to every refugee but with a time-limit for acceptance. There were considerable difficulties in obtaining suitable shipping to transport roughly 150,000 people, and up to the middle of January only ships which brought repatriated PoWs from Rotterdam were available to take Belgian refugees on the return voyage, which had to be made to Antwerp, the only open Belgian port. Organizers had to take into account the fact that the majority of passengers were women and children. In addition, German women who had been in Britain throughout the War were being repatriated to Germany. On 18 February *The Grimsby Daily Telegraph* reported that Mr Shortt, the Home Secretary, had said this was happening where the Advisory Committee had advised in favour. Exceptions were being made in favour of aged people, invalids, and children, but no discrimination was allowed for persons of high social position. However, British born wives and children of Germans were not being sent out of Britain country against their will.

It was calculated that total Government expenditure, including repatriation, arising from the original invitation to Belgians to come to Britain was £3,500,000, plus voluntary contributions. The WRC estimated these as £6,000,000 but it is unclear how this figure was ascertained. According to Home Office figures (PRO. HO 45/10738/261921), repatriation expenses were £242,975 19s. 2d. In fact, rather than resenting this expenditure, British people worried whether the Belgians were being sent back too quickly. Belgians who had been constructed as heroes, then scroungers, were again perceived as victims, normal humans being repatriated too quickly.

Mr C. Smeesters, Belgian Ministry of the Interior, and Chairman of the Belgian Repatriation Committee, wrote to *The Times* (19.12.1918) to thank the British nation. He said repatriation was being organized at the request of the Belgian Government. Everyone felt it was a patriotic duty to return to Belgium and many were also anxious not to add to the difficulties of employment and housing of demobilized British soldiers. The Belgian authorities were arranging hostels at Antwerp and Ostend and there was free transport to people's ultimate destinations on special trains. National relief committees were providing food for all who were out of work. He hoped it would be possible to delay repatriation of those who were resident in devastated areas for a few weeks until the Belgian Government was able to provide temporary accommodation. He concluded: 'I understand that the fears expressed are inspired by the kind-heartedness which is a characteristic of the British race, but I hope these explanations will help to avoid unfounded criticism against the British Government to whom we are indebted for their assistance and repatriation of the refugees.'

Before they left the towns and villages that had given them hospitality for four years, many refugees arranged 'thank you' events; in mid-December a concert was given by the 1,200 refugees remaining at Earl's Court. Also, local Committees gave their guests farewell parties and good send-offs at railway stations. At Grimsby, Mrs G.S. Letten (President of the Ladies' Clothing Committee), Mrs T. Wintringham (who was the supervisor of the country district), and many other ladies were at the Town Station to wish their guests adieu, and the scene at 11.43 a.m. was reported as being 'an interesting one;' there were undoubtedly strong emotions on both sides as guests and hosts said farewell.

After his re-entry into Brussels on 22 November, Albert, King of the Belgians, spoke from the Throne of the hope that Belgium would enjoy complete independence and emancipation from the burden of neutrality. On 6 May 1919, he sent a message to King George, saying:

> The sorely-tried Belgians will never forget the hospitality they were accorded on British soil, the care with which they were surrounded, the spontaneous generosity given so tirelessly to all those whom the invader had driven from their country.

The final Hull report written 17 March 1919, noted that the refugees went as they came, unobtrusively and without form or ceremony. There was, however, a striking difference in their appearance on arrival and departure. They came in misery to a life of comparative peace and plenty, but were going from that to penury and privation. How they would survive the circumstances they would be called on to face – no work, no means and with necessaries at little short of famine prices – distressed those who had become the friends of these civilian heroes. Nonetheless, they were soon forgotten by most of the British people as economic and social difficulties of the inter-war years took their place.

PART TWO

Aid to Continental Europe

While some women were trying to alleviate the sufferings of people of their own and other nationalities in Britain, others began attempting to help on the mainland of Europe. This brought into play a variety of factors which people in Britain did not need to consider, including neutrality, the necessity of working with relief organizations formed by other nationalities, and of being much closer to military action. Military, political and economic circumstances in the various countries of war-torn Europe, together with the geographical location, created different challenges which needed to be surmounted if people were to be helped. In addition, there was the question of transporting supplies as well as workers.

Britain had declared war ostensibly because Germany had violated Belgium's neutrality. German forces quickly occupied the major part of Belgium and Flanders; consequently Allied relief workers could not work in these regions. Here, relief could only be undertaken through self-help organizations, by people from the Central Powers, or neutral nations such as Spain or America. The Committee for Relief in Belgium (CRB), run by the American Quaker Herbert Hoover, with the agreement of Germany and Britain, brought in otherwise prohibited goods, especially food; money raised in Britain was channelled through it. American neutrality was vital for Belgian survival although Belgians themselves provided the means whereby food and clothing was distributed at the point of need. The American Relief Clearing House co-ordinated American relief in France and Belgium and of it Percy Mitchell (1922) wrote: 'The frontiers of neutrality are fluid. They cannot be charted with rigorous accuracy.' We see this in relation to the relief organizations established by American women. Further, while change of national identity on marriage restricted some women's actions, it enabled others, through humanitarianism, to infiltrate the neutrality/belligerent boundaries, directly through care, or indirectly through appeals for funds and workers. Concern for women of other nationalities allowed their sphere of influence to increase to international magnitude.

In war, a national boundary, such as that between France and Belgium, ceases to be as immediately relevant as that created by the presence of an occupying force. This affects relief. However, in the Netherlands, the national boundary was vitally important. In 1905 Queen Wilhelmina pointed out that the Netherlands needed neutrality because none of the great powers could safeguard the Dutch at home or in its imperial possessions abroad (Abbenhuis 2006: 28). Although neutrality did not guarantee independence or avoidance of war's effects, neutrality regulations had to be upheld and breaches prevented. A neutral nation required reliance on internal sources of strength; therefore the influx of needy Belgians created serious difficulties because they sapped resources. British citizens hoping to help the refugees in Holland needed to understand these matters and be circumspect. Britain recognized Dutch neutrality only on 6 August 1914 and could not subsequently violate it with impunity as members of the IWRC and the FWVRC realized. However, the exchange of prisoners in which the FWVRC was involved, leaves many questions unanswered concerning neutrality and Quaker association with the military.

Of the 20,000 Friends, only a few could take a personal share in relieving miseries of war abroad (Hirst 1923: 503). This is also true of suffragists, some of whom worked with the FWVRC. Quakers' experience of relief and charity work went back through generations within families and the doubts and experiences around Boer War aid and the type of relief undertaken were central to their subsequent Great War relief work, personal or family experience and understanding of what happened in places such as Bloemfontein being the background for work later in the century. Further, women's social role within the Quaker network of family and friends was vital to the setting up and success of Great War relief work; the Fry sisters' networks exemplify the significance of this in the composition of FWVRC volunteers. Working through Committees meant that Quakers might be slower to react to a given situation than those who could act independently but the Friends' known relief tradition helped them gain access into countries devastated by war or famine. With wealthy Friends in industry, banking, and several Members of Parliament, useful male networks were already established within Government and diplomatic circles which relief workers used.

Friends' work among refugees aimed at rebuilding people's lives as a testimony against war. They considered it crucial that the refugees' feelings of self-respect and self-reliance should be fostered, rather than that relief should encourage what they experienced as the 'refugee mentality' – the expectation and receipt of handouts without effort. Friends wanted to show their sympathy by fully sharing in the lives of people suffering from the devastation war caused. This was a practical manifestation of their spiritual beliefs, and they hoped that the people they worked among would be transformed by this evidence of caring. Quakers' adherence to principle is examined through their relationship with British and French civil and military authorities. This reveals tensions caused by serving under military control while seeking to keep separate from it and includes discords among the Quakers themselves. Nevertheless, the Quaker reputation for relief work survived.

Suffragists and Quakers shared the conviction that the use of force did not solve problems, but whereas Friends, due to their pacifist convictions, concentrated on alleviating the misery armed forces caused to non-combatants, this belief did not prevent suffragists, particularly those with medical training, from aiding military personnel since their aim was attaining citizenship. Consequently, the main way that suffragists supported relief abroad was through the Scottish Women's Hospitals (SWH) which was formed to aid wounded servicemen. Since shared feminism meant that Quakers continued to assist the NUWSS, any Friend now assisting the suffrage organizations was likely to become involved, even at some distance, in the work of the SWH; Margery Fry was on the Finance Committee of the NUWSS in March 1915. SWH Units served in many countries, but their work in France and Serbia is of particular interest because of their aid to refugees. The speed of enemy advance by Austria and then Bulgaria prevented Quaker relief in Serbia, so instead they helped the Serbian Relief Fund, which had strong suffrage connections. In Serbia relief workers became prisoners, enemy aliens and refugees; the war forced a mass exodus and necessitated an international relief effort.

Rupp (1997) describes the international bonds of womanhood as being forged through a discourse of motherhood and sisterhood. Pre-war connections proved crucial in enabling British women to contact their Continental sisters and provide immediate relief. However, now there was increased emphasis on the effects of war on women, including rape. Concern for mothers and children might in some quarters have reinforced the idea of women's moral responsibility for the future of the world but the response to refugees' need was instinctive humanitarianism *by* women *for* women, children and the elderly. In addition to dealing with the immediate needs of clothing, food and shelter, relief workers tried to provide refugees with some form of continuity with their past and future lives, teaching skills and offering opportunities for employment, promoting refugees' agency by enabling acceptance or refusal of what was offered. Although in many ways, the lives of refugees and relief workers must have felt 'on hold', for many of the latter, the opportunity to go abroad to work was unprecedented and eagerly grasped.

If women were to give aid, they had to overcome the gender implications of various discourses that informed war-time relief work. Although the Victorian ideology of women's moral superiority was a central part of the perceived pre-eminence of English culture, it was intersected by the contradictory assumption of female inferiority which both led to and arose from the bourgeois 'separate spheres' ideal. This explains why the Army Medical Department and the British Red Cross refused Dr Elsie Inglis's SWH and other women's units and failed to help others. Women's perceived inability to fight was one reason for excluding them from the franchise. This hegemonic patriarchal assumption was paralleled by another about the assumed cowardice of conscientious objectors, many of whom were Friends. As Hirst states (1923: 486), Friends resented the assumption that the only national service which deserved the name was that rendered by soldiers. Suffragists and Quakers alike attempted to show militaristic society these ideas were false. The similarities and differences in the ideals and motives of the various groups are depicted in Figure 1 opposite.

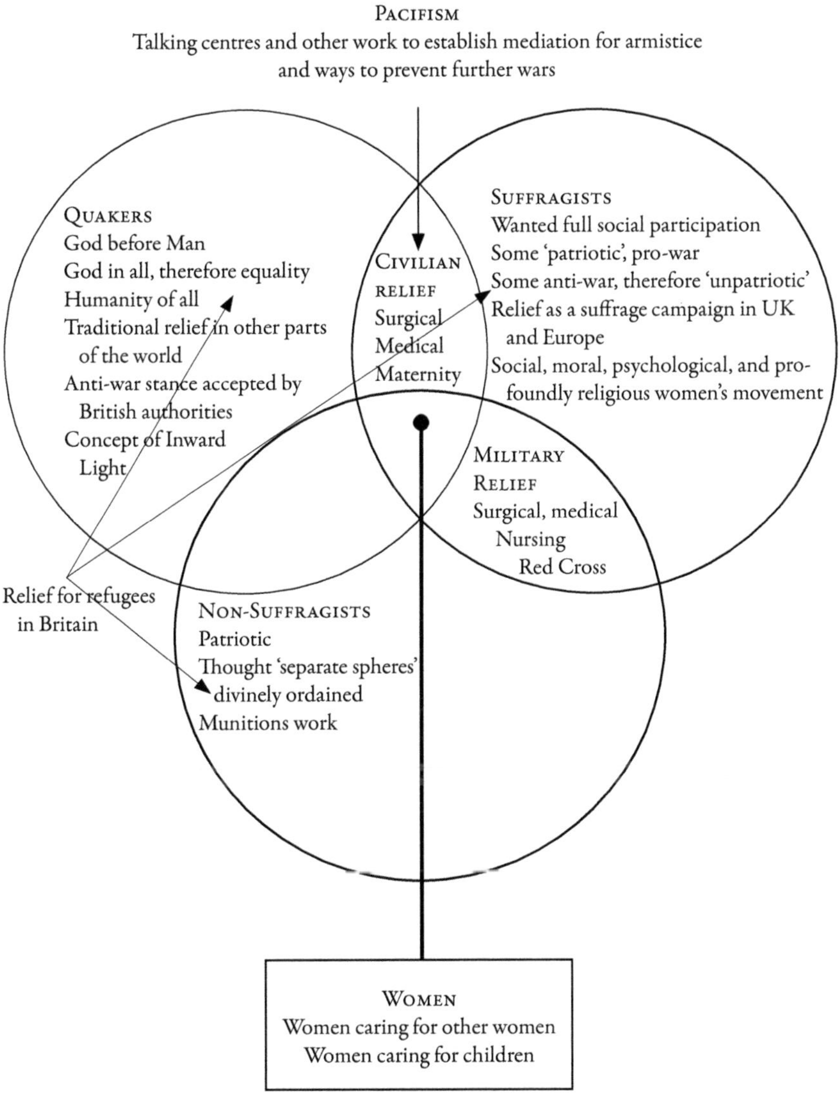

Figure 1. Intersection of women's ideals.

CHAPTER 4

Helping an Invaded Nation: Belgium and Flanders, USA Links

Occupied Belgium

Relief for the Belgians by the Belgians

German troops crossed the border into Belgium as the easiest route into France, which was their main objective. Being neutral did not mean that Belgium had no army, only that its role was different from that of a belligerent nation since theoretically it could not fight the invading army. The occupation was consequently described as the rape of Belgium. As in other countries, there was an immediate economic downturn. On 3 August Jane Brigode, Secretary of the Belgian League for Women's Rights, presiding at a meeting of the Belgian Federation for Women's Suffrage, proposed creating a bureau 'for the centralisation of feminine energy' (*Jus Suffragii*, 1.3.1915). Mme Brigode (born Jane Ouwerx in 1870) was a Belgian Liberal and eminent suffrage leader. Like Millicent Garrett Fawcett, she recognized that women would be thrown out of work and women and children would be the first to suffer. The bureau was intended to find and sometimes create work for the unemployed. Eight days later the Belgian Women's Patriotic Union was founded with Mme Brigode at its head, assisted by Mlle Louise Van den Plas, Secretary of the Christian Feminism of Belgium. The Union's bureau served as intermediary between those who needed jobs and the organizations that might employ them. Suffragists in Belgium were therefore in the forefront of aiding their own compatriots by creating an organization that became vital to the nation's survival.

As the troops swept across the country hundreds of thousands of people became refugees. Wounded men were brought into Brussels and then the German Army arrived. There was an almost complete cessation of industry and shops closed. Private resources failed. The Union quickly became the most important of organizations providing employment for women whose homes were destroyed and who streamed into Brussels from the devastated regions. It established a needlework industry which helped unemployed men as well as women. Clothes, silk flowers and toys were made, using national colours. Knitting rooms were opened and women employed to make garments. Lace makers continued to trade and Mme Brigode appealed for orders and contributions to avert starvation using the IWSA and going *via* a Belgian lady who went to London fund-raising. The IWSA sent £30 to help in the work. Mme Brigode persuaded the National Relief Committee, the *Vestiaire Central*, to understand the importance of its work, resulting in a regular subsidy. During war clothing becomes dangerously difficult to replace and at the outbreak of hostilities the *Division du Vêtement*, one of the many sections of the *Secours* Department of the National Committee, was established. In its first month it distributed 1,617 garments among refugees, but then averaged 442,694 garments per month at the close of 1916. Its activities extended into every village and hamlet of Belgium, with clothing distributed far down into the North of France close to the line of military operations. The *Vestiaire* also bought all the clothes made and distributed them to the needy all over Belgium. By March 1915, the Union employed over 2,000 women. They received 3 frs. 50 c. every eight days in addition to free distributions of soup and help with potatoes and coal. In this way women were saved from begging, and from 'worse evils', by which was meant prostitution.

Food scarcity resulted in prices rising and levels of consumption plummeting. This was partly due to the British blockade, because Belgium needed to import from four-fifths to five-sixths of her food supply, but Germany's submarines also sank supply ships; Belgium's industry and agriculture were exploited for Germany's benefit and the occupation is now considered to have been harsher than under the Nazis. According to official Belgian statistics, civilian mortality rose, 100,000 people dying from war-related causes, although Winter (Wall & Winter 1988: 24–7) considers that there were in fact 146,000 male deaths and that 97,000 female deaths were ignored in the figures.

On 1 September 1915, *Jus Suffragii* carried an article entitled 'Work of the Belgian Women' which stated that representatives of the IWRC had visited Belgium. Although names are not given and it is not stated whether they visited occupied or free Belgium, the indications are that these were American women, and they had gone behind German lines. On their return they spoke 'most enthusiastically of the splendid work being done by women'. They were particularly impressed by the co-ordination and unity of Belgian Women's Relief Committees. They said the calamity in Belgium, being a national one, had developed a national response and allied with the Committee in each neighbourhood were committees of women interested in the feminist movement, who gave work making garments to unemployed women. This was surely Mme Brigode's Union. Its work was subsequently seen and recorded by Charlotte Kellogg and Milton Brown, Americans who, being neutral, were able to visit Brussels and other places in occupied Belgium.

American aid to Belgium

There was considerable strength of feeling in American national consciousness regarding the repayment of a moral debt to France arising from help received in the American War of Independence of 1775–83; this debt was understood as also being due to Belgium since that country did not become a separate state until 1830 when the Belgian Revolution led to the establishment of an independent, Catholic and neutral country.

On the outbreak of the War several relief committees were operated by American and British women for the Allied military and for civilians in occupied Belgium and France despite the fact that America was neutral and Britain at war. In Britain, women's philanthropic role in the public sphere was perceived as essentially 'natural;' their joint endeavours with American women in humanitarian relief for civilians indicate the same gender perception on that side of the Atlantic. The American élite had ties of marriage with Britain's titled aristocracy and shared the same concepts of *noblesse oblige* and philanthropic duty of care. Family ties enabled upper-class women to take a leading share in movements of patriotism and philanthropy on both sides of the Atlantic, bending American neutrality which became meaningless in relation to these joint funds, since whatever the law said, their 'nationality' was pitched on both sides of the Atlantic. American neutrality therefore became permeated by people who were legally members of one of the belligerent nations. This raises issues of the nature of women's identity, the perceptions of nationality and neutrality and firmness of the boundaries created by the legal process of nationhood; in wartime these are significant in relation to the belligerency or neutrality of the nation to which a person belongs and informed the belief that women were more likely to be spies.

The day after war was declared two groups of women met to form Relief Associations. Firstly, British women at the Imperial Club, a British women's club in New York, decided to establish the British War Relief Association. It was the first War Relief Association incorporated in New York City and was primarily formed to aid hospitals and relief stations in England, France and Belgium. Beatrice Forbes-Robertson Hale was President. As the niece of Sir Johnstone Forbes-Robertson she was English by birth, American by marriage. She had been a successful stage actress who continued working after her marriage and was a suffragist, author and lecturer. After her divorce in 1920, Beatrice returned to England, but remained involved with the women's rights movement in the USA. The Vice-President was Mrs Oliver Herford, British by birth and married to a Sheffield-born naturalized American. She was involved in the American Women's Peace Party created in 1915 in New York by Crystal Eastman after the British suffragette Emmeline Pethick-Lawrence and Rosika Schwimmer from Hungary toured America rousing women's peace sentiments. The American Women's War Relief Fund also started on 5 August when a group of American women married to Englishmen and resident in England, met together. Lady Leila Paget was President, Mrs John Astor was Vice-President, and the Duchess of Marlborough was Chair. The foremost concern of this organization was care of the wounded and succour of the women and children left behind to fight a grim fight with poverty. The simultaneity of the foundation of these two Funds indicates deliberate co-ordination. Americans also raised funds for Britain to enable her to carry on relieving her allies thus showing a partiality that belied American neutrality.

The Mayfair War Relief of New York was also formed in early August to supply relief to Belgian refugees. However, like many funds, its aims changed during 1916 and 1917 as events of the war called for a different approach, in this case the battle of Verdun from February to July 1916, and Passchendaele, Third Ypres, in the last six months of 1917. This Fund then extended its activities to sending articles to hospitals and formed a special department to deal with packages for refugees from evacuated regions and for the families of French and Belgian soldiers. While some Committees added the military to their original relief intentions, other Committees did not deflect from their purpose to aid civilians only. The most important of these was the CRB.

Surviving in the Occupied Zone

As the Germans advanced, refugees fled to Brussels from all parts of Belgium and during September there was no flour available in the city. Citizens approached Brand Whitlock, the American Ambassador, to have food imported from England; Burgomaster Max asked Whitlock and the Marquis de Villalobar, the Spanish Ambassador, to be patrons of a relief committee. Discussions were held with the German administration to find means of providing food, the Hague Convention being quoted as stating that it is the duty of the occupying power to feed the population which in reality it did not state but the bluff worked. This was the birth of the CRB, and the British Government gave a contribution of £100,000. As Gay and Fisher explain (1929):

> An official of the British Foreign Office once described the Commission for Relief in Belgium as a piratical state organized for benevolence. This description, however extravagant in certain particulars, has the virtue of suggesting the attributes of an organization without precedent in international relations.

Herbert Hoover had organized the repatriation of American refugees in London, and on 6 October Dr Page, the US Ambassador, suggested that he might organize the *ravitaillment*, the food supply of the Belgians. *Sécours National* was the Belgian relief organization for support of aged people, women and children, and included aid to Belgian refugees made destitute by the war. It did not come under their auspices at first but was dealt with by the Belgian *Comité National*. This was able to distribute food if it could be obtained and restrictions placed by the belligerents overcome. The American Branch of the *Sécours National* was established by Mrs Whitney Warren, the wife of a distinguished American architect. It specialized in providing infants' and children's kits. Contributions of money and clothing were collected and forwarded to the parent institution in France and by summer of 1915 total contributions were $83,000.

Hoover's first appeal for the people in occupied Belgium was made to America and Canada but not to Britain; however, reports appeared in the press regarding Belgian misery. People sent sums directly to the CRB offices in London, totalling up to 26 April 1915, £224,452 9s. 5d. Together with foodstuffs, clothing and contributions from the British Empire, over £784,000 was contributed to the CRB by that date. In November Hoover arrived in Brussels to investigate conditions, accompanied by representatives of the Rockefeller Foundation. They toured occupied France and having seen women gathering refuse to eat from the German camps, reported that people were starving. Toward the end of November Belgium's need was desperate and the Foundation provided supply ships to transport food. It urged that the CRB should extend activities into a strip of France which included the towns of Roubaix, Tourcoing and Lille, where the CRB had its Northern France HQ. By January 1915, 400,000 French people were being fed in occupied areas.

The Women's Section of the CRB was probably the biggest women's organization in America concerned with foreign relief. Its Executive Co-operative Committee included Mrs Carrie Chapman Catt, President of the National American Woman Suffrage Association and first President of the IWSA; Miss Frances W. Sibley, of the Girls' Friendly Society in America; the Rev. Anna Shaw, National American Woman Suffrage Association, and Mrs Arthur Dodge, National Association Opposed to Woman Suffrage.

They therefore enlisted the aid of the great national organizations of women, regardless of politics. The combined membership of these organizations totalled 5,500,000 women supporting relief. One of the CRB Women's Section's activities was to organize a Belgium Flour Fund and using the *Literary Digest* it raised in less than six months enough money to buy 20,000 barrels of flour. It also obtained permission to display appeals for Belgium in every post office. It sent five cargoes of supplies, established sewing camps for Belgian women refugees in Holland and undertook relief work in Poland and Northern France.

In occupied Belgium and Flanders there were 55,000 volunteers working for CRB, and Hoover saw the work being naturally divided by gender. Financing, organising shipments, giving assurances that the Germans were not getting the food, were 'a man's job'. Women's work was providing canteens, undertaking mothers', babies' and children's relief, counselling, and undertaking 'actual executive labour from early morning till late at night … with cheerfulness, sympathy and tenderness'. Charlotte Kellogg was the only woman ever officially connected with the CRB. She was allowed into occupied Brussels in July 1916, to be with her husband, Vernon, the 'ambassador' at CRB headquarters at Charleville, specifically to enable her to record women's involvement in relief and to appeal to American women's philanthropy. This propaganda exercise highlighted the special concern of the Belgians for babies because the model dairy farm maintained by the *Comité National* was now unequal to the demand for milk (Whitlock 1919: 166). Charlotte's role dented the boundaries of this new male world of international relief. Vernon was chief of the mission to Poland, Russia and other places in Europe, in which Charlotte was also engaged from 1918 and 1921, and between 1939 and 1949 she was a director of the Commission for Polish Relief. Vernon was professor of biology at Leland Stanford University; his specialism, especially significant in overcrowded conditions endured by refugees, was lice. Herbert Hoover had been one of his students.

A vast army of women were distributing food and clothes so Charlotte concluded that 'the martyrdom of Belgium was being prevented by its women' (Kellogg 1917) and women's charitable groups such as the Patriotic Union were undertaking the work. Charlotte's book resulting from this visit was published the following year. In it, she did not mention people by name; this was a convention at the time, but it may also have been dangerous for the women to be clearly identified. Madame XXX was credited with the excellence of the organization of the *Comité National* clothing department in Brussels. She used a skating rink for 500 people preparing bundles of cut garments sent out for sewing. Liège also used a skating rink for this type of work.

Comptoirs were like trading posts where goods were dealt with across a counter; there were 20 in Brussels with a few male tailors and many more women, totalling 15,000 workers. The women were divided into groups; each attended one day a fortnight, bringing in their completed work, for which they were paid, and taking home more cut pieces. Workers kept to the same type of work it being considered that specialization helped for the future. There were classes for those not very competent. Milton Brown of the CRB (IWM. USA.2/57) noted that women of all ages and classes of the capital's society worked together, 'women who perhaps before the war scarcely ever turned a finger but for their own pleasure, yet who are now answering the appeal of the suffering of their country and are nobly doing their bit'. Most stuff provided clothes for destitute refugees and gave work to people who otherwise were unemployable, a scheme that helped women to avoid prostitution. Toy making was another industry, but this could be used as a means of resistance to the occupation, colours and styles being selected for patriotic purposes.

Lace workers were central to Belgium's tragedy. Women had tried to retain their workforce, but ran out of materials and a market. A committee approached the CRB with proposals and eventually Britain gave permission for thread to be imported and agreed to take lace for sale so that Germany should not benefit. Lace patterns were also used as a site of resistance, being of ancient designs or related to the current situation; it is hinted that this was the reason some lace-makers were imprisoned. Nonetheless, resistance to the occupation was not easily stopped: women sang Flemish folk songs while they worked. However, Charlotte Kellogg revealed her class prejudice: singing songs prevented 'idle chatter'. Mrs Hoover established committees of American and English women to promote sales during and after the war,

$1,000,000 in net proceeds being divided between the individual workers according to the value of the lace made.

Other towns in Belgium followed Brussels' example. Most striking was the *ouvroir* or workshop at Antwerp. Perhaps unwisely, Milton Brown (IWM. USA 2/57) named the women involved.

> Recognising the splendid achievements of Mme Philippson-Wiener in the establishment of the comptoir system at Brussels, and the merits of that system, Mme Osterrieth decided to operate a comptoir at Antwerp, but also the ouvroir, which is today one of the most remarkable relief institutions in Antwerp.

The aim was three-fold: to provide clothes for the destitute, to create labour for the unemployed, and to engage in social-welfare work as a means of raising morale. Some 27,000 women were enrolled in the *comptoir*. In addition there were approximately 800 girls and women in the shop, cutting, repairing and making up. Antwerp organizers regarded learning different types of work as a 'course' which would better equip each woman for the future. In addition, social work was undertaken through creation of a pleasant environment, and lectures on personal hygiene and domestic economy. Belgian literature and history were also taught. There were singing lessons and talks on music – all ways in which Belgian identity could be affirmed. On fine days a small group of girls had a day in the country; the public library made special arrangements for lending books, banks had special arrangements for savings accounts and the City Hospital allowed a certain number of girls to have baths, using tickets given them at the *ouvroir*, and stamped to show on return that they really had bathed.

In addition to clothing, it was vitally necessary to supply food and arrange child welfare. A special committee, the *Aide et Protection aux Oeuvres de l'Enfance*, was organized in February 1915 to deal exclusively with child problems. Hoover's Report details the problems of keeping newborn infants properly clothed and fed. Pre-war Belgium had approximately 2,250,000 children under 16 of whom 60,000 were in poor families. There were more than 600 orphanages, caring for between 50 to 400 children, or a total of over 135,000 even in normal times. Due to the war an additional

11,000 were being cared for and a further 20,000 were homeless through family disorganization.

Two American funds that focussed on the needs of children were the *Oeuvre Belge du Lait pour les Petits*, with its HQ at Antwerp, and *La Santé de l'Enfance* in Brussels. Branches of these committees were created in the largest cities and towns in Belgium to take care of children in special holiday homes in the country. With the agreement of the Dutch and German authorities, children were sent for three or four weeks' holiday from Belgium to Holland, where both organisations had committees. Miss Marie-Louise de Sadeleer, daughter of the Belgian Minister of State who now lived in New York, forwarded American donations through His Excellency the Hon. Prosper Poullet who had a permanent office at The Hague. No expenses were deducted from these funds, meaning that every cent contributed went towards helping the children.

In a crowded quarter of Brussels Madame X ran a *Cantine* for *Enfants Débiles* (weak infants) where children came from schools each morning at 11 a.m. for a meal. This was organized by the 'Little Bees' society, started five years before the war to distribute children's clothing, and which now took care of about 25,000 Brussels children. When war started the mothers took charge, also establishing a home for over 5,000 refugees. By July 1916, they had 124 Brussels sections. Between 2,500 to 3,000 women, including 400 unemployed telephone girls, helped in the work. The 'Little Bees' provided expectant mothers with layettes and articles required for lying-in including cradles, materials for sheets and blankets, and especially rubber sheets that the CRB was not allowed to import because rubber could be used for military purposes. An American War Babies Cradle Committee had been formed to supply these needs; associated with it were Lady Colebrooke and the Comtesse Marie du Hemptinne. The Committee worked in Belgium and Northern France in conjunction with French, Belgian and British military charities, mothers being visited for ten days after giving birth. Despite it being an American charity, according to contemporary laws the women named as running it were not American. The Comtesse was a Belgian who organized the work at Calais. Lady Colebrooke was married to Sir Thomas Edward Colebrooke, a radical British Liberal MP. She was therefore British and an enemy to the occupying Germans. It is evident that social class eliminated some wartime problems of nationality change following marriage.

As far as possible, weekly menus at the *cantine* were based on the newly discovered scientific analysis of food values and the importance of proteins, carbohydrates and fats. On the day that Charlotte Kellogg visited, 1,662 children were being served, one of whom realized that American aid was a reciprocation of the help France had given America during the War of Independence, 'the gravest crisis of her history' (Clarke 1918). It indicates that Belgian children were being taught the history of France as a background of Belgian history.

Communal *soupes* were directed by men; but women served the queues of people, checking who was 'undeserving' but more usually, 'tragic'. The idea that the first requisite of philanthropy should be the thorough investigation of each case because indiscriminate giving was injurious to the poor, as described by Beatrice Webb (1926: 170–4), was clearly not restricted to Britain. However, this criterion was not rigidly applied under conditions of such obvious need. Occasionally gender divisions of labour also slipped. Charlotte watched an American physician who helped ladle the soup trying to swing his arm back into position, realising that women had been doing the job for 700 days. The following day Charlotte watched women with long wooden spoons stirring 'a great tub full of savory macaroni and carrots – a test in itself for muscle and endurance'. A gentleman in black frock suit and large hat came to look about and keep order. An ageist rule meant that old women who brought young children were not given anything to eat. In Liège directors stood at a long counter, serving, while 65 women rushed to and fro carrying 4,000 portions of soup to people at tables. This sexual division of labour was more usual. Men were the managers on local committees; women did the work.

In addition to gender, class remained imperative. When refugees began pouring into Brussels Madame XX, the wife of a lawyer, felt that some would 'find it torture to be crowded into the big relief shelters' and took five families in with her own. In April 1915, when the Germans took over the Red Cross, effectively destroying it (Whitlock 1919: 423), Madame XX continued to help middle-class people who had become homeless, providing a big house for several families. However, as her funds depleted she appealed to the Belgian Relief Organization to subsidize her work. Charlotte Kellogg visited the house and here came up against the same problem of 'correct' usage of the male pronoun subsuming the female encountered by Whitlock (1919: 265) who wrote, describing people waiting in line to be fed: 'I wish we had a neuter pronoun, it was so much oftener "her"'. Whitlock also wrote of the press-gang tactics of the occupiers who took people for forced labour. He wrote:

> There was another protest, addressed to the American Minister at Brussels, the most touching, in many respects, of all, because it was signed by authorized representatives of all the women's societies in Belgium. It spoke out of the hearts of the mothers of the land, and represented a refined culture beyond the imagination of the Power whose cruelties it condemned. (1919: Vol. 2: 272)

Of the listed signatories the first was Jane Brigode on behalf of the Patriotic Union, followed by Louise van den Plas of *le Féminisme Chrétien de Belgique* and Marie Parent of *la Ligue Belge du Droit des Femmes*.

Unlike Charlotte Kellogg, who only visited Belgium, Miss J.H. Gifford, a Scot, was trapped in Brussels for the four years of war. Based on her illicit diary (IWM. DD. 93/22/1), her writings are in the form of an unfinished book in which she wrote about her experience of surviving on CRB relief. She worked at 'le Castel C.A.' which became a boarding school for English girls in July 1914. On 19 July she visited England, returning on Sunday, the day that Germany demanded passage through Belgium. She must have realized the dangers and consciously chosen to return. When the Germans arrived:

> Only the briefest of diaries could be kept; even these were liable at any time to be confiscated, and, not only that, but the writer ran the risk of punishment according to their contents.

During the first week she was also occupied with meetings of the *Croix Rouge*. Many private houses were arranged as hospitals and she was appointed *Sous-directrice* of Ambulance H, Annexe 31 with 50 beds in one of the village schoolhouses. She began to prepare 20 beds as a convalescent home for British officers in Brussels under Dr Thomson of the British Red Cross.

Miss Cavell, who was executed by the Germans in October 1915, asked her to run it in connection with her nursing home. She assisted the American Legation in repatriating enemy aliens, and commenting about American refugees she noted: 'I find a note in my journal to the effect that the women were often calmer, braver, more reasonable than the men.'

By this time, the provision of food by the CRB had become vital. Eggs were first a luxury, then unobtainable. The Germans took butter and milk; margarine and fats were non-existent. 50 per cent of the younger generation were affected by TB at the end of war. Because of the diet, Miss Gifford became ill and was cared for by friends.

> The CRB kept us from starving, but nourished, no. The black bread was horrible stuff and many of us were ill in consequence with gastric catarrh ... After a time special bread was allowed to those who were delicate as we seldom had enough to eat. How could we? as our supplies depended on what escaped being torpedoed by the Germans.

The wealthy were not badly affected and country people made fortunes from selling their produce. All available odd ground was cultivated; rabbits, hens and goats were kept, but as the Germans insisted on counting these in the supplies, there was little advantage in keeping them, as feeding even hens was a problem. People smuggled in contraband food. The fuel supply was difficult, people were carried off by the Germans for cutting down trees, but fir cones and sticks were allowed as fuel. Clothes were made from blankets and sheets. Leather was requisitioned. British money in banks was confiscated; the British survived by giving English lessons. Miss Gifford taught the Belgian aristocracy and took paying-guests but the food question made it 'impossible'. The sinking of the *Lusitania* made people fearful that relief would cease if American became involved in the war (Whitlock 1919: 406).

In Brussels the British Charitable Society helped enemy alien women whose husbands were at the front or in German prisons. Together with the Victoria Institute and the British Women's Union they provided accommodation and food for British women, mostly governesses. British relief workers hoped that America would stay neutral not only because neutrality facilitated material relief to Belgium and Northern France, but also because it opened the door to mediation. In May 1915, following their Conference at The Hague, deputations of suffragists visited the heads of many nations to plead for an end to the war and for arbitration by neutrals. Jane Addams, the American social worker, visited Woodrow Wilson to plead with him to refrain from entering the war. These British enemy aliens in Belgium were under the protection of the Americans until April 1917, when the Dutch 'who were really excellent', took over. Miss Gifford received visits from Americans, including members of the Legation, Consular and CRB Services whose constant friction with the Germans she found tiring. Miss Gifford said 'Although supposed to be strictly neutral one felt [the Americans] had strong sympathies with the Allies, especially with Belgium and France – if not for Britain as a rule.' When the USA entered the war in 1917 their CRB work was handed over to the Spanish. Miss Gifford's comment that 'The Marquis de Villalobar seemed to have more power than any of the other neutral diplomats' might relate to this American coolness towards the British.

Free Belgium

In free Belgium, which included Furnes, (the Belgian HQ of King Albert), the Yser canal, Dixmude, and Pervyse, there was a movement of refugees fleeing from and returning to their homes according to the proximity of the German advance. This tiny part of Belgium was aided by Funds operating from Britain such as the Committee for Assisting the *Vestiaire Marie-José*. Formed in August 1916, Mme Hymans, the wife of the Belgian Minister in London, was patron. Their aim was to provide milk, food and clothes for Belgian infants behind the firing line in Flanders. Funds were raised by appeals and the sale of Princess Marie-José's Children's book. A Belgian Committee was engaged to make children's clothes, the President of which was Mme Van de Vyvere, the wife of the Belgian Finance Minister.

In September and October 1914, the Society of Friends in London realized that work in Belgium would be closed to them to a large extent because of the occupation. However, at their first meeting in February 1915 the FWVRC General Committee decided to consider the possibility of supporting the work of the Friends Ambulance Committee at Dunkirk and their relief to non-combatants in the Ypres district. Although primarily known for its work with the military, the FAU carried out civilian work in conjunction with the *Aide Civile Belge*, helping to establish orphanages for 200 children at Wisques and Wizernes in the Pas-de-Calais close to the Belgian border, distributing milk to 500 people, and expanding the lace industry with 1,000 women employed. In September 1917, *The Friend* reported that the FAU was working through the whole of uninvaded Belgium and the British area. They had carried out Ambulance work on the Flanders front, including at the Sacré Coeur Hospital at Ypres and the Hospital Elisabeth at Poperinghe. In addition, widespread medical, sanitary and relief work was organized among the distressed refugees and inhabitants whom they took down to Brittany to the Villa St Pierre Hospital on the sea front at St Malo. Their Civilian Health and Sanitary Section operated in a large part of free Flanders, a small section evacuating children from some of the French towns and villages near the lines and another section attached to the Belgian Maternity hospital at Rousbrugge. *The Friend* described their daily round visiting children, watching the health of the neighbourhood for infection, and searching for 'suspects'. House to house visits made them aware that the refugee living in a shanty made out of packing cases may not be a tramp, but a highly educated individual. Shopkeepers spoke Flemish and often fluent English. Hirst (1923: 502) says the FAU aided about 12 hospitals, the majority of which it established and managed including at Dunkirk, Ypres, Poperinghe, and Hazebrouck. 15,000 Belgian refugees were fed and a vast quantity of clothing distributed; lace-making centres created, temporary schools and orphanages established, provision made for milk distribution and for water purification in Belgium. The FAU carried out preparations for very considerable relief work among the civilian population of Belgium ready for when the Germans withdrew. Tatham & Miles (1920: 252–8) record that 20 men lost their lives, others were wounded or invalided and 96 were awarded the *Croix de Guerre* or other decorations. Although most FAU personnel on foreign service were male, women formed approximately 10 per cent of the number. One, Miss K.F. Kinnear, a VAD, died on service with the Unit in September 1917.

Georgiana Fyfe

As Vandenbilcke and Chielens explain (2004), a significant group of refugees desperately tried to hold on to the unoccupied homeland behind the front in Ypres and on the Yser river. People arrived from all over Flanders. Thousands moved westwards and became stranded close to the French border, where they stayed until the Belgian government decided to evacuate them to France in the spring of 1915. About 55,000 tried to remain in Westhoek at end of 1914 but more than 15,000 were compulsorily evacuated and a Scottish woman, Georgiana Fyfe, who worked in the area, was involved in this. The Battle of the Yser is historically important because the Belgian Army was undefeated. Canal locks were opened on 25 October and this meant that the final phase of the race to the sea would be fought around Ypres. There were three main battles. First Ypres began on 18 October 1914, and the Belgians retreated to a line between Dixmude and Nieuport six days later. This was the front's most dangerous sector. Dixmude fell to Germans on 10 November, but because the Nieuport dike gates were opened forming a shallow, effective barrier between the Allies and the Germans, Nieuport remained in Belgian hands all through the war. First Ypres ended on 22 November. Health and safety were major concerns. There was typhus during the first winter, and the government feared civilians would panic with the onset of large scale shelling. The population protested against forced evacuations, and division of families. People with friends in villages behind the front, and those slightly to the east of places of shelter mostly stayed put. The will to stay of the others was so great they could only be manoeuvred very slowly towards the west and the French border. Voluntary and forced evacuations were organized until spring 1918. These facts help to explain Miss Georgiana Fyfe's letters home.

Refugees sheltered on farms and empty properties, or erected ramshackle sheds and barracks. To the British, Belgian and French armies, civilians and refugees were nuisances. However, they could also provide useful manpower and some worked for the Army. In the Ypres salient hundreds were put to work by the French engineering corps and the British Royal Engineers, digging trenches and repairing roads. Women worked in the huge Army laundries. Near Army rest camps, soldiers' shops, canteens and coffee houses sprang up and very young refugees tried to earn pocket money selling cigarettes, souvenirs, and drink. Contact between troops and refugees, especially women and young people, was disapproved of by local religious and municipal authorities. These negative responses created by hegemonic patriarchal institutions foster the lingering impression that refugees are a bad influence and should go away.

As a result of the deliberate flooding in November, relief workers also had to retreat, and a maverick group known as Dr Munro's Flying Ambulance, officially the Red Cross Motor Ambulance Volunteer Corps, moved to Furnes, the base for the Dixmude sector. Georgiana Fyfe (IWM. DD. 86/64/2) joined Hector Munro, a Socialist specialist from Bradford, at the outbreak of war, as *Directrice* of the *Toyers Ecossais*. Her relief work was in and near Ypres although it also took her into Switzerland and France. She began her Belgian Front Relief Fund in October 1914 when a few friends rallied round her and sent her to Belgium. She was a resourceful, energetic, intrepid woman who supported female suffrage, about which she had 'quarrelled' with her friend Robert Fell. He wrote, wheedlingly: 'you always would quarrel with me because I wasn't a suffragette – whereas I was better, one of your many admirers.' She anticipated she would receive a certain amount of help from the Scottish Red Cross but they were niggardly in helping and money was often a pressing need. She wrote on 13 November 1914 to her father: 'I feel strongly that our Scottish Red Cross ought to have supported me to some extent and also our Lord Provost. Did he ever respond to my appeal?' She ran three ambulances that had been rejected by other relief organizations but in 1915 appealed for a new one 'worthy of Glasgow and of Scotland'. Eventually, in December 1917 the Red Cross gave £250 in stores and two Argyll Ambulances. In March 1915 she wrote to Mrs Euing Crawford of Auchentroig, Stirlingshire, her Honorary

Treasurer, that she had about £500, enough to keep going for five months but in April the Fund's income was only 10s. and in September 1916, £7. Donations came from individuals and groups in Britain and America. The American Red Cross frequently made donations; Philip Henry de Ronde of New York donated several times; Miss Clara Hill of New York sent £10 and Mrs J. Young of New York, £1 1s. The American Soldiers for Belgian Babies Fund sent £11 2s. 2d. On 15 February 1917 she wrote to 'My dearest Ethel': 'America is beginning to be very good to us in the way of clothes and I have a splendid lot of boots and shoes in their last consignment.'

On 25 September 1918, Mrs Arthur Gleason of the American National War Work Council wrote for information, her letter conveying a sense of excitement and some urgency:

> Already requests are coming in to me to tell about the babies so won't you please send me post haste all the information I may use on this side to interest people. Any little stories, for instance, like the little girl who was so badly wounded: you had her working in your kitchen while she was convalescing ... My friends are especially interested in the Maternity, so please give me a nice full story about that and I will do my best to get some more money for the babies. (IWM. DD. 86/64/1)

All monies went to relief work, none in personal expenses, which helps to explain how so much was achieved from a fund whose financial position was sometimes precarious. Her work was among the civilian population, but in January 1915 she became officially attached to Army HQ. This is an extension of women's caring role into the military sphere, and conversely an acknowledgement by the Army of some responsibility towards civilians. It may explain why, although she had intended to focus on civilian relief, Miss Fyfe's funds were also used for military aid. She supplied an electric plant to a field hospital for the wounded and huts were provided for soldiers' recreation. When a town or village was under bombardment she rescued civilians who at first were taken to military hospitals. On 28 March, a month prior to the opening of Second Ypres, they:

> evacuated 1,000 from Ypres which is now finally absolutely in ruins. The English Army gave me three big London Buses two miles from the town and a party of volunteers came with me to fetch the poor old infirm men and women and children.

> Such a scene of tragedy I have never seen. I brought away the last three refugees, two dogs and a parrot ... I ought to have five [cars] at my disposal as I am the only one allowed to do the work.

Her letter to her father shows that Ypres' evacuation continued into April and gives insights into life in the war zone just prior to the official dates given for the commencement of a battle. She wrote:

> I have been evacuating Ypres with the help of two cars from Colonel Depage, the head of the Red Cross and it is a matter of hundreds of poor old bed-ridden women and young mothers with babies and no one else to do it as the Army is not allowed to go to Ypres now.

Her committee financed four hospices at different points along the front where the fighting was most pronounced. The largest Refuge was at Hazebrouck, a busy rail junction ten miles from the front. At Hazebrouck and also at Ebblingham the FAU had what they described as 'a car station in connection with evacuation of children from dangerous areas'. Cars were sent up from HQ for the actual evacuations, but when the children had been moved to safety, welfare was dealt with daily. About 3,000 Belgian and French refugees passed through one of Miss Fyfe's hospices in five months. She maintained a maternity hospital in the unconquered part of Belgium at Vincken, with 20 beds, nearly always full, and a children's home. Her records include details of the births she attended, which are sometimes distressing. For example, between 1914 and 1918, 367 women were admitted, and of the 344 babies born, 14 were dead, four were *sexe inconnu* and five *non delivrée*. No effort was made to record details of the fathers. Many mothers named their babies George or Georgette, after her.

In addition, four Scottish 'Firesides', either wooden huts or abandoned buildings, were available where women and children were given food and clothing and cared for in illness; Red Cross nurses and nuns helped her. She also worked with Mr Jacacci and Mrs Hill of the Franco-American Society for the Protection of Children from the Front. Her headed notepaper contained two additional addresses: the Rockefeller Foundation at New York and the War Refugees Committee in Berne where she had a Swiss Committee connected with the Foundation.

During quiet periods of warfare she persuaded mothers to allow their children to be sent to areas of safety. They were more willing when there was shelling and also when gas was used during Second Ypres in April and May 1915. St Joseph's Home received Flemish-speaking children who were to be transferred to Switzerland and she evacuated 1,341 Belgian children from the war area into France and Switzerland, frequently escorting them herself. As it was intended to restore the children to their homes when peace came, very careful records were kept.

In Paris she had a committee of four young men who cared for the children while she rested, and returned them to the station in time to catch the train. Once she took with her Mlle Widemaus, the daughter of 'the Chief of the Belgian Army who died lately' but the journey proved too much and the 'desolate little girl' was ill in Paris with a heart attack. The Army there was very helpful. 'Even Hotel Edouard VII takes us at "Military Prices".' When in Paris, she spent two days seeing different Committees and was usually given free medicines, bandages, and other supplies 'which our own Red Cross won't send me'. In January 1916, her father died and she temporarily returned home.

Elisabeth, Queen of the Belgians, at the outbreak of war installed a children's hospital in the Royal Palace where the children put little Belgian flags on each bed (Whitlock 1919: Vol. 2: 177). She was patron of Miss Fyfe's hospitals and was present to see each group of evacuees off on their journeys to safety, although this could be problematic. On one occasion they:

> had to catch a night train at Calais at 7 o'clock and the Queen was still with me at 4 o'clock. Our cars tore along and we caught the train and did not get to Paris until next morning at 8.50 although we were due at 5 a.m.

As well as donating personally to the Fund, the Queen helped with fund-raising, making a direct appeal to 'the generous womanhood of America' for the 'unoffending civilian population – the aged, the infirm, the women and the children' (Hoover 1959: 10).

In November 1917 over 4,000 refugees passed through Miss Fyfe's hands. This was Third Ypres, Passchendaele. In December a little girl named Suzanne was buried for 56 hours in the rubble of her home and dug out by six soldiers. This event affected many people, including a Dr Porter Smith (IWM. DD. 86/64/1) 'who helped me in my Hospital at Hazebrouck during the last stand there'. He wrote in 1918 'Very few people in England fully realize the awful hardships and tragedies of the refugees in France and Belgium.' Sir Philip Gibbs (1933: 83) is even clearer, writing: 'the soldier suffers less than the women and non-combatants. His agony perhaps is sharper, but the wound of the spirit is hardest to bear.'

Miss Fyfe was awarded the *Croix de Guerre* and the *Ordre de Leopold*. Although not much is known about her after the war, in early August 1919 she received a permit to go to Cologne and report to the British Armies of the Rhine so it appears her work continued during the Armistice. Nonetheless, the British did not acknowledge her work, and she is now virtually unknown.

Baroness de la Grange

Living in the same area of Flanders and known to Miss Fyfe was Clementine de Chaumont-Quitry, Baroness de la Grange, the most aristocratic of these women. A widow, she chose to stay in her Château La Motte au Bois, near Hazebrouck, acting as hostess to Allied military, leaving only in March 1918 during the Germans' final advance. In this way, as with the Victoria League women, she was using social means to political ends. In 1929 she published *Open House in Flanders* based on her diaries of the war. Although entries mainly concern her family and cementing the *Entente* with English military guests of her own class, her descriptions of refugees emphasize the meaning of war to those who are meant to be protected by its prosecution. For example, on 30 April 1915 she recorded that the fighting at Ypres resulted in thousands of inhabitants who had been living in their cellars now being evacuated towards Poperinghe. On 10 October 1915 when enemy outposts reached the Forest of Nieppe that surrounded the château, the Baroness described the pathos of the refugees' flight. Sometimes they had no shoes; some had walked 20 miles. A paralysed old grandmother sat on a red velvet easy-chair in one cart. In another, a young woman holding a baby had by her a glass case containing her bridal wreath; a struggling young calf was tied behind. Flemish carts were usually three-wheeled and frequently ended in ditches. Most refugees were trying to get to St Omer and Hazebrouck but at the end of the month she realized they were trying to get to Dunkirk and Gravelines instead, many dying on the way, or being made prisoner by the Uhlans. This term relating to a mounted soldier from Eastern Europe was applied to German cavalry to emphasize their barbarity. American aid was channelled through Emily Sloane, an American, who during the war married the Baroness's son Amaury. In October 1914 she returned to New York where she had an office collecting funds for French soldiers and sending consignments of clothes and first-aid outfits. In December Emily helped found the Lafayette Fund as a result of 'gratitude for the assistance of France to the American Colonists in revolutionary days'. Yet despite this, she asked for information which would help her try to change American public opinion which was not always very favourable (Grange 1916: 97) due to a reluctance to become involved in European affairs. On 28 January 1916 the Baroness and Emily together visited the Hazebrouck Auxiliary Hospital No. 6. This was without an operating table and Emily proposed getting it from American charitable funds. On 16 April 1917 she left France with Amaury who was on an official mission to encourage French co-operation with the American aviation service. Her task was again to collect goods and as a means of raising money she showed lantern slides of the devastation. This new form of technology aroused much interest and was a useful fund-raising aid which Francis Birrell used for the FWVRC at a boys' school in Vermeiul, Normandy on 17 July 1917. That month Emily sent word that provisions and clothes would be arriving soon at Hazebrouck having previously organized a regular supply of clothes and provisions to be sent to the 17 prisoners from the village who were then in Germany.

Bombing from aircraft was a new form of warfare and is mentioned frequently. Margery Boot of the Canteen à la Gare at Doullens, between Arras and Amiens, recorded how the Germans tried to bomb the railway line. The Baroness first heard of bombing raids when the post-office and station at Hazebrouck were bombed on 11 October 1914; she wrote about German aeroplanes over Paris and victims of the raids. Miss Gifford also reported civilian injuries and how, after the fall of Antwerp people fled to

Ostend which the Germans bombed. Being an important rail junction with links to Liège, Paris and Calais, Hazebrouck was a frequent target. However, danger also came from Allied aircraft. Charlotte Kellogg described German anti-aircraft batteries trying to shoot them down during her visit to a toy factory and how 'one of the aviators ... threw his bombs' within 'a few hundred meters of the Molenbeek Station'. On 15 October, when the Germans entered the town, a curate helped Miss Gifford obtain lodging in a Convent but the Allies bombed the station nearby. There was another bombing raid on 26 December 1916 when 17 bombs were dropped from aeroplanes on Dunkirk 'while the market was in full swing'. Casualties from such attacks were taken to local hospitals. But planes could also be used for helpful purposes. In July 1915 Amaury left his Cavalry Corps to become a pilot, and on 6 December 1915 he threw leaflets down onto Lille laundries giving addresses of some of the refugees whose families were unaware of their fate. He chose laundry as a camouflage, because white paper showed less against white sheets, and he felt that washerwomen would spread the information quickly.

Emily Hobhouse

The Baroness remained in France and to a large extent at her château, whereas Emily Hobhouse, working independently as in the Boer War, travelled throughout Europe during the early part of the European conflict. When fighting began she concentrated on supporting women's efforts to mitigate the effects of this further man-made catastrophe. She distributed leaflets and in early 1915 addressed open-air meetings with Vernon Lee and Isabella Ford. Her friendship with Ruth Fry, daughter of Sir Edward who supported her Boer War efforts, suggests concern with Belgian refugees and enemy aliens; Fisher (1971: 236) records that in March 1915 she set off via Dieppe to go to Paris with 'the Quaker Relief Detachment' but her name is not included in Ruth Fry's list although Hobhouse definitely worked with Friends in Paris and Vienna after the Armistice. In the summer of 1915 she decided to go to Switzerland and Italy to rouse women against the war. In June she saw in Berlin the German Minister von Jagow, an old friend, who arranged for her to go to Brussels, but constantly accompanied by Baron Falkenhausen she was not allowed to speak to the Belgians. Emily's efforts show the importance of internationalism, indicating how friendships can survive and be used for humanitarian purposes, even when the friend becomes an 'enemy'. Charlotte Kellogg wrote that the 'whole city seems turned into a kitchen', a fact which could not have been lost on Emily. She was allowed to interview the manager of the communal soup kitchens and learned that there was insufficient food and an increase in TB, coming to the conclusion that the British blockade was responsible for the high infant mortality (Fisher 1971: 246), 'exactly the sort of conclusions the Germans desired her to form'. Afterwards, she visited Antwerp, Malines, Charleroi, Aerschot, Cambrai, Liège and Louvain, finding the latter not as badly destroyed as reported in British newspapers. She was also able to contact Dr Elizabeth Rotten, Secretary for the Berlin Committee for the Relief of Foreigners whose reports were printed in *The Friend*. Emily also visited Dr Weiler's sanatorium and Ruhleben Camp for Interned Civilians. Prisoners whose records survive about this visit apparently misinterpreted her remarks, suspecting her of immorality with her escort, or of spying. Focus by YMCA visitors on the cultural and educational activities organized by inmates blurred the fact that this camp was on the Berlin race-track, and civilian accommodation was five or six men to one horse-stall. Described as a mischievous pacifist by an official in Lord Robert Cecil's office, Emily 'lectured' Grant Duff on prisoners' conditions but he dismissed her concerns. For some reason it was more important to believe the Germans than a woman of British nationality. She suffered the whistle-blowers' usual fate of being treated as the perpetrator of the crime when she inadvertently left on the Consul's desk a letter to Dr Aletta Jacobs who had arranged the International Congress of Women in April 1915; revelations about her contact with the 'enemy' from this letter raised the question of whether she should be interned. She suggested a scheme for exchanging German and British civilians over military age but this was not accepted by the Foreign Office although other people were exchanged. On her return to Britain she tried to see first Sir Edward Grey, and when her approach was ignored, Lord Robert Cecil, Minister of Blockade, to talk about the camps, eventually writing to him on 3 November, stressing her humanitarian interest.

The letter was not answered. She published a report about her visit in the *Daily News* of 4 September 1916, illuminating 'war in everyday garb, stripped of glory – war in its ultimate effect upon a civilian population in misery and broken lives'.

After Emily Hobhouse's return, Mrs Pethick-Lawrence invited Sylvia Pankhurst and members of the WIL Executive to her home to meet her. Described by Pankhurst as a frail, elderly woman, this partly reflects her view of a woman 22 years older than herself, Emily was aged 55. She had not played an active part in the suffrage movement, although she described herself as an ardent supporter of women's rights. She strongly disapproved of the militants' tactics, but neither had she joined one of the constitutional societies. Brian Roberts (1991: 270) hints it may have been due to Millicent Fawcett's attitude to her Boer revelations. Now it was considered 'impolitic' for her to be invited to the WIL offices; Catherine Marshall's tone as she introduced Emily was deprecatory and the atmosphere hostile. Emily reported on the work attempted by the headquarters committee of WIL at The Hague on which she had worked from its inception. She described her visits to Germany and Belgium and what she had done to present the authorities with details. There was an antagonistic silence when she finished and Catherine Marshall, as Secretary, indicated to her that the committee did not accept her as representing the British Section of the new international organization founded at The Hague. This was a disgracefully churlish reception by women who called themselves internationalists to a woman who had shown fearless integrity in the cause of peace. Emily left quickly. This incident, as with the Boer camps, was underwritten by conflicting definitions of patriotism in war. The suffragists repudiated her because she was too radical and broke the rules. They were law-abiding and used to negotiating constitutionally although some would soon discover that they had crossed an unseen line and were harassed by the police who searched their premises. She had been stripped and searched and Sir Edward Grey had refused to see her, although he knew her. They blamed the victim – it must be her fault. They kept saying that when the Government really trusts you they don't treat you like that. These women had their political training under Millicent Garrett Fawcett and probably believed she, not Emily, had given the true version of the Boer Camps. As Pankhurst said

(1987: 384–5), they had not yet learned that obedience to conscience is of greater value than subservience to authority, but harder to achieve.

Mrs Fawcett's understanding of patriotism is still contesting the Socratic version which seeks to make the country the best it can be in an international setting. Emily Hobhouse acted this out, challenging her so-called 'internationalist' British WIL colleagues and the government. As Lerner says (Humm 1992: 325, 327), describing women's agency: 'The true history of women is the history of their on-going functioning in that male-defined world on their own terms.' Emily did not fit the stereotype of acceptable femininity in war-time, being regarded as an unpatriotic thorn-in-the-flesh of the British political and military, even lecturing on the foundation of a League of Nations prior to the Armistice, which was unacceptable. Brown (2003: 176) argued that wars, particularly the Great War, accelerate social development. In this instance it accelerated the erosion of civil liberties. Hobhouse's contact with friends who were now officially her country's enemies resulted in changes in the Defence of the Realm Act so that others could not follow her example. However, this moved her into domestic and foreign politics even more than during the Boer War. She was influential, although ostracized. Nevertheless, she showed what one woman with determination could do in a humanitarian cause.

CHAPTER 5

Dealing with Difference: Refugee Relief in France

Suffrage relief

During the first week of August there was fighting in Alsace. As production changed into war preparations people were laid off and an economic downturn was created throughout France. French suffragists immediately set up workshops for the unemployed (*Jus Suffragii*, 1.5.1915). As parts of France were occupied, civilians helped each other, also wounded troops and civilian and military prisoners-of-war. Wives and families were left unsupported and became homeless when their villages and towns were destroyed. Mme Gustave Kahn, wife of the literary theorist and poet who claimed to be the inventor of free verse, formed a society for helping such families. It promptly received 5,000 applications from refugees who had fled from the invaded districts and were now without homes and clothing. They included the wife of a doctor, the wife of a now penniless lawyer and an old father with seven sons at the front and two who were prisoners. In November 1915, the society appealed through *Jus Suffragii* for money and clothes.

The first of the Scottish Women's Hospital Units, formed by Dr Elsie Inglis in August went to France in December 1914. Elsie Inglis had qualified as a doctor in 1892 and then left Edinburgh to get experience as house-surgeon at the New Hospital for Women in Euston Road, London. This hospital, founded by the first English woman doctor, Mrs Garrett Anderson, had only women on its medical staff, and therefore was in the forefront of progress in all that concerned women who were interested in medicine. On 13 August 1914 Dr Inglis told Mrs Fawcett she proposed forming hospital Units. Most women doctors were suffragists, but rather than use 'Suffrage' in the title she named the Units the Scottish Women's Hospitals in order 'to get all women to help'. Mrs Fawcett (1924: 214) said the SWH became almost a world movement; by October 1918 they had raised £428,905. Behind Dr Inglis's patriotic, humanitarian idea was a suffrage campaign designed to show that women were capable of using their medical and surgical skills in wartime. In addition to promoting the cause of women doctors and other professional women, it would show they could be near the front without becoming hysterical. Inglis explained to Mrs Fawcett that 'Wherever people see the Union Jack with the [suffragist] red, white and green flag below it, they'll know it means efficiency and kindness – and intelligence.' She continued:

> I cannot think of anything more calculated to bring home to men the fact that women can help – intelligently – in any kind of work. So much of our work is done where they cannot see it. They'll see every bit of this ... (WL. GB/106/7/MGF/89/94)

On 2 December 1914, Miss Mair, President of the Scottish Federation of the NUWSS watched as six nursing sisters, three orderlies and two cooks left Edinburgh for London. They paraded before Mrs Fawcett in the London offices, joined members from other parts of the country, including seven doctors, and were seen off from Folkestone by Dr Inglis *en route* for Royaumont Abbey. Formed for military relief they also helped thousands of civilians, their hospital helping the inhabitants of local hamlets deprived of medical aid, including a man dying of cancer, and a French girl seriously wounded in an explosion in a munitions factory in Compiègne. Outpatients numbered 1,537 civilians. Despite the condition of injured servicemen, the death rate at Royaumont was only 1.82 per cent. Among the 527 non-combatants it was higher at 4.37 per cent reflecting the hardships suffered by civilians and the more vulnerable age groups (Bowden in Crofton 1997: x).

Dr Inglis's desire that men should *see* what women were doing was being achieved. A frequent visitor to Royaumont, where he carried out some of his research, was Professor Weinberg, the leading gas gangrene infections scientist. He recognized the unique contribution the Royaumont women were making (Crofton 1997: 213) 'to further the work of the women's movement', a comment that denotes considerable respect for their medical work. Laurence Binyon (1918: 245–6) wrote of the Royaumont women: 'If any male doubt the capacity of women to organize, administrate, and create a cheerful order, let him go to Royaumont.' In addition, women university students at Girton and Newnham sent £1,800 to the SWH for a Unit of 200 beds for the wounded at Troyes. The next month an X-ray ambulance car, equipped under the supervision of Mme Curie and Mrs Ayrton was on public view at Bedford College. It cost more than £1,000, had its own dark room and water-supply and was under the direction of Dr Agnes Saville of Harley Street. There were different ways of making women's work visible.

Quaker relief work: starting again

In London Dr Hilda Clark, who was in practice in the East End, was anxious about the mothers and children behind the fighting line in France, knowing they would be without medical care. Hilda Clark had previously rented rooms in Mary Sheepshanks' Bloomsbury flat, as had Catherine Marshall (Pye 1956: 15). She now lived with Edith Pye, a senior nurse, aged 38; both were members of the FLWS. These women were among the younger members of the relief movement. Catherine Marshall, born in 1880 was 34; Dr Hilda Clark was 33; Mary Sheepshanks was the oldest of the group, now 42.

Edith Pye recorded that on 4 September Hilda Clark expressed her 'concern' for relief work in the devastated areas of France to the Meeting for Sufferings, reporting that despite the danger of smallpox, cholera and typhoid among the refugees, non-combatants were not being helped by the French Red Cross and suggesting a relief mission. This action is normally attributed to the Quaker MP T. Edmund Harvey, another FLWS member, whom Hilda Clark involved. As Scott explains (1964: 18), a 'Quaker concern is the conviction that a particular task has been laid upon her … by God'. It may be unwanted, unsought, but insistent. Once the Meeting is assured that it is 'in the Life', it will give the Friend complete support. In this instance, the Friends War Victims Relief Committee (FWVRC) was resuscitated. Originally formed in 1871, women had served abroad with it but it had been dormant for some years. Members were immediately appointed and met that day to consider and take action on relief work in Holland and medical and nursing assistance to non-combatants in France. Belgium was also in their brief but on 23 September Friends decided it was impossible to do anything even in free Belgium until the Germans left, although the FAU worked in the unoccupied zone, as we have seen.

Hilda Clark enlisted Harvey's aid, and they gathered a group of young people who wanted to share the dangers of the battle zone, but without bearing arms. 'Ted' as he became known to the workers, had been warden of Toynbee Hall from 1904 to 1911 and was in put charge of the FWVRC Mission in France. Hilda Clark wrote to the French Red Cross and the *Union des Femmes de France* to get information. By the following week, they had learned that although Paris was full of refugees no extra help was needed, but despite the dearth of medics in country districts it was difficult to discover which French Authority was responsible; consequently there were delays caused by what British relief workers saw as French inefficiency. In order to get permission for their work, on 26 September Edith Pye went to Paris where she was able to see M. Léon Bourgeois, a member of the Government, who was greatly supportive from then on. M. Renache at the War Office, and M. Appel, *Président* of the *Comité du Sécours National*, welcomed their scheme and military permission to enter the war zone was received by telegram. The French Government recalled the service given more than 40 years earlier and gladly accepted the assistance of builders, doctors, nurses and other workers for the homeless people. By 7 October the situation had radically worsened. Doctors and nurses had fled from Reims and there were none in Bèaume where there were also many wounded.

That day, the FWVRC Executive decided to ask Ruth Fry to be on the General Committee and on 14 October she was appointed Assistant Secretary and worked from a basement room near the Angel, Islington. Aged 36, and with no formal training for the job, she served on volunteer selection committees, and was the director, manager and co-ordinator in London of the Friends' work in each country where a mission was established. As Bernard Carter wrote (*Friend*, 4.5.1962): Ruth Fry became:

> A sort of generalissimo-cum-quartermaster general ... responsible for a vast programme of supplies, administration, personnel management, public relations, fund-raising, leadership and inspiration, on behalf of a complex of projects the like of which had never been known in Quaker history before.

She also had to ensure that selected workers, who were not all Quakers, would be sympathetic to SOF pacifist ethos and practice in order to facilitate smooth group working and maintenance of Quaker reputation. Networks were central to the raising of personnel. David Garnett and Francis 'Frankie' Birrell, a Cabinet Minister's son, fringe members of the Bloomsbury group, and friends of Ruth's brother, Roger, were among the workers who went to France in June 1915. Birrell, a pacifist whose absolutism was not put to the test because he was exempted, became a member of the General Council of the UDC in 1920. According to Garnett (1955: 58), one of the reasons that Birrell was accepted for the Mission was because he was a useful person to have as a 'powerful friend in case of need. Moreover it would impress the French Authorities on whose goodwill the whole work of the Mission depended.' David Garnett wrote that he and Francis Birrell were:

> interviewed by a number of leading Friends who did not seem to like us, but were not prepared to veto our joining. The only one of them who was at all favourable to us was Miss Ruth Fry, Roger's younger sister.

Friends' previous relief experience had raised anxieties about links between their work and the military, and caused conflict between what Quakers saw as obedience to God *versus* obedience to human authority. Quaker Queries, by which Friends examine their testimony, in the eighteenth century had included the inquiry as to whether they were 'in any way concerned in the militia' (Jones 1966: 53), and traditionally there had been no question about what the response should be. Subsequently the Query was amended to bearing 'testimony against all war', but in the Boer War, even this threatened the continuance of the work. Keeping civilian relief separate from military relief was difficult when the boundary was crossed by the humanitarian instinct. Further, being under the control of the military made complete civilian/military separation impossible and there was much soul-searching at the outset over whether an Ambulance Unit should be formed to aid the wounded soldiers.

Lady Mariabella Fry wrote to *The Friend* on 14 August saying she thought that most members would not have joined the Red Cross because 'it is so entirely under military control and we cannot consistently with our principles share in any help especially destined for the army and navy'.

However, not all Friends agreed. As Kennedy indicates (1884: 243–5), from 1888 an alliance of influential Quakers, especially John Wilhelm Rowntree, guided the British Friends towards new forms of religious and social activism and away from the sole authority of the Bible. Their mystical and egalitarian concept of Inward Light, which was a democratic stab at political freedom, allowed them to accept social concerns of the wider world, including aiding the victims of poverty, injustice and war. It also forbade inflicting injury since 'that which is of God dwells in all'. Nevertheless, acceptance of individual interpretation of God's will through Inward Light, despite normal Quaker scrutiny of this by peers, meant some men joined the Army and some Quaker women undertook Army relief. Rachel Alexander of Worthing, Sussex, a friend of the Fry family, and her sister Jean, Ruth Fry's playmate, aided non-combatants, directing a factory for women embroiderers at Châlons-sur-Marne but Rachel also opened a canteen at Bar-le-Duc under the auspices of the *Comité Britannique de la Croix Rouge Française*; its aim was to provide hot and cold meals and drinks to soldiers. The immediate test of Mariabella Fry's opinion occurred when Philip Noel-Baker, the Quaker Vice-Principal of Ruskin College, Oxford, suggested an Ambulance Corps to operate under the protection of the Red Cross. Although the Ambulance bore the name 'Friends', and was run first by Baker and then other Friends, it was not an official SOF organization. Whether or not to join the FAU became a matter of conscience significant to FWVRC workers in France in 1915 when direct appeals were made to them to join.

At last, the first Friends' volunteer relief expedition left on 5 November 1914. There were three doctors, eleven nurses, several of whom were midwives, one medical student, two qualified chemists, one sanitary inspector and 14 men such as chauffeurs and orderlies; not all were members of the SOF. Indicating how impossible it was to keep totally separate from the

Plate 2. Showing some of the first FWVRC workers, wearing their uniforms bearing the Quaker star, at Victoria Station leaving for Paris, France, 1914. (Photograph courtesy of The Religious Society of Friends in Britain)

military, the 'mission' was officially placed by the Minister of War under the *Service de Santé* of the Army, under the direction of the *Directeurs des Étapes et Service*. By May 1915, there were approximately 70 workers but more were needed.

Châlons Maternité

The *Préfet* of the Marne wanted provision for refugee expectant mothers and gave for a maternity hospital part of the *Asile des Viellards* at Châlons-sur-Marne which housed homeless old people and younger, epileptic women whose medical condition not being understood, were thought to be mad.

The *Asile*, like the British workhouse, was an instrument of social control of those thought to be inveterate nuisances. Châlons was in the area of the Battle of the Marne, which, although brief had devastated many villages, the Germans destroying everything in their wake as they retreated. Châlons had been occupied for only nine days, and therefore suffered very little, but refugees from a wide area crowded into it. The type of relief needed was consequently different from that in Britain and Holland where refugees found safety in foreign countries with no war damage.

On 25 November Hilda Clark, Dr Dyson Holdsworth and the advance guard arrived at Châlons. With military assistance, one Friends' group prepared the foul and infected building and disinfected, repainted, and chased 'dirt with legs'. There was no hot water and only paraffin lamps; the American Red Cross paid for installation of electric light in 1917. The domestic staff were female 'imbeciles' selected by the Director of the *Asile* as being best able to help. In December Hilda Clark asked Edith Pye to assist in the *Maternité*. Despite the high esteem in which Edith Pye was, and still is held, Miss Charis Barnett who worked with her wrote that everyone except Callwell, MacColl and possibly Marjorie Rackstraw disliked her. Rackstraw was a member of the Fry network; now aged 26 she was Deputy when Margery Fry, Ruth's older sister, was Warden at Somerville College, Oxford, and had helped at the Birmingham Settlement while there. On 9 December the first baby was born at the *Maternité* although the hospital actually opened on 14 December. The French authorities paid all costs, including food for the patients and staff.

Châlons was 15 miles behind the fighting line and here the Friends' medical work was centred despite being subjected to shelling, for example on Christmas Eve 1914. The patients, 'good and solid French housewives' (Pye 1956: 19–28), were some of the 2,500 refugees from the ruined villages, but others were victims of troops' abuse. Hilda Clark described how a dazed and bewildered little girl of 13 was brought into the *Maternité* by her mother in March 1915. A drunken soldier had brought her home. Hilda told Edith that the baby was not due for some months but did not explain the pregnancy and leaves it open whether rape was carried out by French *poilus*. Despite Quaker 'plain speaking', probably certain things could not be written about this, even between such close friends as Hilda and Edith who were both in the medical profession. Brownmiller (1975: 41–5) quotes Toynbee describing the swath of horror cut by the German Army as consisting not only of burnt houses and destroyed villages, but multiple and gang rape in Northern France, Flanders and along the Franco-Belgian border. Brownmiller (1975: 35, 64) argues that gang-rape is a method of male bonding, by which all men keep all women in fear. It is the act of a conqueror and the victim is chosen not because she is representative of the enemy but 'because she is the enemy – a woman'. Confirming the latter part of this statement W. Owen Stephens, recorded that in January 1918 there was attempted rape in Ham by British 'Tommies' leaving the next day. And in Sermaize in July, Stephens (1921: 92, 189) wrote: 'I have just had a Harvard graduate say to me "wait 'til we get into Germany. We'll 'put it to' their women and girls."' One result of this war against women was that there was greater sympathy for unmarried mothers. Hilda described how one, Marie M., was brought in from a shed measuring about 12 ft × 14 ft where seven men and women and six children slept. It was the conditions of the shed itself that shocked, not the fact of an unmarried mother.

The Châlons *Maternité* was important as indicating to the French officials immediate proof of good faith but it was only a small cog in an immense wheel of which Hilda Clark was the hub. If Hilda was unavailable for an emergency, the military hospital's offer of help was accepted or later, a worker co-opted a member of the French Army Medical Services working at the station. At one time, members of the English *équipe* were the only members of the public allowed on the station platform. However, qualified midwives normally managed the midwifery with statistics comparable with the best maternity hospitals in Britain. At the end of August 1915, the Châlons *Maternité* had to be evacuated due to the German advance. It was from here that Edith Pye won her decoration for rescuing children from Reims while under bombardment, with FWVRC workers evacuating children to safety. It was reopened later and in 1919 the fully functioning maternity hospital was handed over to a French committee, as *La Maison Maternelle de la Marne*. Harvey's wish that it would be worthy of the Society was fulfilled when the formal transfer of the *Maternité* took place on 17 June 1922 with M. Léon Bourgeois, former French President and now *Président* of the Commission on Assistance and Supplies, remaining its

Président d'Honnneur until his death. After the war Bourgeois was President of the League of Nations Council and became known as the spiritual father of the League. As a memento of the transfer a statue of a mother and child, entitled *Marne, 1914–1919*, was sculpted, perhaps by Ethel Pye who worked in France in 1917. Brayshaw (1921: 338) recorded that 1,000 babies were born in the Châlons *Maternité*.

Adjusting to circumstance

To operate their work, the Friends received contributions and 'untiring personal service' from Quakers and non-Quakers. They were entrusted with a share of the administration of various funds that were collected publicly. According to Brayshaw (1921: 331), these included the *Manchester Guardian* Fund, Treasury grants, Lady Forster's Australian Fund, and after the war Save the Children, Imperial War Relief and the Russian Famine Relief Funds. It appears, therefore, that their attitude towards the collection of money had softened in view of the scale of the war. It was also clear that complete separation from the military was impossible. The help the Army gave at Châlons was reciprocated by the Friends elsewhere. For example, in the Somme FWVRC workers carried wounded British and German soldiers to dressing-stations and made them tea. As early as October 1914 Dr Clark indicated the difficulty of keeping civilian relief separate. Mlle Senard of the French Red Cross reported they were unable to cope with the wounded who were suffering more than the British because of lack of preparations. Dr Clark's conclusion that work among non-combatants could best be introduced by offering to assist in care for the wounded and her suggestion to use the Château de Compiègne appears diametrically opposed to the Quaker desire not to get involved with the Army but is explained by the dilemma of conscience created by a French Army surgeon's appeal for Friends to erect an emergency hospital with costs being met by the *Service de Santé*. As the Quaker Mission had accepted their work in France under the direction of the *Service* it was possible such orders might be repeated. The Field Committee decided to comply, but since the prime aim of the Mission was to alleviate civilian suffering, they thought those at

Home might have difficulty with their decision, taken on the basis that it would assuage pain and save lives in exactly the same way as that suggested by Dr Clark for Compiègne. Their explanation highlights how very thin the dividing line was between civil and military life on the field – civilian hospitals were evacuated for wounded soldiers, and military engineers built shelters for the homeless, so it could even be said that Quakers' work of building huts for refugees released the military to fight.

In January 1915, refugees were streaming into Compiègne where an offshoot of the suffragist Women's Emergency Corps (IWM. France 5.1/15), the Women's Emergency Canteens for Soldiers, was using the Orangerie for food and sleeping quarters for the 'old people and mothers with young families' as they made their journey to Paris, 'though Paris has long been so congested with refugees that they could not possibly be allowed to remain there'. The Canteen Corps was started by Mrs Wilkie when WEC wanted to close it down. Two ambulances evacuated the wounded from barges to hospitals during the summer of 1917; they helped Belgian soldiers in Paris and shipwrecked sailors, and carried out refugee work in devastated towns at Noyon, Compiègne and Villers. Winifred Stobart, the Acting Hon. Secretary of the Emergency Canteens (IWM. France 5.1/29), revealed the potential dangers of living so close to the Front. On 8 March 1917, one of their workers, Mrs Gartside-Tipping, 'was shot one night when returning from the Canteen, by a French soldier, who afterwards turned out to be a well-known Apaché'. Her funeral was at Compiègne and the General commanding that sector laid the *Croix de Guerre* on her coffin. This Corps is also recorded as being run by the *Dames Anglaises*. However, it is probable that the term was applied to any group of English relief workers. Edith Pye wrote (Pye 1915: 8) that due to the absence of medical aid for civilians, visits of the English doctor were clamoured for. She continued: '*Les Dames Anglaises* with the star upon their arms are often stopped on the road and asked for a visit.' The 'star' was the black and red Quaker insignia. Although, as Brayshaw says (1921: 330), it became known all over Europe, because it was in the German colours of black, white and red and the grey uniform was similar to the Germans', Garnett (1955: 81) thought this may have contributed to problems between workers and the French people. Miss Barnett found it excited much comment.

In March 1915 Margery Fry took over from suffragist Hilda Cashmore and was in charge of the mission's relief work until 1917. For the first few months of the war, Margery Fry had Belgian refugees living in her house in Birmingham, and helped organize the use of disused Army huts elsewhere. In France her work covered first the Marne and Meuse area, and later all the FWVRC work in France including helping to find homes for refugees from Verdun in Haute Savoie. Committee work had led Margery to believe that giving as a kind of first aid must not be continued except in the relation of friendship. When she arrived at Sermaize-les-Bains there was much 'first aid' relief necessary. The relationship between giver and receiver caused her anguish, largely because charity work in Birmingham had been to the working-class, now it was to 'those of her own nation', the middle-class. Consequently (Jones 1966: 95, 97), 'to the ordinary peasant woman she remained an eccentric, well-intentioned foreigner'. She found working with the French authorities was satisfactory, but trying to persuade French farmers to share equipment with other farmers whose implements had been destroyed caused angry scenes. Birrell said farms were run on uneconomic lines due to the subdivision of their land, but he was instrumental in changing this by the simple expedient of working regardless of the boundaries.

'Frankie' Birrell missed the intellectual stimulation of his friends, so political discussions with his father by letter were important. The situation was made worse by the 'imbecility of Friends' talking to him about the 'ineffable goodness of the Creator'. He enjoyed the company of the French peasants and in the absence of French teachers taught their children and organized the purchase of books in Paris through Jane Harrison, a classicist Newnham friend of his mother, who died in March 1915 from an inoperable brain tumour. Jane Harrison was a suffragist and one of the most celebrated thinkers of the day. She was herself scarred by the war; her brother was killed and her first child stillborn. Birrell wrote on Sunday 22 July 1917 that the 'War created a gap in my life – it feels futile'. But he acknowledged it was worse for those fighting. It was a 'reign of utter unadulterated stupidity' that looked like continuing. He wondered what hope there was for the world and linked this with his objection to the grand narratives of 'war, religion, democracy and all the great influences of the last 2,000 years'. Nonetheless, Birrell undoubtedly would have agreed with Hilda Clark's sentiments when she wrote in May 1915 (Pye 1956: 31–3): 'How stifled by lies and hatred one feels especially in all the news from England'; and in July, 'If one did not feel so entirely remote from the earth it would make one very homesick. I sometimes wonder if one will ever really feel anything at all or always be numb.' Nonetheless, Hilda was able to refresh herself through music, writing to Edith from Sermaize on 17 May 1916 that they had a feast because a good band spent 'all its spare time practising in the woods by La Source and the *chef de musique* has found in the regiment quartered in the next village a celebrated pianist of the Paris Conservatoire who is a *simple soldat*', but whose captain got him leave occasionally and 'brings him to play on our piano'. Such things eased the spirit, and improved Hilda's uncertain health.

The continuation of relief depended on the co-operation of British and French authorities; Frankie Birrell's presence, and Ted Harvey's status as a Liberal MP contributed. Nevertheless, the British authorities' attitude towards the Friends' work was ambivalent. On the one hand, although in December 1915 the British War Office had recognized the work in France as important to the war effort, and therefore liable for exemption, the fact that despised pacifists did it meant difficulties continued. They were abused by individual officials, and regulations designed to limit the escape of 'slackers' were over-zealously implemented causing delays to the work and goods being held back by customs. Some French people, including those the workers came to help, derided them as *embusqués*, taking advantage, or being uncooperative. Other problems related to the spy panic. In January 1915, when Ted Harvey and Mark Leicester visited Paris their movements were hampered by precautions against German spies thought to be numerous in the French Army. Nevertheless, when they offered further assistance they received a cordial welcome although this was ambiguous. Their plan had been for additional medical work, but the Military Authorities were unwilling to admit any need for sanitary precautions, which included burial, and were therefore unhelpful; yet in contrast, in March 1915 the Third Army gave the workers free petrol and lent them horses and carts. Harvey considered Quakers' presence and help stimulated the French to aid the victims, which implies that refugees were not helped as much as they might have been. The National vote of 12,000,000 francs under discussion in the *Corps Legislatif* was partly owing to the presence of Friends in France and the French Government voted maintenance allowances for homeless refugees. Further, in Paris in April 1915, 150,000 frs. were voted for the Friends by the Conseil General for wood for huts, and for furniture if they chose. The money was to be entirely in their hands and paid over to them, not to Paris ladies who offered to furnish the huts and were counting on this money to carry out their promise (Pye 1956: 29).

Coping with difference

One of the most damaged villages in the area was Sommeilles. It had a population of about 370 and stood on the brow of a hill with a glorious view. At first when Friends visited in February 1915, they could not find a home standing. Someilles and Vitry-le-François, where Joffre had his HQ, co-ordinated work in what remained of the other devastated villages, but Sermaize-les-Bains, formerly a town of 4,000 people, was the overall administrative centre. Having lost 900 of its 1,000 houses, its devastation particularly shocked all who saw it, being not much more than heap after heap of debris. Sermaize had roughly 400 refugees from the town crammed into *La Source*, a disused spa hotel near the sulphur springs a mile outside the town. Despite its almost uninhabitable condition, two women members of the medical *équipe* settled in *La Source*. Caring implies involvement, not detachment, and Quakers felt they gained the confidence of the people by living with them and were anxious to restore people's independence and self-respect. By means of camp beds, much soap and water and the Mayor of Sermaize's help, a corner was made sufficiently habitable for them. Their work was to be largely maternity and childcare, although district nursing was carried out, and sick people were helped whenever necessary. A few men remained in the town, over age or not strong enough for military service, complicating an already difficult problem because they were unoccupied. However, Pye (1956: 27) hoped when the sugar refinery was re-started, some would get employment. By March 1915, a little wooden cottage hospital had been erected, with two wards, and a verandah for TB patients. By May 1915 there were eight Quaker centres at various places.

Proximity to the fighting and the size and geographical position of France meant that different places had specific needs. For example, relief workers might have to deal with totally destroyed buildings, or damaged but partly standing ones; stock, agricultural implements, harvest and seed corn might be burned or standing crops lost. These problems were magnified by the scarcity of male labour and horses, and further complicated by the loss of furniture by pillage and fire, and overcrowding in what shelters there were.

In addition, these conditions created different types of refugees. In South Africa Kitchener had identified as separate refugee categories the families of burghers who had surrendered, dependents who were actively engaged in passing information to the enemy, families from farms used as sniper's posts and others from farms used as food depots. These apparent motives for refugeedom led to discrimination in food rations in the camps (Fisher 1971: 114). In contrast, Quakers identified different types of refugees according to their need, recognizable by their situations and helped accordingly. Other utterly destroyed villages where parties worked included Soudan, near Fontenelle in the Aisne, and in January 1915 another group of nearly 20 workers started in Fère Champenoise. This had not suffered much and so became their HQ. Villages for miles around were half destroyed and relief was given only to villages in this state, except in Fère Champenoise itself where a few *émigrés* from other districts received clothing and blankets. *Émigrés* were *réfugiés* who fled before the Germans into safer areas of France; they sometimes became mixed with troops and might be helped by *cantines* intended for the military. However, the need of these people was not as great as in Châlons, because here they were lodged with relatives. Labour needs were met by casual day-labour or sometimes *émigrés* were able to give a day or two. In June 1915, the suffragist Suzanne Day of Dublin went out to join the workers in Bar-le-Duc where there were about 3,500 *émigrés*. They were sent by the Government to any Department of France that could receive them and theoretically needed only temporary help, but in February 1915, Hilda Cashmore, who had been at Châlons for some time, found that about 2,000 had refused to go because they had large families of little children or were awaiting the birth of a baby. Living in deplorable conditions, they needed such basic things as clothing and also medical assistance. To minimize the danger of infection and disease, Friends established a special branch of the Municipal Dispensary with a fully-qualified nurse. From Bar-le-Duc May Staveley, one of Margery Fry's Somerville friends who had also worked at Birmingham Women's Settlement, reported that (FEWVRC. M2 28.9.1915) 'accommodating refugees in the first rush of invasion was great and mortality among children quite terrible'. At that time there were 4,000 refugees in Bar and although clothes had been sent out, warmer ones were needed for winter, especially for boys, and blankets.

At Vitry-le-François and Sermaize there were fewer *réfugiés*, but more *sinistrés;* these were people who had lost their possessions and homes, but who remained in the same place. In these circumstances sanitation work was needed, including drainage and sewerage. The final group were *rapatriés*, people whom the Germans sent from the occupied areas back into unoccupied France, *via* Switzerland; of these the FWVRC Field Committee for France recorded in December 1915 that a 'large number were insane and others had TB'. Frequent mention of 'insanity' indicates the degree of trauma to which these people were subjected; shellshock and gas were not limited to the armed forces, a fact not generally acknowledged. There was, in fact, another group of refugees although they were not identified by a special name. These were people who needed temporary help when coming to visit their wounded or sick relatives.

The inrush of *émigrés* into some towns caused an artificial but marked rise in prices. Ruth Gaines (1918), an American relief worker in the area, explained that the amount of *allocation* to which *rapatriés* were entitled was calculated by the mayor according to number of children and other 'rules'. This provided a bare subsistence: adults were given the same as soldiers' wives, 1.25 frs. per day, but this did not take price rises into account and left nothing over for other necessities such as blankets or warm clothes. Rents had risen and the parish priest at Waives, three miles away, spoke against landlords' greed. Many refugees were lodged in the remains of houses ruined by the bombardment, and in farm buildings not fit for habitation, yet the owners were asking extortionate rents from people who received this meagre Government allocation. Necessities were sold by the Quakers at cost or less but refugees were exploited by local trades-people, so M. Chavaillier, an ex-Mayor of Bar-le-Duc, opened a market in which vegetables, butter and eggs could be bought at the cheaper Paris prices. Suzanne Day wrote (1916: 132): 'Perhaps it is the misery of their surroundings which leads so many people to speak of, and treat, the *émigrés* with contempt.' As she pointed out, the conditions were bad because the buildings had been infested with vermin for centuries before the war. There was no water, and no sinks. Shelters were overcrowded. In the Rue des Dues at Bar the Friends found 27 people living in a single room, and 'one frankly verminous domicile shelters 100 people under its roof'. Although 'the spirit of the French nation is indomitable', and some people gave what help they could to those who had lost everything and fled to another part of France, others treated refugees with contempt, or ignored them. Stephens (1921: 290) said the French did not help each other: 'The Midi people don't care what happened to the people in the North because their homes were safe.' Further, Suzanne Day pointed out (1916: 138–9) that 'Women suffered the worst of all humiliations' and some were only helped when they discovered other refugees from their own town. This helps to explain why, as Pye says (1915: 7), Friends organized quite a large out-patient practice among *émigrés* and arranged that a district nurse visit them.

To deal with these differences, from the beginning the FWVRC work among civilians was divided into four categories, each with its own *équipes*. Despite an apparent rhetoric of equality between the sexes, Quakers were influenced by the nineteenth-century ideal of caring womanhood and their presumed inability to undertake certain tasks and innate capacity for others. Therefore on the whole Agriculture and Building were staffed by men, Relief and Medical by women. The latter implies a considerable extension of women's role in view of the struggle they had had obtaining medical qualifications, but male doctors had been enlisted, meaning there was an opening for women. However, men dealt with male workers' matters. In March 1919, Harvey was pleading for at least another 50 male workers and Margery Fry was asked to go to Paris on matters relating to women. Photographs, however, show women helping with the building of wooden huts erected as homes for villagers and workers. In Plate 3 Miss

Plate 3. Miss Jowett on the roof, tiling, with David Garnett, Sermaize, 1915. (From the Francis Birrell Papers, University of Sussex. Courtesy Mr Jack Lander)

Jowett is on the roof, and another woman is inside the hut. Birrell, who was described by Garnett as a 'tousled gnome-like creature' because of his size, told his father that 'magnificent females' did heavy work that was beyond his strength.

The building *équipes* began by attempting to rebuild the destroyed buildings. At Thieblemont workers erected a new type of house with brick walls at the request of the Department. Another group at Vitry-le-François built small wooden huts for the peasantry, designed by Granville Streatfeild, the architect who was also responsible for the design used by the Friends in Holland. In France, Mrs Streatfeild arranged the hut-building between Vitry and Sermaize. The *Préfet* agreed to supply the timber free, so a one-roomed hut 13 ft-square cost only £3, approximately £129 in 2009 values. Members arranged workshops and French carpenters, some of them Territorial soldiers who were paid a current wage, were engaged in making these wooden shelters. Refugees, who may have included some of the men whose idleness concerned Edith Pye, and were not of an age or strength for the Army, also worked under Mr Streatfeild's instructions. This work at Dôle and Vitry was so successful that later in the war the *Préfet* at Marseilles asked for two or three men to give instruction in hut building for Serbian refugees who had been brought to France, but there were insufficient men to let any go. However, W. Owen Stephens (1921: 290), who worked with the Quakers in France and went out to do building work, was frustrated by the fact that the money the Government had promised had been used for what he considered unsatisfactory purposes. 'They don't give it to us. They rebuild the churches and construct monuments to the heroes of France.'

The agriculture *équipes* dealt with problems arising from the fact that cows, sheep and poultry had been taken by the Germans. They looked after poultry and rabbits and did all kinds of horticulture. Brayshaw said (1921: 339) 25,000 chickens, rabbits, sheep, pigs and cattle were transported to France and 900 tons of grain threshed in one year.

Woman's traditional role is evident in maternity welfare and in family-centred aid dealt with by the relief *équipe*. Relief work started with families being visited and food, clothing and bedding distributed. As was so often the case, women needed some kind of occupation to alleviate boredom and help support themselves. Various cloths were provided and women were taught skills such as embroidery. Their work was sold, in this case some going *via* the Fry family network to the Bloomsbury Group's Omega workshops, with profits being returned to the makers. The intersection of the Quaker network with Bloomsbury and through Margery with that of Somerville College, Oxford, and the Birmingham Settlement, was therefore significant in relief to France. In addition to those already mentioned, one of the workers at Châlons was Mildred Pope who had been Librarian at Somerville prior to Margery Fry taking that post.

Dealing with war-time bureaucracy

As the work expanded a Centre was established at the *Hotel Britannique* in Paris which J. Penrose Whitlow, a member of the FLWS, Norman Angell and Mark Leicester helped inaugurate. When visas were given only as far as Paris, authorisation was needed from the French HQ and/or a letter from the *Service de Santé Militaire* or the *Infirmières Visiteuses* before workers could proceed to their destinations so they stayed at the *Hotel Britannique*. Regulations about passports changed frequently, visas needed special permission from the French Adjutant General, and permission from the War Office for each individual worker. Women as well as men might encounter problems.

However, although some French authorities were co-operative, particularly Léon Bourgeois and the Prefect of the Marne, and although sometimes the military were very co-operative, they could be obstructive. For example, in February 1915 there was a crisis; the military would not provide any more *carnets* because in November 1914 37 staff had been sanctioned and they were abiding by that number, despite the increased work. To make matters worse, the maternity work at Châlons risked being closed because visas were being refused. The Prefect was told and his aid enlisted. Visits of Ruth Fry and William Albright, planned in July 1915, could not be made because permits could not be obtained. Another difficulty was that when workers wanted to return to France the military authorities asked them for some authorisation from the Red Cross. Ruth Fry wrote to George Innes (FWVRC Box 1.3.1), Secretary of the Field Committee: 'So far the Red Cross, whom we have approached, cannot see their way – and I am not surprised – to giving us any papers of this sort, as our work does not really come under their jurisdiction.' The Government was tightening the noose around 'slackers'. Under the Derby Scheme of August 1915, men serving with the Friends faced having to decide whether to return to England to register but were advised that someone else should register them. Returning to France might be impossible because passports were being withheld and probably no more would be granted until the Military Service Bill passed into law. The problems resulting from conscription were becoming acute, not only for male workers, but also because of the implications and associated difficulties for women. The Ministry of National Service refused to grant passports to trained women unless a recommendation to do so was received from one of the Government offices. Nurse Hanna was stopped, but subsequently allowed a permit. It became difficult to obtain nurses, and Ruth Fry had an interview with Mr Shortt of the Ministry to acquire the necessary recommendation. But the situation was paradoxical.

> After it was recognised that conscientious objectors with tribunal exemption might have passports, it was suggested by the National Service Department that the work might be carried on exclusively by men. Even the suggestion that this was not wholly suitable in the case of a maternity hospital was denied by a responsible official. (Fry 1926: xxiii–xxiv)

In January 1916, the Meeting for Sufferings considered the matter of exemption. The Meeting did not take votes, but sought to obtain a consensus referred to as 'the sense of the Meeting'. This time it was that to give witness to their peace testimony, Friends should appear before the exemption tribunals. On 6 January Asquith introduced the Military Service Bill. In March 1916 W. Shewell of the Field Committee corresponded with M. Pizot, the Secretary-General of the Marne, who sent a letter of appreciation of the FWVRC work to the French Minister of War and copies were sent to the various Field groups and to London. Ruth Fry negotiated with the British authorities on behalf of the conscientious objectors to gain exemptions and also dealt with issues of nationality. This worried Birrell, who knew she was apt to get 'fluttered' in a crisis. In July, as the Battle of the Somme was decimating the armies of both belligerent sides, conscription threatened to turn the FAU from a voluntary relief organization into an alternative form of conscription. The FWVRC Field Committee thought men would be morally obliged to return to England unless exemption was gained on the grounds of being occupied with work of national importance, but the Home Committee disagreed.

There was considerable correspondence (FWVRC Box 1.3.1) about the difficulties resulting from wartime bureaucracy between Ruth Fry and George Innes. The groups worked in areas under the control of the Third, Fourth and Fifth French armies, and authorizations were needed from the appropriate authority to allow workers into specific areas. Innes thought

Ruth inept, underlining words several times in red, the word 'not' being particularly subjected to this treatment. In one instance Ruth wrote back: 'Yes, but you said you only needed three days' notice to get the permits, and we thought the need was urgent. I send you a wire about the imminent arrival of a worker, and confirm it by letter.' Implying some of this effort was superfluous, Innes replied: 'Why send the wire?' Nevertheless, he created unnecessary work for her. Frequently Ruth wrote to say someone was coming, then George complained he had never heard the name before. In June 1915 she wrote regarding two workers, Jewson and Sewell, saying she had written to them direct about their money, 'as I have told you repeatedly'.

There was also antagonism between Ruth Fry and other workers. In the Clarks' case this may partly relate to suffrage. Edith Pye and Hilda Clark were both members of the militant WSPU (Holton 1996: 171) as well as the FLWS, whereas Fry does not seem to have had suffrage links and may have disapproved of militancy. Records imply Ruth Fry's workload was too heavy. She served on other organizations' relief committees, making visits to the war-torn countries where Friends workers were based, including Russia, depleting what Jones describes (1966: 95) as her limited physical resources in what was certainly not the 'subsidiary role' she seemed destined to play as a child. Whatever the reason, Field relief workers felt London failed to support them properly (Holton 2007: 221). Antipathy between Hilda Clark and Ruth Fry grew. Hilda complained her letters were not acted upon and Alice shared Hilda's opinion of Ruth's obstructionism and poor management. Hilda Clark's mother, Helen Bright Clark, thought her daughter 'insufficiently diplomatic about the difficulties she was experiencing with the London headquarters ... and advised other family members to share the typed copies made of her letters only with her inner circle' (Holton 2007: 219).

Problems also arose because the selection process was not infallible. Two male workers were sent home, but one later repented of his unidentified misdemeanours and returned to France on probation; the other joined the FAU. No records exist regarding the selection of volunteers except that separate gender-specific Selection Sub-committees interviewed volunteers. The letter to Birrell dated 16 June 1915 saying they had been accepted and were being sent to Aimes, reveals the selection process as one that candidates had to 'pass' despite being volunteers; integral with this was the depth of their pacifism. Francesca Wilson was turned down because Ruth Fry felt she was looking for excitement. They did not receive training, nor were they necessarily given work for which they were qualified. Birrell and Garnett were accepted as agricultural students but both were sent to do hut building although Birrell did agricultural, and later, administrative work. On the other hand, C. Richardson and Theodore Tawell were both farmers sent out to do agriculture, and did it. Volunteers were at first unpaid, which meant they were from middle-class families who could afford to support them: workers even paid for their own travelling, equipment and maintenance. Birrell wrote home for money, usually £10, several times. However, in exceptional cases, and often for doctors and nurses, an honorarium was given. In October 1914 ten well-qualified nurses had gone out to France and been given £3 per month expenses. Such women found their volunteer status difficult to maintain and knew that other organizations, such as the SWH who were at Royaumont, Yvetot and Paris, did give remuneration. The Friends consequently decided to pay £52 per annum.

Nurses were usually needed, but women taking Cookery Diplomas were not so necessary. Skilled mechanics were also vital, although difficult to obtain. Recruits were given a medical examination to ensure physical suitability, but George Innes wrote:

> We recommend that the medical examination should be more stringent in future … This arises on account of two or three of our members not being sufficiently strong for the continuous hut erection which they came out to do. (FWVRC Box 1.3.2)

Women helpers needed to have a strong physique and to be French-speaking. The Executive Committee at Sermaize recommended that suitable candidates with knowledge of French should be helped to secure necessary midwifery training. Innes asked Ruth Fry whether Miss Briggs' French was good enough to enable her to talk to the children she would be dealing with. If not, it was hardly worth her while coming out. In July 1915, due to the amount of administrative work on the field, it was decided to have one volunteer who could type to concentrate entirely on this work.

There were few suitable candidates, and, being able to write shorthand, Stanley Jackson was given a trial. Were they looking for a man? Perhaps this delayed filling the post. As recently as 1896 Octavia Hill would not have a woman secretary, considering this to be a man's role. But where this could have been a gender problem, the Women's Selection Sub-committee proposed to limit recruits by a decision that smacks of religious intolerance. Their Secretary sent a letter to Dr Clark stating they were not in favour of accepting Roman Catholics. The Field Committee responded firmly: 'We feel that membership in any religious body outside the Society of Friends should not in itself be a bar to acceptance.' Nonconformists and atheists were accepted with no apparent objection.

Attempts were made by the Home Committee to match candidates with current needs in France but the time lapse between requests and fulfilment was one cause of misunderstanding between Home and Field. On 20 September 1916 Hilda Clark wrote to Edith Pye (Pye 1935: 35):

> Things have got so wrong between us and the London Committee that if I could be sure of getting out again I should try to get back to see them as soon as the other doctors come. We hoped our difficulties with the Authorities were over but I am rather afraid they are not ... The London Office appears to have forgotten the existence of the two doctors for whom I was waiting so anxiously – one of whom I know was ready to start last Wednesday.

The importance of maintaining Quaker reputation was highlighted when, in August 1916, a particularly serious problem arose. Dr Hilda Clark reported on an interview with a representative of the special military police in Châlons, indicating that as a result of a communication from Dr Albert Wilson, the Grand Quartier General of the French Army HQ staff, the police were making an enquiry as to the exact objects of the work and the character of the workers. The Prefect of the Marne confirmed this confidentially. It appeared that the workers had been accused of pro-German sympathies and propaganda. This was related to endemic spy-fever, exacerbated by Quaker behaviour. The accusation seriously menaced all their work in France, because the military authority acted on the slightest suspicion. The work remained in jeopardy, and several privileges were withdrawn. Cecil (Cecil in Fry 1926: ix) said that permission to work in France was

Plate 4. Quaker Monthly Meeting, Maurupt, France. Ted Harvey on his feet, 1915. (From the Francis Birrell Papers, University of Sussex. Courtesy Mr Jack Lander)

granted on the strict understanding that Friends abstained from pacifist propaganda or proselytising and were told that the New Testament was a 'very dangerous' book. However, as van Drenthe discusses (1999: 19), such work was propelled by the combined and mutually reinforcing discourses of humanitarian sensibility and revivalist Protestantism. Consequently, they distributed tracts to the French people. The Committee were not prepared to prohibit this but felt that distribution of religious literature should be confined solely to giving copies of the Gospels. They advised that members should not hold classes for religious instruction.

Birrell and Garnett give additional insights into the Mission's religious life. They found the regime oppressive due to religious meetings and the Quaker obsession with sin, a close watch being kept on workers. 'Sin' meant sexual morality. As Garnett (1955: 72–3) pointed out, and Foucault (1979: 304, 312) was later to theorize, this transformed sex into discourse and enabled Friends to talk about sex with impunity – the only way this was possible, 'intensifying people's awareness of it as a constant danger, and this in turn created a further incentive to talk about it'. At this time the sexuality of 'mad' men and women and those who figured as having 'unnatural' sexuality came under scrutiny by authorities whose dividing practices enabled control. Birrell's homosexuality was criminal at this time and he did not really begin to settle until Garnett left in the winter of 1915. Garnett was the object of his desire, but as his son Richard Garnett said in 2005, he was 'leaned against' rather than 'leaning towards' same-sex relationships.* The Friends' 'striving for sainthood' with its 'inherent hypocrisy', their 'gatherings three times a week', combined with 'lack of understanding or knowledge of the Bible', irritated Garnett and Birrell. They failed to accept, as Hirst explains (1923: 522), that the Society's peace testimony was not based merely on the recorded teaching of the New Testament, although in full harmony with this, but grew inevitably out of the conception of the Inward Light.

Censorship was another problem. Quakers held the right of free speech and some members wrote letters mentioning the coming and going of troops. The military censor discovered three instances in one week and recurrence meant being withdrawn from the area. Expressions of political opinion in letters conveyed through Army Post were also forbidden. Letters could be sent by ordinary post but they were also liable to censorship which Charis Barnett may not have realized when she deliberately used this method on her way to Châlons because she wanted to mention place names. In April 1916 it was planned to 'discuss our position with regard to the expression of political opinion and the right of free discussion at the next General Meeting'. By November this problem had not been resolved and the Executive Field Committee despairingly recorded in Minute Book 2, 'We don't want to have to appoint a camp censor.'

* In conversation with the author in July 2000.

Birrell's letters and the magazine he edited, *Reconstruction*, also indicate discord between the workers themselves. The strain of working and living in shattered buildings which shook from the constant gunfire and other wartime conditions exacerbated tensions but were not the prime cause. Although as Ruth Fry explained (1926: 16), 'men and women worked together equally, as has long been the Quaker habit' women's representation on committees was a still further cause of discontent, partially solved by the introduction of proportional representation. The size of équipes was another factor but Birrell said (Sussex: Birrell Papers. Box 1.27) Sermaize was at the root of the unexplained friction. The arrival of Americans, some of whom were Mennonites, caused further trouble due to their desire to 'do things in a big way'. Home/Field relationships had been difficult in the Boer War and, as indicated, were so again, probably exacerbated by the general lack of understanding at home of the conditions of war encountered by everyone serving abroad. The desire of the Home Committee to retain control resulted in a Field challenge, with Birrell playing a key role and changes being made to the workers' satisfaction. However, the omission of some names, including Birrell, from Ruth Fry's list of workers is perhaps indicative of clashes over control. The fact that (Holton 2007: 220, 219) she fails to mention in *A Quaker Adventure* that Alice Clark, Hilda's sister, took on the secretaryship of one of the France sub-committees, hints at retribution rather than forgetfulness.

In the last year of the War an influenza pandemic swept around the globe. It started in mid-June in England, and Francis Birrell and some other workers were affected by it in France. He referred to it as 'Spanish flu'. In November there was some kind of recurrence they now referred to as the stomach 'grippe'. The wife of the *Sous Préfet* of Verdun and her children caught it and some people, including relief workers died of it. There was a further recurrence in February during the Armistice, not alleviated by the fact that for the first time for two years Birrell was able to have something for breakfast at Sermaize. He told his father that the whole world was 'seedy'.

The Armistice and after

For Margery Fry, now in her mid-40s, leaving Sermaize was worse than leaving Oxford and she remained nostalgic for her years in the Marne. She feared being 'jammed back' into Birmingham. The 'gap' for Margery, was on leaving Sermaize. Jones wrote (1966: 107): 'she never lost her almost savage nostalgia for her life among the people of the Marne'. She wrote to her brother Roger: 'The sheltered selectness of an old maid's establishment doesn't suit me as well as a milieu where everyone lives and speaks with brutal plainness.' The Bristol Union of Women's Suffrage Societies almost persuaded her to stand for parliament as candidate for West Bristol but her loss of sense of purpose was eventually restored though her prison work. Many women's limited pre-war life-styles expanded during the war, and contracted after the Armistice.

Quaker work was valued by the French authorities; towards the end of the war the Friends began work in the Somme and later were asked to go to Verdun. In the late summer of 1919 (Brayshaw 1921: 338) 'the work of the British Friends was merged with that of their American counterparts to form the Anglo-American Friends Mission' and the French authorities handed over the area to the east of Verdun to them. They continued building wooden houses, and 'helped to clear fields and to plant and harvest crops in addition to contributing large quantities of seed and equipment'. Relief workers faced the winding down of their work and return to civilian life. Dr Courtauld, who worked for three years with the Royaumont SWH Unit, found it 'a grievous business finishing it up and severing connections with one's fellow workers. But the experience will always be something worth remembering'. Nevertheless, this 'gap' was postponed, since she undertook new work in Caudry, near Cambrai, with the American Fund for French Wounded 'which now really means work among the refugees'. The FWVRC Mission ended its work in France in 1921, its stores and equipment being sent to Poland and Vienna where Hilda Clark and Edith Pye were working. Greenwood says that Ruth Fry retired to Norfolk after the war (1978: 210), but this is an inaccurate description of her subsequent life. She visited the United States in 1918 and 1934, and in addition to producing and distributing peace pamphlets, published *A Quaker Adventure* in 1926 and a *Life of Emily Hobhouse* in 1929. Her 1930s output indicates considerable preparation in the earlier decade and she became treasurer of the War Resisters' International from 1936 to 1947. Seeking to prevent another such period of killing and pain, Ruth Fry, Dr Hilda Clark and Edith Pye (*Times*, 28.4.1962) all promoted the work of the League of Nations.

CHAPTER 6

Dealing with Neutrality: Suffragists, Quakers and Government Links between Britain and Holland

Organization of Dutch relief

As in the other countries that have been considered, in Holland the first people to suffer from the war were the wives and families of mobilized men, over 400,000 of whom between the ages of 20 and 40 were conscripted. H. van Biema-Hymans, President of the National Council of Women of the Netherlands (NCWN) explained in *Jus Suffragii* (1.3.1915) how in early August Aletta Jacobs, the first Dutch woman doctor and President of the National Society for Woman Suffrage (*Nationale Vereeniging voor Vrouwenkiesrecht*) appealed to branches to organize relief committees. On 10 August Queen Wilhelmina convoked representatives of existing local relief committees, social workers, representatives of trade, industry and agriculture, and the NCWN to a meeting at The Hague, when a Royal National Relief Committee (RNRC) was established; suffragists were not invited. The NCWN was thereby given official recognition and called on to represent Dutch women, although as Biema-Hymans' report states, it had no branches and while it could disseminate ideas, was not a suitable body to organize relief. Further, since the RNRC decided only to negotiate with the official local committees, other women's organizations such as the suffragists were further sidelined. Nonetheless, the NCWN, through its RNRC delegate, who was in charge of the supply of food, clothes and material for the refugees, and was possibly Biema-Hymans herself, acted as liaison between it and suffragists. Aletta Jacobs confirmed this sequence of events when she described how women's relief committees began more quickly than men's but then joined the General Committees so that men and women worked together for refugee relief. Despite apparent exclusion from the RNRC, Dutch suffragists served on official relief committees as well as their own.

During the early months of the war, when thousands of refugees were pouring across the Channel into Britain, even greater numbers were flooding neutral Netherlands, overwhelming villages and straining resources. In the first weeks approximately 100,000 Belgians took refuge in the Limburg and North Brabant provinces and during September it was reported that 1,000,000 Antwerpers had fled to the Netherlands. This, according to Abbenhuis (2006: 96) prompted the first large-scale Dutch humanitarian response. British suffragists and Quakers were involved soon afterwards.

Quaker First Aid for Holland

On 4 September the FWVRC Committee in London established a Belgium subcommittee, to which Dr Hilda Clark was appointed, to consider relief work in Belgium and the Netherlands. By 8 September the Dutch Consul had told Committee member William Kennedy that there was great distress and the Ambassador advised the SOF to contact the English Minister at The Hague, which they did. They also decided to ask Henrietta Thomas to enquire into medical and nursing conditions next time she repatriated German women. Later in September Ted Harvey and Dr Dyson Holdsworth visited the offices of the RNRC in Amsterdam, sitting in on a meeting. They visited a warehouse where clothes and goods were stored and were then taken by their 'hospitable' Dutch friends to see an internment camp at Oldebroek where there was an artillery training camp with adapted cavalry stables housing 200 civilian Flemings and about 1,000 French-speaking Walloons, mainly women and children, from Visé and Liège (*Friend*, 9.10.1914). The presence and help of nationals of a belligerent country were thought to be unwise but they were given a 'courteous welcome' although visits were normally discouraged. This camp (vluchtoord) and others were purposely sited far from the frontier to avoid possible involvement in other countries' wars. Harvey and Holdsworth became aware of the strong determination to preserve neutrality which Ruth Fry connected with tension and nervousness that a German invasion was imminent. Some of the refugees complained of the cold and of wet feet because it was raining. The FWVRC sent £100 for boots.

Harvey reported everything was 'perfected to a high degree', a strange way of describing such accommodation, and surprising considering the Dutch Consul's statement of great need. However, the camp commandant, Dr Muller, may have misled them as he did a Dutch delegation, who were not shown round the camp, saying that nothing was needed except skittles and some clothing. Harvey said Muller was a 'good Protestant', and seemed bamboozled by the fact that the stables had been renamed for Dutch and Belgian Royalty. Philip Burtt of the FWVRC saw another side of Muller in July 1915, describing him as an autocrat on his high horse. On their last day, Harvey and Holdsworth learned that some babies had been rescued from burning houses by German soldiers and sent across the frontier. Harvey suggested women Friends establish a crèche for under-3-year-olds; Edith Pye agreed and later sent warning about 300 destitute Belgian babies and orphans on Dutch soil. Apart from this, the men advised waiting until it was possible to work in Belgium itself. However, in October the RNRC appealed to the Friends on behalf of the babies, so Gulielma Crosfield, FLWS President, went to Holland to arrange housing and care. Her report indicated that all was not as perfect as the men had thought and mentioned difficulties which might indicate disagreements between Walloon and Fleming.

Suffragist relief of Flushing

The race to the sea by the contending armies threatened Belgian people's chance of escape from danger and the siege of Antwerp from 26 September increased panic to reach the coast. Aletta Jacobs explained to Mary Sheepshanks that while the richer refugees could afford to go to England, the poor, or those who delayed their escape, were left behind in Holland. Children became separated from their parents, many people were sick or crippled and mothers gave birth wherever they happened to be at that undeniable time. Emphasizing that wars do not promote women's rights she added (*Jus Suffragii*, 1.11.1914) 'those poor Belgian refugees demonstrated who it is who have to pay the bill of the war. It was the mothers and children, children and women, without end.'

At the beginning of October over 500,000 Belgian refugees crossed into the Netherlands. This number of homeless and unemployed people tripled or quadrupled the populations of some towns and villages overnight, despite lack of sufficient food and shelter and resultant sanitary problems. By 11 October Roosendael's few thousand inhabitants were swamped by 30,000 refugees from Antwerp; the incomplete sugar refinery was opened to shelter 1,600 people. The vast influx of 80,000 refugees into Flushing by land and water caused enormous difficulties, increasing its population of 20,000. Miss Stickney and Ellen Walshe of the IWRC encountered the chaos while escorting parties of German girls through Holland and contacted Mary Sheepshanks for help. They described people thronging the roads, sleeping in the open and trying vainly to get food. Roads were also crowded with about 200,000 Belgian cows, some being driven by their owners, others trying to find a peaceful field. At the Armistice, cows were important throughout Europe.

Mary Sheepshanks' office received Ellen Walshe's appeal at midday on 13 October. By the evening, four railway trucks containing bread, chocolate, condensed milk and biscuits were shipped out. Edinburgh barrister, leading pacifist and suffragist Chrystal Macmillan directed operations, obtaining the consent of Government Departments to export food that was forbidden by blockade regulations and gaining remission of dues and/or special help from Customs and Port Authorities, railway and shipping companies. This is the first of two occasions when women broke the blockade, the other being during the Armistice.

Arrangements to relieve Flushing were made without the funds to support them, but Mary Sheepshanks was sure the money could be raised later. Consequently, the IWRC was the first organization to alleviate the suffering. She visited the Belgian Minister, who gave £500 from the Belgian Relief Fund. On 14 October Miss Walshe's report was published in the Press; daily consignments of food were shipped for a fortnight, totalling £2,000 in value, and a further £1,200 in cash was donated. The next day Miss Walshe returned to Holland with Miss Boileau and Mary Sheepshanks to ascertain what had already been done and what further help was needed;

they discovered that 'everything' was wanted, 'including baby clothes for the many new-born infants'. It is probable that many of these births were premature in view of the conditions of flight of their mothers.

Dutch women had organized relief committees and established one in the station. Two members of the local committee, Mrs Van Raalte and Mr Niftick, took the visitors to see the refugees. In an incomplete factory little 'rabbit hutches' were assembled from planks for 2,000 refugees to crawl into on hands and knees. Schools were used; one had been turned into an impromptu maternity ward for 30 mothers being cared for by Belgian refugee nuns. Barns, mills, sheds, workshops, a coal shed with straw on the floor and an empty circus tent also gave shelter. Tarpaulins were stretched out for people to shelter underneath. Such conditions held potential for smallpox, cholera and typhoid epidemic. One family of four generations particularly saddened the visitors: a woman had her 82-year-old mother with her in a shed, plus a daughter with her newly born baby for whom the woman begged some milk. The little town of Bergen-op-Zoom had an influx of 25,000 refugees, mostly women and children. The Mayor wired for help in obtaining 'all baby articles'. However, internalisation of Edwardian mores required silence on some subjects. The emphasis on new-born babies obscures mothers' distress at giving birth in public places. Heavily-pregnant women are not mentioned, nor those who suffered miscarriages as a result of their ordeal. The vulnerability of newly-born babies meant liability to acute suffering and even death under traumatic conditions of flight and survival. Problems for menstruating women are never indicated and that of non-existent lavatories are only hinted at by phrases such as 'attempts at modesty'. The towns and villages of the area visited by the suffragists normally totalled 343,000 inhabitants, but there were now 543,000 refugees to care for. Nevertheless, they were assured that the Dutch would rather bear the burden than drive their guests back into Belgium. This was, however, questionable.

On 17 October, as a further response to this unparalleled disaster, the British women chartered a small ship and set out across the Scheldt. The Netherlands Government had instituted war buoying on 4 August so that the buoys and lights secured their boundaries. As Abbenhuis explains (2006: 87), only trade ships were allowed to use the river during daylight hours and the waterway was closely monitored by the Dutch who feared that Britain would send troops up-river to support the Belgian war effort. Ships were escorted by Dutch pilot boats. The women visited Breskens and Sluis with supplies sent by the IWRC. They visited Hansweert, normal population 1,200, which had 2,000 refugees living in the village and a further 15,000 on barges. The scale of the disaster is indicated in the following table of approximate figures printed in *Jus Suffragii* in November that were obtained at random from the burgomasters reports' showing that in this area the population increased by about 60 per cent in a few days.

Table 3. Numbers of refugees in some areas of Holland. *Jus Suffragii*, 1.11.1914

Area	*Inhabitants*	*Refugees*
Province of Zeeland	300,000	500,000
Flushing	20,000	30,000 to 50,000
Middelburg	18,000	7,000
Sluis	1,500	8,000
Aardenburg	1,500	5,000
Breskens	800	2,000
Hansweert	1,200	17,000
Total	343,000	589,000

Mary Sheepshanks' comment that 'a new chapter in international relief work [had been] opened by the bombardment and fall of Antwerp' shows her perception of the significance of these events. Chrystal Macmillan visited Rotterdam, Amsterdam, Breda, Flushing and outlying towns and villages, consulting Dutch Relief Committees. At Flushing school buildings were packed and people had crowded into windowless coal sheds near the station. Dutch soldiers were reported as protecting them with guards. Since the Dutch military did not take part in the war as belligerents, they became responsible for security and defence, monitoring the refugees who were a security threat (de Rooij in Abbenhuis 2006: 16) because they represented an uncontrollable chaos. The authorities regarded them as a nuisance because they took food supplies, clogged the transport system and were a drain on the public purse. By September 1918, they had cost 42,000,000 frs. Abbenhuis (2006: 98, 101) explains that any woman who associated with troops was likely to be labelled a prostitute who would 'compromise' them; all women were therefore a potential threat to public order. Nonetheless, refugees were reported as being looked after by 'kindly' Dutch soldiers.

Recognizing that a small nation like Holland could not cope with this influx, the IWRC determined to inform the British Authorities and public in the hope of getting further help. They poured out information to the Press. Mary Sheepshanks wrote to Sir Edward Grey at the Foreign Office on 20 October, describing her visit, the steps already taken and the urgent necessity of bringing refugees from Holland to England for humanitarian and, intelligently, also for military reasons. Her letter indicated the resentment of the Dutch that they had been left to care for over 1,000,000 refugees compared to the 'small share' taken by Britain in mitigating their calamities. Eleanor Acland explained to readers of *The Englishwoman* (July–September 1915: 122) that while England had taken between 200,000 and 300,000 refugees, about twice as many were in Holland.

Mary Sheepshanks was seen at the Foreign Office by Francis Acland, Under-Secretary for Foreign Affairs and Eleanor's husband, who wrote to Sir Edward on 20 October, stating 'I have known her for years to be reliable and not given to exaggeration'. Acland's note also indicated the difficulty the LGB had in dealing with the present influx into Britain, because the existing means of accommodating refugees were congested. In other words, where could more refugees be housed if brought from the Netherlands? Acland had 'explained to Miss Sheepshanks that … I would put her letter before you so that it might, if you thought right, be brought before the Cabinet'. Grey then forwarded it to Herbert Samuel intending this should happen. Samuel was President of the Board of Trade, a member of the War Cabinet, and in charge of the reception of Belgian refugees into Britain. Cahalan (1982: 120–2) states that a Cabinet discussion probably took place on 21 October. If so, it was motivated partially by the suffragists' efforts.

In fact, a report dated 14 October (FO 369/671/59417) shows that the Foreign Office recognized the question of Belgian refugees in Holland would shortly become acute. There had been a steady influx of about 500 a day during the previous two or three weeks and 10,000 were brought over from Ostend after the fall of Antwerp, some in transports, but the rest arrived in any available craft and settled on the East coast. The possibility of an invasion of spies among them practically decided the LGB to refuse to take any more for the present. It was also recognized that the situation could no longer be dealt with departmentally but must be considered by the Cabinet in all its bearing and some policy agreed on.

Mary Sheepshanks' confidence in her fellow-suffragists, and in the response of the general public was justified. By 1 December £4,502 had been donated to the IWRC for the relief of Belgians in Holland. Hundreds of cases of clothes were dispatched; when the Dutch organized the food supply, money was sent instead. However, showing the Friends' larger resources, by March 1915, they had received £36,261 13s. 9d.

The Quakers also wrote to Sir Edward Grey to urge the Government to act. This reinforced Mary Sheepshanks' moves. Sheepshanks reported (*Jus Suffragii*, 1.12.1914):

> It was at first proposed to send a number of workers, and many volunteers came forward from the NUWSS ... but it was found that Holland could only use its own helpers, so their services were not required abroad.

There were so many refugees due to the fall of Antwerp that FWVRC members Mrs Henry Hodgkin, Gulielma Crosfield and William Kennedy planned to go immediately to the Belgian frontier and arrange temporary shelter. Ruth Fry thought that the invasion of refugees into Holland made invasion by the German Army less likely and British help more acceptable. Mrs Crosfield also had interviews with Samuel and Acland who discussed a scheme for sending Belgian refugees to Ireland which they hoped the Friends would organize. Sir Edward informed them the Government had offered £50,000 for relief of Belgian Refugees but the Netherlands Government had refused it as prejudicial to their neutral status. In the absence of peace, what was needed was accommodation in another country.

On 9 November the Quaker MPs Percy Alden and Arnold Rowntree, with Seebohm Rowntree, and E. Richard Cross went to Holland at Herbert Samuel's request. Cross had been Chairman of the urban side of the Land Committee appointed in 1912 by Lloyd George. Cross was a member of the Fabian Society Research Department which oversaw Leonard Woolf's scheme for the League of Nations (Vernon in Chapman and Manson 1998: 156–7) and in late 1914 he founded the Council for the Study of International Relations with 'Goldie' Lowes Dickinson and Lord Bryce. These men were members of a network of what Hamilton calls 'talking centres' planning for a future international peace-keeping society of nations. Matters discussed included settlement of international disputes, continuous mediation, establishment of a permanent international council of conciliation, who delegates should be, and how appointed. Helena Swanwick, the economist J.A. Hobson, Willoughby Dickinson, Arnold Rowntree and Robert Cecil, together with members of the UDC and people who later formed the Bryce Group or the 1917 Club, were in nodes of this network. Figure 2 depicts some groups of such people who are known to have met together, and links between them can be traced through individuals' names; names of facilitators or relevant organizations are given in capitals. This was a significant area of liaison between Quakers, suffragists and others who met in different people's homes, including that of Mary Agnes Hamilton, who was assistant secretary to the Land Inquiry. Hamilton (1944: 136), whose mother's family were Quakers, named Richard Cross as 'the master mind in working out ... the plan for a league of nations'. Their close connection with influential men like Maynard Keynes, Leonard Woolf and Ramsay MacDonald contributed to the League's foundation, even though the form it took did not match their proposals. Cross, Arnold Rowntree and others were therefore attempting to organize an international system leading to permanent peace while coping with the refugee crisis. Together with Seebohm Rowntree and Alden, they visited Flushing, seeing the conditions in which refugees were living, exactly as the suffragists had seen earlier. They were informed that the Dutch government did not want the refugees to return to Belgium because this would play into the hands of certain Dutch Burgomasters of German proclivities who made poor provision with the idea of getting the refugees to return because the

Germans wanted them for their Army. This was the military reason Mary Sheepshanks had given Grey.

The British Government took until 21 November to decide to begin transporting Belgian refugees from Holland. Philip Burtt asked Cross, who was acting as adviser to the FWVRC, to try to arrange an interview with Herbert Samuel. Samuel had to get Admiralty permission for ships, and then authority from the War Office, both dilatory because of other priorities. Percy Alden tried to organize on the Government's behalf to bring over a total of 20,000 Belgians. He returned to Holland in December with Mary Godlee, another Quaker suffragist, to see if he could arrange things from there. Miss Godlee's Report to the Executive resulted in £10,000 being sent by the Belgian Consul to The Hague for general relief. Money could be transferred and accepted if the right channels were used. By December Belgians were being brought to England at the rate of 1,000 or 1,500 per week. From the first week of January the Government made arrangements to increase the number to a weekly total of 2,500.

Although they felt there was not much else they could do, in December contacts between the Dutch and British suffragists and Quakers meant the Friends sent £50 to help establish a Mothers' Home at Middelburg, about 12 miles from Flushing. This indicates previous Quaker-suffragist women's collaboration and personal association which may have partly arisen from work done by Josephine Butler and the Quaker Elizabeth Fry in the Netherlands. Already the Friends had set up a home in Flushing where 70 babies were born up to May 1915. They liaised with other Committees already working there including WEC and the IWRC. At Middelburg the suffragists had met Mrs Anne Bollë, President of the local Suffrage Society and now Treasurer of the Provincial Relief Committee, who was known to Mrs Crosfield. The Mother's Home was discussed on 15 December and Chrystal Macmillan was invited to the meeting. She prepared a statement highlighting the overcrowding, exposure and lack of sanitation in Holland. Gulielma Crosfield wrote to her friends and to the Burgomaster, to see whether a Home could be opened under their care. Through such actions the women being helped could regain some respectability instead of retaining their status as outcasts. The IWRC appealed in *Jus Suffragii* (1.1.1915) for more Belgians to be brought over. Mary Sheepshanks explained that

Figure 2. 'Talking centres' network involved in League of Nations and ILO planning, showing Leonard Woolf, Ramsay MacDonald and Lowes Dickinson as key figures.

the Belgians' sufferings were growing worse despite all the Dutch could do, so they had sent over 700 cases of warm clothes and money to buy food; 100 sheep's carcasses received from the Government of Victoria had been forwarded for Christmas dinners. In February Mrs Crosfield was authorized to go for another visit, this time with another suffragist Quaker, Edith Bigland, who, with her husband Percy was also participating in the discussion network with a group of about 20 people, including those who were to form the League of Nations Society.

Dutch neutral status was hard to maintain. The temptation to join in and be allied to one side was very great. Neutrality was suspected by both sides, and subjected to harsh restrictions and indignities. Ruth Fry thought Holland's determination to keep at peace called forth respect and admiration. The Dutch placed strong emphasis on humanitarian activities as a method of staying out of the war, increasing the value other nations placed on its neutral status. The discourse of the Dutch as 'hospitable' and 'kindly' adopted on both sides of the belligerent lines assisted in this. The Dutch facilitated food shipments to occupied Belgium; in February 1915 the government agreed to exchange sick and wounded PoWs between Britain and Germany across the Netherlands and the first exchanges began almost immediately (Abbenhuis 2006: 109–10). The Dutch Minister of Foreign Affairs also permitted civilians imprisoned as aliens in Germany and Britain to move to the Netherlands where they lived like other refugees. Some people being helped were Belgians who had escaped from occupied territory. Ruth Fry (1926: 101) identified 'fugitive Belgians' being given assistance by the LGB including a girl escaping from Antwerp with her brother and cousin.

Friends helped in the humanitarian activities. Firstly, by December they were providing portable wooden homes; secondly they created industries in the refugee camps such as knitting for the women refugees, and thirdly, they arranged for refugees to be brought to England and assisted in prisoner exchange. Van Drenthe and de Haan (1999: 14) claim that caring power is a productive principle that calls up responses and refugees were not passive recipients of these actions. They had the power of choice: whether or not to attend the workshops, to ask for separate huts, or to co-operate with relief workers, even to go back to Belgium.

Camps and wooden huts

Most civilian refugees returned to Belgium fairly quickly, helped by what Nagtegaal (2004) describes as the 'gentle insistence' of the Dutch government stimulating their return. Abbenhuis (2006: 99) explains how, from 18 October, civic representatives from Antwerp met refugees in Breda, Roosendael and Bergen to assure them that Antwerp was safe, but also gave them the opportunity to travel to Britain. People who remained were mainly those who could support themselves, the *pauvre honteux*, 'deserving', middle-class people who had lost everything because of the war, and poverty-stricken Belgians. The Dutch Government gave the middle-classes a small allowance but took no responsibility for those who had nothing. These 'undeserving' refugees could go to camps or back to Belgium. Some mayors refused to feed refugees if they stayed. Indeed, General C.J. Snijders, the Commander-in-Chief, did not classify Belgians as true refugees, probably seeing them, in to-day's terms, as 'economic migrants'. He wanted to close the borders in November 1914 to prevent Belgians from entering. As in England, Jewish refugees were cared for by Jewish organizations, and children without their parents and 'maladjusted' refugees were cared for separately.

In May 1915 over 100,000 refugees remained in permanent camps which had been built by the Dutch Government. According to Greenwood (1975: 198) Friends were unable to get relief workers into camps until June 1915 when four women were sent out. However, Miss Vulliamy and other workers were there in March dealing with transport of the wounded, and hut building. The Quakers established a Dutch Field Committee to administer the mission's increased work; meetings were held in Rotterdam, Utrecht and The Hague. For a while no new workers were sent when the atmosphere became unsettled and it became difficult to keep up refugees' courage. Food conditions were hard. As ever, Quakers' desire for plain speaking could cause difficulties and on 16 November 1915, Ruth Fry (FWVRC Box 9.3.3) wrote to J.W. Barry that workers should be 'even more careful of expressing opinions on any controversial matters in Holland ... for the whole of our work might be undone otherwise'.

By 4 August 1915, Friends were working in three of the four main camps, Ede, Uden and Gouda, and were anticipating going to Nunspeet, which, with a capacity of 13,000, was opened at the beginning of November for the 'undeserving' or 'undesirables'. Miss Vulliamy, Miss Pim and Mary Rees arrived at Nunspeet on 12 October. It was an unhealthy place with earthy roads paved with discarded sheets of asbestos. Here, and at Roosendael, soldiers guarded prostitutes' quarters and rooms where refugees suffering from disease were placed in quarantine (Abbenhuis 2006: 99). The use of guards in both instances seems heavy-handed and indicates what Nyak and Suchland (2006: 469) describe as 'gender violence', the acts and practices that systematically target and discipline a marginalized group to dominant political structures and practices. Many issues are raised by this action, for example, how and by whom were the women identified as prostitutes? It was understood that desperately poor women turned to prostitution as a survival mechanism. Prostitution was a threat to the sanctity of the family and a sin and cast female sexuality as powerfully active. By segregating these women from the space of the camp, sexualized as familial but also under guard, the authorities had effectively created a doubly guarded brothel of Belgian prostitutes. The Minister of Internal Affairs urged mayors to send prostitutes to this isolation barracks to prevent troops visiting them. Further, what diseases were the refugees suffering from? Were they the men who consumed sex? There was clearly fear of weakening the population by spread of illness and thereby increasing the threat of invasion. Keeping Dutch neutrality secure was the over-riding factor.

On 17 April 1916 the Dutch Field Committee, meeting at The Hague, listed 22 women and 16 men working in Holland. At Ede, which was between Utrecht and Arnhem, there were four women Friends and three men. The refugee village was about three miles outside the village and was something of a show camp intended to hold 10,000 respectable refugees. By 1916 it was controlled by Colonel J. Mingels, the specially appointed Government Commissioner. According to *The Times*, 28 March 1916, it was a 'model of town planning, although only temporary'. The residential buildings were barracks with accommodation that 'seemed in every way adequate to the requirements of simple folk'. Older people had separate quarters and a crèche was provided for infants. Friends' industrial work at

Ede was typical of that carried out elsewhere; men, taught by men, learned skills such as brush and shoe making; dressmaking and house-care classes were given for and by women in separate workshops. Some tasks were chosen because the skills could be helpful on repatriation.

Uden opened on 20 December 1914 for 5,400 people. It was designed for respectable poor and better class refugees. Nevertheless, there were unspecified problems. In April 1915, H.P. Enkey at the British Government Commission for Transportation of Belgians to the United Kingdom, was told that people were in such fear of being sent to Uden that a number were running away and going to live in Flushing, leaving huts unfinished. However, Enkey arranged for the men to finish the houses, staying with their families in the Strand Hotel until the work was done. *The Times* correspondent visited Uden in March 1916 and found 4,000 refugees there. His evaluation was typically middle-class, expressing pleasure that each area was named after a Belgian river and dormitories after distinguished Belgians. This may have been done to make the refugees feel at home and therefore to prevent possible disturbances. It was as if the authorities were trying to recreate a small part of Belgium that had not been violated, but it could have served the opposite purpose, reminding them that living in a Dutch camp was not the same as being at home. Inevitably, the refugees wanted more huts. Nonetheless, many babies were born there and day-care facilities were provided so women could work; there were separate buildings for men's smoking, reading and recreation. The ideology of domesticity and appropriate roles for men and women was obviously identical to that in Britain. However, food shortages, which resulted in riots in Amsterdam on 14 June 1916, affected cookery classes' capacity to obtain ingredients. A further problem was when in March 1917, a number of 'roughs' came into the camp from near the frontier and stole things from the Scout club rooms and in May the rooms were again broken into.

Mary Rees (Wilson: 1944), who went out with other workers in September as Grace Vulliamy's assistant, suggests cogent reasons for discontent:

> The girls always seemed busy doing the work of the camp – it was the boys who were at a loose end. It was very gloomy for the refugees. The camps were run by the

> Dutch military and guarded by sentinels. They couldn't go out without a pass. We made a great difference to them.

In May 1916, Grace Vulliamy became worried about food the refugees were receiving. Australia had offered to send bacon, but there were fears that the Germans were getting food meant for civilians. In 1915 the kitchens had 150 kilos of bacon to put into the soup but now had only 57 and whereas nine sheep had been boiled on a meat day, now only two were available. The refugees' physical condition suffered. Further, the winter of 1916–17 was intensely cold and on 2 February 1917 Grace Vulliamy told Ruth Fry that bedclothes were frozen to the walls and floors were sheets of ice. That month at Ede and Groningen there was meningitis, which Grace referred to as 'spotted fever'. Those refugees still at Ede were due to be moved to Nunspeet, but this was delayed until the isolation period was over. Although records state Ede closed in the spring of 1917, Friends' work continued there until at least September. Quakers attributed the success of the work in Holland to Grace Vulliamy who had initiated relief there, starting at the vluchtoord at Ede, going on to Gouda and finally Uden. Friends' concern to help the refugees equip themselves for a return to their homeland gave hope, indicating the possibility of a new life and giving meaning to their activities. This was also true of aid to refugees in Britain and elsewhere. Van Drenthe and de Haan give this as the first requisite of 'caring power' in action (1999: 19). The camps provided a place to stay, but the Quakers gave 'psychological and material support ... not just by visiting and talking with them, but also by arranging religious and secular education ... and a job'. This fulfilled another requisite for caring power to be effective.

As an alternative method of relieving the overcrowding in Holland, by January 1915 Percy Alden had plans to erect a town of transportable wooden three-roomed huts, each with land for cultivation. The work was to be entirely carried out by Belgian workmen, with timber bought in Holland and paid for by the Friends Committee; workers in camps in France were already making equipment. The cost of this was between £50,000 and £100,000 and an advance of £1,000 to £2,000 was needed. Fred Rowntree had interviews with the Dutch Authorities, including the Prime Minister who approved Alden's plan. Fred Rowntree was an architect from Scarborough who, with two other men, employed Belgian refugees to create prefabricated buildings for re-erection during the war. The first scheme was to be of 20 huts at Flushing, with the possibility of a similar scheme at Gouda. There were 100 men working at cottages at Amersfoort and here the Society's huts were to be marked to distinguish them from those erected by other societies. Baron de Tuyll of the Danish Committee, which was also building refugee houses, wrote to Grace Vulliamy on 31 March 1915 (FWVRC Box 9.3.5), his letter indicating their friendly relationship and a sense of humour regarding the difficulty of contacting her during working hours.

> Dear Miss Vulliamy.
> Juffrouw 9155 Haag. Is Miss Vulliamy there? No, then is her secretary available? Oh well. This is each morning the beginning of my daily task. When are you to be found, except in the dark?

He had heard that besides the ten houses being sent to Gaasterland on Monday there were ten more nearly finished and asked if these could also be sent to Gaasterland where they were badly needed. He continued:

> Mr Buyse has promised to have 30 houses ready in a month's time but I greatly doubt it. As you know, the way these women are housed in the Brickworks is shocking and it is a great pity Mr Buyse put a stop to our work. However. We wash our hands like Mr Pilate.

The Repatriation Committee's scheme for housing was partly at Elisabethdorp, near Amersfoort. Eleanor Acland received a report from M. Buyse who confirmed that £1,000 had been granted, eight huts erected and 129 people homed therein. However, infantile mortality was high owing to generally bad housing. One of the Repatriation Committee members, Mrs Chapin, offered to hand over hospital equipment worth £2,000 to £3,000 at the end of the war if the committee could now free £2,000 in order to provide huts in Holland for the women and children. Eleanor Acland, who made at least two visits to Holland, the first in December 1915, and another in May 1916, offered to go to Holland with Mr Burke to study conditions. £2,000 was immediately allocated for the erection of moveable huts in Holland.

Eleanor Acland's opinion of Mr Buyse was completely different from de Tuyll's. She wrote in the *Liberal Women's Review:*

> I hope all our members will ... remember the name of Omer Buyse, who has been the prime mover in the creation of this colony of Elisabethdorp. He is one of the finest friends of women in this or any other country whom I have had the luck to meet ... Other people seeing these soldiers' wives in their former misery said that they were of a low type; but Omer Buyse believed in them and his faith has been amply justified. May I add that ... that there are still many women begging for houses. So if any reader of the Review is moved to send even a small donation to the LWSU [Liberal Women's Suffrage Union] office it is by no means too late.

Fred Rowntree and Ruth Fry visited Amersfoort in August 1915. They found the camp cruelly overcrowded with families of interned soldiers, some housed in a granary. Old people and children suffered particular hardship as refugees. In November Grace Vulliamy wrote about the miserable condition in which the children arrived, very insufficiently clothed and with next to nothing in the way of shoes and stockings. Each month 500 children arrived from occupied Belgium for a short holiday in Holland and a Dutch lady donated money to buy shoes. Grace asked Ruth to send £8 worth of shoes for children aged 10 to 12. She said the Belgians in Elisabethdorp seemed to regard the Quakers as their friends although they stole from them when they were out of the way and then blatantly wore what they had stolen. She thought this was a national characteristic which did not alter their genuine affection. Ruth Fry, who attended Repatriation Committee meetings as FWVRC representative, reported on 2 December 1915 that Amersfoort and other centres still needed suitable accommodation for women and children. Women might pay 4 frs. a week for a small space partitioned off in a garret, a situation that left them financially strained because the wives of interned soldiers only got a grant of 75 c. a day and 25 c. for each child. In January 1916, there were 200 children living in 'Village Elisabeth', the houses built by the SOF and the Belgian Repatriation Committee at Amersfoort.

In contrast to these big camps, Gouda could take only 2,000 refugees. By 1 November 1914 it held 1,444, with some sheltering in a boat and others housed by private societies. By February Quakers were working in Gouda and considering building huts there. Originally the Netherlands Government thought refugees should be cared for privately and the camp at Gouda was opened after a local refugee support committee arranged for a Commission for Supervision to administer it. In December the camp was given official Government approval. Kraaijestein (2004) says that the remarkable thing about Gouda vluchtoord was that it was the result of private initiative. Nevertheless, this encouraged serious shortcomings, which apparently the authorities ignored. On 3 May 1916, Grace Vulliamy and Harold Ellis had an interview with M. Poullet, Belgian Ministre des Beaux Arts at The Hague, who was in charge of the supervision of war relief charities. Perhaps indicating that M. Poullet was not really bothered about the refugees, her report stated:

> M. Poullet was not at all au courant with any of the affairs in Amersfoort. He was surprised at our opinion of Gouda (poor) ... Poullet wanted us to remain as long as possible at Ede because he didn't think the Dutch would spend the money in employing the unskilled girls as we were doing. Further, he hoped we would go to him at any time and keep him au courant with all our work in Holland. (FWVRC Box 9.3.2)

In 1916, the Glasgow Corporation sent James Stewart and Alexander Walker to report on the Repatriation Fund houses at Amersfoort and to visit Gouda. Stewart was a member of Glasgow Town Council; Walker ran the Glasgow Belgian Relief Committee, and was a City Assessor; both men were Repatriation Committee members. They arrived at Flushing on Friday 4 February and left on Monday evening. First they visited The Hague and then Amersfoort where the Friends had erected 20 single-storey wooden cottages, and were completing a large one to be used as a school. Close to these the Repatriation Fund had erected ten huts and two-storey ones were being completed. They decided that the Friends' house should be built in future and suggested they ask them to look after their property to avoid overlap. Gouda developed in two parts, one with wooden cottages built by the SOF and with other wooden buildings serving as classroom, workshop, hospital, library, church and kitchen. But there were 1,700 other refugees including about 700 children housed in old Victorian 'tomato-houses'. Three were set up as dormitories, two for recreation and another as a dining room. The conditions were horrifyingly unsatisfactory, with internal cardboard divisions providing families with their only privacy. Stewart and Walker heard an unverified rumour that the Friends would discontinue their work at Gouda and remove their cottages unless something was done. The site had been let to the Government under terms that did not allow it to terminate the over-high rental. Furthermore, the Chairman of the company that owned the greenhouses, Mr de Schepper, was also the Chairman of the Commission of Supervision of the vluchtoord. Perhaps he agreed with Amsterdam that destitute refugees were 'Belgian Vermin'. The remarkable thing about this camp therefore appears to be the profit motive. Questions were asked in the Dutch parliament. Phillip Burtt's 6 July 1915 report to Ruth Fry from Rotterdam, indicates de Schepper's priorities were more social than humanitarian. The Friends had arranged to start on Wednesday, but 'everybody including our own ladies went to the circus' at de Schepper's invitation. However:

> He is a splendid man and has given a fine tone to the whole camp. The ladies appealed for his help in regard to subsistence and equipment and as he realised how much we are doing and giving up for the work here he is arranging to equip one of SOF's houses at Gouda with all we want and the ladies are to obtain their supplies of food from the general camp store at no cost to us ... De Schepper presented a clock to every one of SOF's tenants as each house is complete. Mrs de Schepper is supervising the Rockefeller needle class. (FWVRC Box 9.3.3)

Nonetheless, there were clearly some difficulties between the Commissioner and the Friends. In February 1916 they closed their workrooms and in August decided it was useless to reopen unless the authorities really welcomed them. On 6 October 1916 Eleanor Acland asked Ruth Fry about Gouda. Père Hardy, a Repatriation and WRC Committee member said he had heard it was to be evacuated but Eleanor thought this was unlikely because of the 'famous contract'. Problems continued and on 1 February 1917 the SOF wrote to de Schepper telling him their houses were being moved. They thought the Belgian Relief Fund or the Dutch government should bear the cost, as it was on their recommendation that the houses were placed at Gouda. Gouda closed in 1919.

Stewart and Walker's visit revealed three complications; firstly, the uncertain definition of refugee and the likelihood of 'sponging'. Some Belgian wives and children were voluntarily leaving Belgium for Amersfoort to be near their 'military internee' husbands, termed such rather than PoWs because of Dutch neutrality. Were these families genuine refugees? It was decided they were. Secondly, refugees knew the Friends were British but thought the Belgian Repatriation Fund was an institution of the Belgian Government. This related to the third problem concerning the release of Fund money to aid civilians and resulted in co-operation between the WRC, the British National Committee for Relief in Belgium (NCRB), the SOF, and the Repatriation Fund.

In March 1916, the Belgian Minister asked the Repatriation Fund to build more wooden huts at Gouda and Eleanor Acland (PRO. MH.6) wrote asking for the 'residue of that amount which we understand has been transferred to Havre to be allocated by the Belgian Government. We want £50,000 for proper housing of Belgian refugees in Holland.'

Between 1 January and 30 June 1916, the Repatriation Fund raised donations of £5,098 9s. 10d. but this amount was insignificant compared with resources available to the Belgian Relief Fund which worked in seven camps in Holland. As the response was to allocate money for soldiers' families only, she requested a further £25,000 for refugees, pointing out that this would meet the wishes of those in the British Empire who had subscribed to the original Fund. The Minister suggested that the Repatriation Fund should make another appeal. At that time the only Belgian Relief Fund records showed £100,000 being contributed for people in Belgium *via* the CRB on 24 October 1914. Since there were no published accounts Eleanor Acland pointed out that people would wonder what had happened to the money and ask why give more? She said the remaining balance of between £600,000 and £400,000 should have provided ample relief; but only the Belgian Government could explain where this money was.

Although the figures are not clear, Eleanor's further actions shed light on the issue. She enlisted the aid of Mr Goode, the Honorary Secretary of the NCRB and through him, Mr Hoover of the CRB. She wrote on 11 May 1916:

> M. Buyse has received 450,000 francs for soldiers' families, but the problem of housing and other refugees was untouched. Mr Hymans thought that money was a 'sacrifice' the Belgian Government were very willing to make. I said very little as I felt that you and Mr Hoover could take the matter up better. Personally, I do not see that the Belgian Government make much sacrifice in disbursing sums which are only a small part of a Fund subscribed by British people for immediate relief of Belgians ... You have a very strong case for pressing for a real account of the disposition of that whole Fund, if Mr Hoover cares to take the matter up. (PRO MH8.6)

Eleanor Acland also wrote to M. Berryer, the Minister of the Interior, about the problem of the *pauvres honteux*. The *Committee des Hommes pour les Sinistrés Belges* at The Hague had appealed to her Committee to provide dwellings for people whose houses in Belgium had been destroyed. She reported to her Committee that Berryer had promised on behalf of the Belgian Government to provide the first 20 houses. Berryer's reply indicates a reneging of this promise and continuing reluctance to release either information or funds for the work in Holland. He said the Belgian Relief Fund was not only for Belgian refugees in foreign countries but for the 7,000,000 in Belgium. Although he supplied a list of organizations the fund had contributed to, he gave no indication of amounts donated, or proper accounts. This shows a comparative lack of anxiety on the part of Belgian authorities for civilians outside Belgium, unless wives and families of soldiers, and even then concern was minimal. It also shows the need for public accountability by the recipients of Fund money.

Nevertheless, as a result of Stewart and Walker's visit the Repatriation Fund decided to work at Gouda. The Liberal Women's Suffrage Union contributed to the Fund, sending out parcels of clothing and paying for the building of a hut at Elisabethdorp for refugee families and families of interned Belgian soldiers. Elisabethdorp was only one of several camps where the Repatriation Committee built houses. On 8 June 1917, Eleanor Acland, who lived in Kendal, Cumberland, and was coping with her child's illness, wrote to Ruth Fry trying to arrange a meeting at her sister's home near where Ruth lived. She asked for information about the interned soldiers in Holland and admitted that her committee were not 'in the thick of it as your people have been. I feel as if your people know so much more about the work than I do'. Indicating the extent of this between-Committees co-operation, she added (FWVRC Box 9.3.5): 'Vulliamy says your work is practically self-supporting. If so, an appeal seems unnecessary.' In 1917, the *Liberal Women's Review* described the transformation at Elisabethdorp:

> Once there was nothing where Elisabethdorp now stands save sand-dunes and low oak-scrub; within a year appeared rows upon rows of gaily painted houses, a communal bakery, communal workrooms, butchery, coal supply, etc. ... There is also a village school and church, and all these buildings are moveable and will be moved in happier days to Belgium.

On 17 September 1917 Eleanor Acland contacted the *Fonds du Roi Albert*, the Belgian Official Reconstruction Committee, confirming the gift to them of equipped and furnished huts including 64 at Gouda, 19 at Amersfoort and 18 at Gaasterland. The Repatriation Committee wanted to remain responsible for their upkeep and control while in Holland and she hoped to contribute towards the cost of moving them to Belgium, but could not guarantee to have sufficient funds when the time came.

People exchange

The third activity in which Friends were involved was the transfer of civilians to Britain and the exchange of prisoners. In February 1915, having acted as the representative of the LGB, Grace Vulliamy was appointed Liaison Officer between the Dutch and the British, transporting the wounded from Germany to England. The SOF first asked Vulliamy to help them when starting industries for Belgians in refugee camps. She organized specialized embroidery work as employment for women and was involved in the provision of clothing for 3,000 refugees. It is tempting to think that one of the two women shown standing in Plate 5 might be Grace Vulliamy but their identities are unknown.

In March 1915 she learned that the LGB had consented to send all relatives of workmen wishing to go to England to the Uranium Hotel at

Plate 5. Belgians sewing in an internment camp in Holland. (Photograph courtesy of The Religious Society of Friends in Britain)

Rotterdam where the LGB kept 600 to 700 working-class people, until they were able to leave. She thought this would make their task easier, as they could then concentrate on the better classes. In April the Friends asked her to start a Hostel at Flushing so she used the Strand Hotel as a shelter for 70 better-class people prior to embarkation. The work done by Miss Vulliamy and Mrs Enke there so impressed the wife of the Belgian Consul General for Holland, Madame Goffart, that she was anxious to continue it. When the numbers crossing to England made this amount of accommodation unnecessary, a hostel called the *Home Belge* was maintained where educated Belgian girls could be taken for a short time, because Flushing was not considered a suitable place for homeless girls. Mr and Mrs Armstrong, British residents, helped supervise the Home, but a Quaker was put in charge when they left.

The 'workmen' were the 'Invisible Army' of coal and iron, railway and other skilled workers the Belgian and English governments were anxious to get out of Holland and Belgium. Their removal was always conducted furtively because of the discrepancy between stated and real aims in order to safeguard Holland's neutrality and so that it could continue. It was, as Cahalan says, recruitment dressed in the garb of relief and it is presumably this to which Grace Vulliamy was referring when she wrote to Agnes Conway saying she did not want her name known because of the 'secret' work she undertook for the British Government, which she would write about at the end of the War, but which she failed to do. However, even more secret was the process of getting people out of occupied Belgium. In order to appear to be in control the Dutch prevented a shipload of refugees from leaving on 6 December 1914, but allowed them to sail the next day. On 15 March 113 specially chosen workmen were on the boat from Flushing to Folkestone which became responsible for accommodating the Invisible Army for different lengths of time although delays led to men slipping away. Alexandra Palace was reopened to receive them. Miss Mercer (IWM. Belgium.2.4/4) said Lord Lytton was the only one who seemed to realize that 'you couldn't keep these men hanging about even two or three weeks'. By March 1916 over 12,000 men and 17,000 women were transported on specially chartered boats.

When the LGB withdrew its official involvement in the transfers, Friends' participation was more necessary. In October the Foreign Office asked them to send representatives every month to the German frontier to meet British civilians being repatriated from internment in German camps such as Ruhleben. Grace Vulliamy organized their reception at the Belgian-German frontier on their journey to Flushing, housing them and transporting them to England, sometimes escorting them herself. Records show this work began prior to October, for that month the Aliens Committee asked for three Belgian children aged 4, 6 and 8 to be brought to England, suggesting that Grace Vulliamy might look after them on the boat. However the 6th and 7th of the month had to be avoided, as she took part in regular monthly exchanges on those dates. There were also additional emergency exchanges. These involved train journeys of eight to ten hours, two or three times a week.

The dates are, however, inconsistent, for Ruth Fry records that the first train was met at Boxtel on 6 November 1915. She describes (1926: 116) 'A motley crew – gentlemen, jockeys, negroes and naturalized Britishers', and the strong camaraderie between them. Their women, children and ill and maimed people were also on the train, incapacity being a qualification for release. Sometimes they were too ill to continue their journey and there were 'so many insane that a mental nurse had to be added to our staff to care for them on the journey'. It was, she said, 'nerve-racking'. On 6 February 1916, a party of 67 British civilians left Germany, 17 being released prisoners from Ruhleben and the rest women and children 'expulsed' by the German authorities. On this occasion a large proportion of the women were described as being of an undesirable character and expressed their regret at having to return to England (FWVRC Box 9.4.5). It was also reported that all returning civilians complained of their treatment at Ruhleben partly because they were forced to make munitions. This confirmed Emily Hobhouse's report.

On arrival at the Dutch frontier, food was provided by local people and served by Friends' workers Mary Rees and Mrs Rozelaar who listed names and addresses during the journey to Flushing to help the Consul at the port and expedite the sailing. Other workers were John Barry and Dorothy Whiting. The arrival of trains was unpredictable and on one occasion Miss Livingstone met the train at 3 a.m. and still managed to give hot drinks to everybody who wanted them. On 6 November 1915, the workers were notified that the train was to be four hours late, because it was to be held up at the frontier for examination. It arrived at 11.45 p.m. and although the 'Boxtel ladies, and SOF workers from Uden and the Dutch Commandant and soldiers had good things for us' the refugees had nothing since leaving Ruhleben at 7 a.m. and needed water. They were weak and sick and when examined by the doctor, one was not allowed to travel further. The sea passage was often rough, making caring for the people particularly arduous. At Tilbury the Red Cross took charge of the invalids and the rest were taken by the Central Charities Committee, who arranged accommodation for the homeless. The Quakers gave further help to those who had not lived in England for years.

In January 1917 Grace Vulliamy told Ruth Fry that civilian prisoners from Ruhleben had been coming through almost continuously but at uncertain times. When there was no boat immediately sailing for England they needed accommodation for unknown periods and some kind of entertainment, but also strict disciplinary measures to prevent drunkenness. Some of her work was under the auspices of the Red Cross who, in 1917, owed her quite a lot of money. A total of 7,800 wounded German PoWs were repatriated in this way, and 4,700 British soldiers. Although she wrote that the first batch arrived on 29 December 1917, in fact one party of 57 arrived at the Hook of Holland on 7 October 1916, where, according to *The Times*, they were welcomed by various dignitaries and 'Miss Vulliamy of the Society of Friends'. *The Times* named her again on 21 December 1917, as one who *since the beginning of the war* had 'done excellent work in connection with the transfer of the sick and wounded' (my italics). Grace Vulliamy wrote to Eleanor Acland on 21 December 1915 asking whether the Repatriation Committee could do anything to help.

Among those helping Grace was FLWS member, Howard Rowntree. In September 1916, the Home Committee decided Rowntree should go to France, despite the fact he said his present work was his right work. This was an allusion to 'Inward Light', envisaged as 'that of God' which spoke to each person individually. Rowntree's absence would be a serious loss to Miss Vulliamy and the Dutch Sub-committee because he had won the confidence of the Dutch authorities and his knowledge of the work was significant. Nonetheless, he was sent to France, but returned to Holland several months later. Grace Vulliamy was thinking of leaving to take up more urgent work in England, but because of the problem of handing over, the complications caused by constant change of workers, the difficulties of travelling and the civilian prisoners, she was uncertain. Miss Vulliamy intended to be in Holland for three weeks but stayed for over four years.

It has proved impossible to ascertain whether Grace Vulliamy was a member of the Society of Friends or of a suffrage society, although her family had links with both. On the outbreak of war she joined WEC, organising the meeting of refugee trains at London stations and Alexandra Palace and arranging refugees' accommodation. When WEC moved to Bedford College in October, she was appointed Organising Secretary and when it started co-operating with the LGB she went to Flushing on the Government Commission working with Mr Reyntiens and Dr Farrer transporting 1,200 refugees to the UK. The Government Commission closed in November 1916, but the work continued through the auspices of the British Consul-General in Rotterdam and in that year 2,224 refugees were brought over. Grace Vulliamy resigned from WEC in March 1915 to work under the LGB but worked with the FWVRC simultaneously. Her assistance in the transfer of military personnel, which was publicly acknowledged in *The Times*, is a grey area, since it is unlikely the SOF would have been happy with such close involvement with the military, but they can hardly not have known about it. Nonetheless, it extended women's role out of the domestic and nursing, into a completely new military area.

Grace Vulliamy's work of caring was complex, and is an example of how such work enables women to think of themselves in a new way, acquiring new public identities and gaining agency, as van Drenthe hypothesizes. Vulliamy's identities include relief worker with WEC and Quakers, civil servant with the LGB, and undercover agent. She was described by Francesca Wilson (1944: 6) as 'an attractive woman always in a whirl of activity and excitement' who 'brought stimulus into the lives of the interned officers who were often let out on parole'. She had an interesting time welcoming prisoners who escaped from Germany, or were returned on an exchange basis and 'brought flirtation to a height of perfection rare with the English ... an art'. Such flirtation was a way of gaining acceptance in the man's world. In June 1917, her work was officially recognized. The Prince Consort of Holland, President of the Dutch Red Cross Society, presented her with the Dutch Red Cross Order for her services with the exchanged prisoners of war passing through Holland. In September 1917 she finally left the Friends to work under the British War Office arranging for British PoWs who were to be transferred from Germany and interned in Holland. She then acted as British Red Cross and YWCA representative in Holland. At the request of Major General Sir John Hanbury Williams she organized the first temporary Hospital for sick or wounded PoWs. She was Sir John's representative in meeting all PoWs at the frontier, making arrangements often for over 300 and telegraphing to England to warn of their arrival. Major-General Onnen, Dutch Military Officer in charge of PoWs interned in Holland, arranged her attachment to the Dutch Medical Service as liaison officer until the Armistice. Grace Vulliamy crossed the North Sea over 40 times, ten of the ships being later torpedoed, mined or captured. She remained in Holland to assist repatriation.

Abbenhuis (2006: 35) says the balance of conflicting great power interests in the Netherlands was chiefly responsible for keeping Holland out of the war. The Netherlands' humanitarian work was important to both Germany and Britain; therefore Quaker and suffragist relief workers and particularly Grace Vulliamy were instrumental in helping to maintain this balance, reaffirming and renegotiating Dutch identity as a neutral, humanitarian nation.

CHAPTER 7

Relief Workers Become Refugees: Serbia and the Balkans

Working in Serbia

Serbia's war, which began and ended at different times from that in Western Europe, can be summarized in three periods. The first was from July 1914 when relief work was possible; the second was from October 1915, when Serbia was invaded by the Austrians and Bulgarians, causing an event that became known as the Great Retreat. The third phase began in the autumn of 1918 when Serbian troops drove back the invading enemy armies. The British people were told that they were indebted to Serbia because its resistance drew Austria's strength away from the Western Front. Molly Hamilton was among those who were undeceived by this, considering that Serbia was the 'arch-villain' of the piece (Hamilton 1944: 67, Gilbert 1995: xxi), a view also expressed by Ludwig Wittgenstein to Hilda Clark in Austria in 1919 (Pye 1956: 40). Nevertheless, Serbia was already exhausted by the Balkan Wars when on 28 July Austro-Hungary declared war and the next day began to bombard Belgrade.

In addition to the French SWH Unit, Dr Inglis planned a Serbian Unit which was adopted by Robert Seton-Watson, a respected historian and member of the House of Commons Yugoslav Committee. Significantly, two people in the Press offered help and by early October the remaining task was to get the necessary money (WL. GB/106/7/MGF/89/94). The Serbian Unit with Dr Eleanor Soltau in charge reached Kragujevatz on the Balkan front in January 1915.

The Hon. Mrs Evelina Haverfield, a militant suffragette who had been imprisoned under the 'Cat and Mouse' Act, was a Unit member. She helped launch the Women's Emergency Corps and then organized an ambulance corps in France which she left to go to Serbia where she established field hospitals, dressing stations, fever hospitals and clinics. By the end of the war Dr Inglis had established 14 fully equipped surgical field hospitals serving with most Allied armies except the British, which underscores British misogyny. They were supported by suffragists more than any other form of relief, raising nearly £500,000 in voluntary contributions. It is ironic that, by attempting to force women to 'go home and keep quiet' British militaristic patriarchy paradoxically positioned them to undertake relief on an international scale that was not limited either by imperialism, wartime alliances, race or time. This applied to the SWH, but also to those women who specifically went abroad to help refugees, such as the Quakers in the Netherlands and Russia and later in countries such as Germany.

At the same time that Dr Inglis was forming her Hospitals, Madame Mabel Grujić, the American wife of the Serbian Secretary of State for Foreign Affairs, came to England to appeal for medical personnel and urgently needed supplies. She had lived in London for seven years, leaving for Belgrade in January when her husband took up his appointment. Mme Grujić returned to Nish, the second largest town in Serbia, on 13 August taking eight surgeons and nurses including a Red Cross medical orderly, Flora Sandes, and an English theatre nurse resident in America, Emily Simmonds. When Simmonds and Sandes returned to England on the expiry of their three-month contracts they campaigned for Serbian relief. Lord Northcliffe, who was on the WRC, printed their appeal in his *Daily Mail*, raising £2,000 in three weeks. On 30 January 1915 the *Evening Standard* printed the Serbian Government's request for more women physicians to be sent out at its expense. The British War Office remained intractable.

Mme Grujić's press reports led to the formation of the British Serbian Relief Fund (SRF) in September. It started in the Serbian Embassy with an improvised and honorary staff and became the officially recognized British Relief Fund for Serbia which meant other British Funds working through it. SWH nurses and doctors worked for the SRF; both organizations were started by women and the units were staffed and administered mostly by women. Reports about the SRF were printed in *The Englishwoman* and SRF printing was undertaken by the Women's Printing Society. The SWH partly funded it, and suffragists such as Lady Cowdray and the journalist

H.N. Brailsford were Executive Committee members as was the Friend Percy Alden. Lady Grogan, whose husband served as a military attaché in the Balkans, selected SRF personnel. It was formed primarily for the troops as long as they were defending the country but the rapidly changing situation meant that both SWH and SRF helped civilian refugees, children and prisoners-of-war. During the first year of the war the SRF had five complete units in Serbia and in August 1915 made appeals for its Orphanage in Nish. It became deeply committed to caring for civilian refugees and the education of Serbs in Britain, some of whom Margery Fry was responsible for selecting. Seton-Watson became Honorary Secretary (FWVRC Boxes 9.5.1 and 9.5.2) and Sir Edward Boyle, Honorary Treasurer; both spent some time in Serbia. SRF members included two members of the House of Commons Balkans Committee: St Loe Strachey, editor of *The Spectator*, and G.M. Trevelyan. Trevelyan, a historian, believed that History was an essential element in the public culture of any civilized nation and was sympathetic to the suffragists' cause. Late in 1914 he visited Serbia, and published an article in *Jus Suffragii* (1.4.1915) entitled 'Serbian Women in Wartime'. He explained that although the Serbs had been ruled by Turks for several hundred years, there were no harems and now 'the educated women of the small middle class are learning to work together in the manner of modern women's movements in Western Europe'. The 'Serbian Sisterhood' had organized several hospitals 'doing fine work among refugees from North West Serbia who fled from the Austrian advance last November'. SRF contributed to other Funds and organizations working in Serbia; one was the Archbishop of Belgrade's refugee fund which in turn helped the Sisterhood.

Friends' work in the area preceded the Great War. In 1903 Noel Buxton and his brother Charles Roden Buxton had established the Macedonian Relief Fund and been instrumental in feeding 6,000 people who became refugees due to the Greek uprisings against the Turks at places such as Skoplje (Uskub). In 1914 the brothers were in the Balkans on a mission to secure Bulgarian neutrality when an unsuccessful assassination attempt by a Turk resulted in Charles being shot through the lung; he was not fatally injured.

The Friends helped non-combatants during the Balkan Wars and raised about £12,000 for Ann Burgess' Mission for relief of thousands of Moslem refugees in Constantinople. When it was again reformed in 1914, the FWVRC planned to work in Serbia, but events made it impossible, so they loaned workers to the SRF. In spring 1915, the SRF borrowed Theodore Rigg and Robert Tatlock and financed seven named workers, and an unnamed volunteer already working in France, for work in Serbia. Co-operation between the two societies was cemented when, in November 1915, Ruth Fry and William Albright of the FWVRC joined the SRF Executive. Ruth Fry's written list of members indicates Committee concern for gender equality, showing 17 men and 17 women, excluding the Chairman, Vice-Chairman, Honorary Secretary and Honorary Treasurer, who were all men. The borrowing arrangement continued after the Armistice when the SRF asked Ruth Fry whether the FWVRC would allow workers to be under Dr Clemow, the SRF Administrator in Serbia, and if so, how such an arrangement would operate (FWVRC Box 9.5.3). Clarification would prevent later problems.

The first SRF Unit was a surgical hospital of 56 people established at Skoplje on 17 November 1914 under Lady Leila Paget, the wife of the British Minister in Belgrade during the Balkan Wars when she had also undertaken relief. In February 1915, the second SRF unit of 47 persons under Cornelia, Lady Wimborne, also went to Skoplje. This Unit joined with the Red Cross to form a 'typhus colony' during the outbreak as did the Wounded Allies Relief Committee's (WARC) Unit, which was sponsored by the SRF and also formed in February 1915. The WARC Unit sent a fully equipped fever hospital of 200 beds to Montenegro with four doctors some of whom were women, and about 20 nurses. In April Lady Paget and Flora Sandes were among the 16 victims of typhus, returning home temporarily to convalesce. On her return to Serbia, Sandes was cut off from her hospital and joined a Serbian Army Ambulance Unit, becoming a combatant soldier and taking part in the Great Retreat. Her military identity was not approved of by the SRF whose Executive in July 1917 passed the motion moved by Lady Grogan and seconded by Ruth Fry that 'no member of the SRF Staff should assume rank in any foreign army without first obtaining the consent of the Executive Committee'. In contrast, Dr Constance Slater, on the medical staff of the WARC Hospital at Kragujevatz, reported in *The Times* (29.10.1915) that their chief physician, Dr Aspland, also female, had been awarded the honorary title of Major in the Serbian Army. That the SRF exercised some control over the WARC is shown by the fact that in January 1916, the Executive approved the appointment of Dr Lilias Hamilton as doctor to refugee camps in Corsica. It is clear therefore that there was considerable co-operation between suffragists, the SWH, the FWVRC and the SRF but Quaker pacifism was less dominant in WARC.

Many hospitals had arrived in Serbia by this time and, as there had been no fighting since December, the surgical units found themselves with little to do. Mrs St Clair Stobart, who commanded the Third Serbian Relief Fund unit which was entirely staffed by women, landed in Serbia in April 1915, and at once began to utilize her medical personnel for the far greater needs of the civil population. She put up a wayside dispensary by the hospital camp, where 12,000 people were treated in a few weeks, and established six others in country districts during the summer.

For ten months Austria left Serbia alone, but nonetheless, on 13 August 1915 Robert Tatlock reported that distress was greater than in France, since the Government even distributed food. Some volunteers from Sermaize, mostly women nurses, went out. Tatlock, Rigg and Robert Fitzpatrick wanted to investigate agricultural needs in North-West Serbia where there were large devastated areas. Although the Serbian Government was suspicious of offers of help because many foreign societies in Serbia were reputed to do little, the men thought Quakers might be accepted because of their work in France. Lady Grogan advised them that there was greater need in Montenegro but Lady Paget in Serbia contradicted this, so William Albright discussed the best course of action with Bertram Christian, Chairman of the SRF, and they agreed that Friends should go to Monastir, the former name of the present-day city of Bitola, Macedonia.

During the summer, which they were warned was the lull before the storm, the SWH London Committee equipped two more units, one for Mladenovac, the other for Lazarevac (Krippner 1980: 91). Over 600 British women doctors, nurses, VADs and orderlies were then in Serbia, some under canvas. In addition, there were numerous independent medical women and relief workers who were attached to Serbian hospitals and relief organizations, such as Mrs Hardy, and Mme Christitch's unit at Valjevo. Although in Lady Paget's Unit most of the surgeons were men (Krippner 1980: 103), at one time 50 British women doctors were working in the country; of these, 14 were in Mrs Stobart's SRF unit. The Press was soon to refer to them as 'noble ladies', never as 'British refugees' as they had named other British women.

The second phase of the war in Serbia began when the Austrians attacked from the north and north-west, re-taking Belgrade on 8 October 1915. On 23 September King Ferdinand of Bulgaria ordered the mobilization of his army on the Central Powers' side outnumbering the Serbian Army by over two to one. French and British divisions were sent from Gallipoli to help but fell back on Salonika, where many were subsequently interned. On 30 September, rather than surrender, the Serbian Army began its Great Retreat to the Adriatic coast across the mountains of Montenegro and Albania in the depths of winter. Being a victim is less than heroic, despite the fact that retreating armies are sometimes depicted as heroes; in this the British and the Serbs are alike. Nonetheless, retreating civilians convey implications of carelessness, lack of foresight or preparation and therefore of unworthiness. Hundreds of thousands of people fled south to Salonika but most of the peasantry, including women carrying babies in cradles, thousands of boys and some relief workers retreated with the Army, huge numbers dying in the attempt. This bedraggled, starving multitude struggled across the narrow mountainous tracks to Durazzo and Valona from October 1915 until early 1916. The Serbs were exploited by their traditional Albanian enemies, exacerbating the already poor relations between them. In the Albanian town of Elbasan (Burgess 1963: 101), the inhabitants 'turned indifferent faces towards all pleas for help' although they were willing to exchange a crust of bread for the refugees' overcoats or boots.

By October, therefore, relief in Serbia had become impossible due to the fresh invasion and Friends decided to assist the SRF Hospital for the time being and allocated funds. On 1 October Sir Ralph Paget visited Colonel Ghentchitch at Kragujevatz to urge him to ensure the safety of the foreign units. Sir Ralph had told the medical staff a rapid retreat might be needed, but they were unhappy about abandoning their patients and stores, saying they had not been sent out to retreat on the first approach of danger. On 12 October Bulgaria invaded Serbia from the east and on 17 October Lady Paget approached the French and British Army commanders in Salonika to ascertain whether they should evacuate from Skoplje and if so, whether they would receive help. The answer was evasive. Skoplje fell to the Bulgarians on 22 October. When Sir Ralph got to Skoplje his message to Lady Paget had not arrived and she was still there. She and all her staff decided to remain with the hospital and allow themselves to be taken prisoners by the Bulgarians in order to continue to care for the Serbian wounded of their own hospital and of the other hospitals abandoned by their staffs. She was allowed by the Bulgarians to distribute the hospital stores of food and clothing to all destitute refugees irrespective of nationality.

Heads of the Units had assembled at Vrnjatchka Banja and although most wanted to stay, for those who wanted to leave 30 or 40 carts were needed. The military commandant at Kralievo said he could spare none. On 2 November they got ready. Bread was unobtainable except by military order and other food was scarce. The railway station was blocked and the roads terrible, cars got bogged down in mud. Even if they managed to get out of Serbia, WARC staff reported there was no food or transport and no ships calling at Giovanni de Medua. Among the refugees were SRF nurses and doctors who left Kragujevatz on 25 October. One was Dot Newhall, a sanitary inspector with Mrs Stobart's Unit who had been on the Mons retreat. Their attempt to escape through Albania was unsuccessful and on 15 November about 120 British and French personnel left Mitrovitza for Ferizovitch in Serbia by train with Colonel Mihailovitch. The Colonel's peremptory military order to go to Ipek and out through Montenegro was not understood at the time but eight days later the Serbian Army was destroyed in the Battle of Ferizovitch. The SWH personnel, suffering from freezing cold and hunger, because they needed ten days' supplies but had only been given enough for two, now retreated across the snow-covered Albanian mountains.

British women had now became prisoners of war and about 100 relief workers, 50 or 60 of whom were women, escaped by way of the mountains, despite physical injury, lack of food, inadequate clothing and the winter conditions. The route from Ipek was a rising mountain path, barely two feet wide, a high rock wall one side and a precipice on the other, covered with snow most of the year. After eight to ten hours' marching the path emerged from the gorge and went up in zigzags reaching the summit over 5,000 feet above sea level. Sir Ralph Paget reached Velika 14 hours after leaving Ipek, going on to Andreieviza and then Podgoritza. Landslips and bridges were washed away, hostile aeroplanes followed them and the Units struggled through a heavy snowstorm. Their retreat lasted six weeks and included stopping at the Patriarchate Monastery to spend a night in the stables. Dot Newhall scandalized the monks by hanging up her washing nearby.

Finally they reached Scutari where they were given empty houses as preferable to beds in the hotels. Food was a problem: the shops refused to take paper money. They tried to set up a soup kitchen for the soldiers and refugees to alleviate the misery, starvation and squalor. When the refugees reached the coast their sufferings did not end. The Ministry of the Interior failed to keep their promise that all refugees would be fed with Army food and many lay on the shore dying although there was food available. When Flora Sandes and her regiment reached Durazzo she found Emily Simmonds cutting through red tape to feed those without food, and escorting mostly women and children in allied ships across the Mediterranean. Some well-meaning people gave the survivors food their bodies could no longer process and many more died. At Gerdalitza Florence Maw arranged transport of thousands of stranded refugees. They were further mistreated by authorities entrusted with their care even as they were taken to Corsica, Corfu, Italy, North Africa and France according to whether they were troops or civilians.

Rigg and Tatlock who had retreated with the Army to Scutari and Durazzo were assigned to help refugees and were assisted by Mr Kamenarovitch, a member of the Yugoslav Committee. Tatlock called his experience of the Retreat his 'Hours of Darkness in Albania', and exposed the discrepancy between newspaper reports of the invasion of Serbia and the actuality of refugees' position. It was estimated that 100,000 soldiers perished on the retreat although whether this figure included prisoners is unclear. However, Marrus estimates 500,000 civilians took part, 200,000 of whom, including a large proportion of young Serbian boys, died. This is an enormous increase over estimates made at the time of 50,000 civilians, this figure including the boys. Serbia practically became a nation of refugees – one-third of the population of barely 3,000,000 were uprooted; typhus killed over 150,000, including a quarter of the Army; 10 per cent of the population were sent to Hungary or Bulgarian camps. In 1915, troops of the Central Empires interned 150,000 civilians. As a result of this and the death of so many of its men, Serbia became a nation of women, children and the old. Marrus (1985: 48) states there had never been such a scale of refugee movements. In co-operation with the Friends, the SRF despatched agents to the Albanian coast where they aided both military and civilians; for two months the SRF was the only private relief organization and on its own resources organized relief for 10,000 people.

On 29 October *The Times* reported that Lady Ralph Paget's Unit at Skoplje had arrived safely at Monastir. The five London Units were reported as safe but there was continued anxiety for members of the SRF Units under Dr Clemow. From November the Friends sent out flour, milk, clothing and blankets for the refugees in Montenegro; and through the SRF a Mme Vesnitch arranged a special press appeal for funds for women and children refugees. Did the FWVRC recognize how dire the military situation was? On 4 November 1915 Ruth Fry told George Innes in France (FWVRC Box 1.3.2) he would see from the Minutes that the Committee was generally in favour of women going to Serbia but she wanted to wait to hear from Theodore Rigg's party. She added: 'Dr Clark's friend, Miss Courtney is anxious to go.' Courtney was one of a group that went first to Salonika in December 1915, just after Serbian resistance against the enemy advances had crumbled, and then to Corsica.

On 17 November, as a result of the Austrian offensive, Mr Cathcart Wason asked for reassurance in the House of Commons concerning the 'safety and honour' of the British women; this is partly a euphemism for possible sexual abuse. Lord Robert Cecil replied that he had only been able to ascertain that the WARC and British Farmers' Units (also sponsored by SRF) might be in Bulgarian hands, but there was no reason to believe that the ladies of the SWH at Valjevo or the staff of the WARC would be badly treated. Gallantry towards 'ladies' was still presumed. On 3 December *The Times* reported that Dr Lilias Hamilton and four nursing staff of WARC who had started for Monastir two weeks earlier, had arrived at Salonika; also that 37 members of the SWH had reached Podgoritza in Montenegro. Dr Helena Hall described how, on arrival there the Turks showed them 'wonderful kindness', providing accommodation in harems and giving presents on departure. On 22 December another report, indicating the reporters' stunned reaction at the ladies' stamina, stated that a party of British nurses, who had passed through Rome *en route* for London, must have walked 200 miles through Serbia, Albania and Montenegro. They had left Scutari more than a week previously but had to wait at Medua until a steamer arrived that could take them to Italy. At least bread was available at Medua, with bacon and tinned meat recovered from the sunken ships.

Sir Ralph had learned from Rome that the American sailing ship *Albania*, then at Durazzo, would call at Medua a few days later and, despite the risk of Austrian submarines, embark the foreign medical mission women and any men debarred from military service. However, when it failed to arrive they boarded an Italian cargo boat on 17 December and thence back to England. More SWH members, including Drs Chefney, Laird and McVea from the Kragujevatz, Meadanovatz and Lazarevatz Units arrived in Turin towards the end of December.

After the Retreat the SWH cared for thousands of refugees. Brayshaw (1921: 339) says the Friends also 'took important parts in rescuing refugees but their work here, as in other areas, was handed over to other bodies, in this case the SRF'. This fails to describe accurately the co-operative nature of the work, especially since at least 12 Friends lost their lives. As Hirst explains (1923: 500), Friends worked under SRF helping refugees on their arrival in Albania and at Salonika, and on their further journeying to Corsica and southern France.

Dr Inglis and some of her staff were captured when Kruševac fell to the Austrians on 9 November. They were allowed to continue their work although this meant 20 people dining, sleeping and washing in one room. However, Inglis refused to take charge of a hospital of women with VD, a decision she found difficult since she acknowledged it undermined the solidarity of women (Krippner 1980: 160). Undoubtedly thinking about the morality of prostitution, Krippner says it was 'neither a callous nor a purely moral standpoint'. Inglis wanted to focus on the Serbian wounded, saying the VD hospital had been opened not for the women's benefit, but to protect German soldiers from infection. There was, notwithstanding, the moral issue of using the funds for the purpose for which they had been collected which, when the War Charities Act came into effect in August 1916, became a legal requirement. Nonetheless, this incident shows how vulnerable the 'women caring for other women' ethic was when women were involved with military relief.

Their repatriation began on 4 February 1916, with the help of the International Red Cross and the American Embassy. Following their arrival at Southampton Elsie Inglis began forming a Russian Unit and undertook a publicity and fund-raising campaign. Lady Cowdray gave an 'At Home' for people to meet Dr Inglis and the Crown Prince of Serbia was present.

Serb sufferings were compared to those of the Belgians by Hannah Bellows, Hon. Secretary of the Friends League for Women's Suffrage (Lunn 1997: 51). She wrote on 6 March 1916 to Mr Christian, Chair of the SRF (FWVRC Box 9.5.6):

> In the winter of 1914 in England we thought the Belgian nation a pathetic and pitiable spectacle, but their sufferings are nothing to those of the Serbians, who have been driven this way and that and had no rest practically for four years.

Corsica

In January 1916, the Foreign Office proposed forming refugee colonies in Italy but the French Government offered hospitality 'on its own soil'. This meant Corsica, Algeria and the south of France. However, shipping arrangements were poor. Mr Patterson's Report to Lady Grogan said that while the French fed and cared for refugees on French vessels, this was not so on Italian ships; Italians regarded refugees as 'very distasteful' and tolerated them only if they passed through the country. Between January and April 1916, about 3,000 refugees passed through SRF hands at Brindisi. On board a French boat with M. Grujić, Mr Bosanquet and Miss Simmonds, Hannah Bellows sent an explicit description to Mr Christian in London. At Gallipoli on the Gulf of Táranto, the Italians made them 'tranship refugees to two boats in the port' but there was 'no bread on the new ships' so the British party arranged food. One ship was 'so crowded that some refugees couldn't lie down for the six days of the voyage'. To make matters worse, there was only one latrine but the Italian doctor did not realize how serious this was and hardly ever went near the refugees (FWVRC Box 9.5.6). Emily Simmonds saw to both food and illness; she discovered three suspected cholera cases who were taken ashore. On arrival at Messina the ship was put in quarantine but no food arrived. Then boats came out charging extortionate rates for necessities. Hannah Bellows demanded to see the English Consul and went ashore but could not find him. Neither did the Serbs help their own: Theodore Rigg wrote from Marseilles that the Serbian authorities were not treating their refugees well. Food distribution was haphazard and some days hardly any was given. However, the French made improvements once John Bellows arrived although what steps he took to achieve this are not explained.

As a result of the occupation, relief to Serbia was therefore mostly undertaken beyond its boundaries. Most civilian refugees were taken to Corsica and the Serbian Relief Committee of America took sick people there. Up to 14 January over 1,500 Serb refugees arrived in Corsica. In the third week of January 3,000 refugees brought over from Medua and Durazzo to Brindisi were mostly 'of the better class' and about a quarter were women and children. When the SRF asked for more workers in January 1916, Ka Cox, Margery Fry and Maurice Wilson (Francesca Wilson's brother) went out. Ka Cox is best known as being a friend of Rupert Brooke, but she was also a close friend of Leonard and Virginia Woolf and Molly Hamilton, and was instrumental in providing a venue for one of the talking centres, planning future peace.

When the SWH women arrived at Ajaccio they asked Henry Dundas, the British Consul, to help obtain necessary supplies. Instead, he wrote a malicious letter of complaint to the War Office. Dundas did not like efficient women and complained that the Administrator 'Miss Culbard, a suffragette ... is at the bottom of all the discontent'. The fact that she was labelled a 'suffragette' confirms the negative impact the militant movement had on some people. However, Sir Edward Boyle, Head of the British Mission, who provided practical help, wrote supporting the SWH work and a dismissive note about Dundas was penned by a War Office official on the back of one document. *Jus Suffragii* reported in January 1917 that the SWH Unit was responsible for all the medical organization of Corsica, in particular for the 2,000 Serbian refugees. The main hospital was at Ajaccio, with several outlying dispensaries. A French General at a recent inspection had complimented Dr Mary Phillips on the hospital organization.

However, Authority on too many occasions showed disregard for relief workers and refugee alike. For example, the *Préfet* at Ajaccio treated not only the refugees, but the accompanying SRF representatives with scant courtesy. Refugees were immediately taken to military barracks, convents, large houses, and the penitentiary. They needed, but did not get, change of clothing. Washing and sanitary arrangements were poor and local medical services unable to cope. According to Wilson (1944: 2), the French dumped them into huge barracks and fed them, but did little else. Refugees were also unhappy at how the French treated them afterwards. An attempt to celebrate the most important Serbian national festival, the Sava (FWVRC Box 9.5.2), 'was sternly repressed and ended in many tears'. There were problems of dormitory accommodation, lack of privacy, the medically unfit being put with the others and the 'herding together of middle-class with peasants'. Sir Edward Boyle wrote:

> Although from one point of view the better class people have the first claim upon us, from another stand-point it is the peasantry who feel most acutely the treatment accorded to them. Many have already escaped into Ajaccio from the penitentiary at Chiavari.

The SRF workers were dissatisfied with the accommodation the French had provided in Ajaccio for interned civilian men broken down in health, and found and furnished several flats for the families of Government servants, *sous-préfets*, police, and families of officers at the front and, most numerous of all, school teachers of which there were 70, making it possible to have a pupil-teacher ratio of 1:1. In January 1916 Kathleen Courtney was in Corsica (Alberti 1989: 59), and on 30 January the first batch of 1,700 refugees arrived at Bastia where she played a significant role as *Directrice* of a hospital. She wondered why there were so many boys and was told that the Serbian Government had ordered all boys over 14 to leave the country. It was said that 36,000 boys started on the retreat, but only 7,000 reached the coast. Amongst about 2,000 refugees there was only one complete family. The *Préfet* agreed to the SRF taking refugees from his public refuges and housing them; he would pay the Government allocation direct. The SRF hired the ground floor and two floors of bedrooms in the Schweizerhof, a pension hotel at Ajaccio, where they had about 90 refugees, including a staff of five Serbian servants. By the middle of January, thanks to Miss Bankhart and two SWH workers, Miss Green and Miss Begg, it was running smoothly. Miss Courtney (IWM. DD. Courtney. 32. 28.2.1916) tried to find houses for women and children, the Serbs selecting the families but she used her right of veto when they selected 'women expecting babies in a few weeks to go several miles off'.

The SRF shipped out clothing for the refugees but Margery Fry was infuriated that it was not sorted by cheap labour at home first. It included (Wilson 1944: 75) 'all the discarded wardrobes of England and America' and 'hundreds of thousands of exquisite baby garments – in a land where there was scarcely a child under four years old'. Damp cotton petticoats arrived to clothe the many ragged boys. The Executive suggested that a cargo of men's clothing sent out for civilian refugees could be used instead for the Serbian Army, whose condition was deplorable. Miss Bankart started an *ouvroir*.

By February Sir Ralph Paget was unwell, no longer able to control matters and returned home. Sir Edward Grey agreed to Sir Edward Boyle acting as Commissioner for Serbia. The Friends (FWVRC Box 9.5.3) therefore worked under him in Salonika and Corsica from the end of 1915 until 1919. His evaluation of them was that they were inspired by high seriousness, and had a measure of capacity greater than that shown by the average voluntary worker. Having a body of relief workers with a viewpoint their own had caused certain occasional difficulties for the administrator, but much was done that otherwise would have been impossible. This was qualified praise, but praise nonetheless.

The French authorities intended Corsica to receive between 4,000 and 5,000 refugees but early in 1916 there were over 9,000. Kathleen Courtney thought it a mistake to take them there because it lacked sufficient resources. She said the French Red Cross:

> is proving a broken reed and now find they know nothing and expect us to do everything. If the reed would break completely and disappear it would be comparatively simple. (WL. KDC/C1/1–4)

She thought the French nurses were careless of their patients. A little boy was brought into the hospital in a state of collapse but they were prepared to leave him for the night with only one of the orderlies to sleep beside him. She got a hot water bottle for him because his feet were so cold and sat with him.

Kathleen Courtney was a member of several British relief committees, and had been Honorary Secretary of the NUWSS from 1911 to 1915 resigning over the issue of the Congress at The Hague which she helped to organize. She was therefore a founder member of WILPF and also President of the British section, WIL. Her split from Fawcett was distressing and she became frustrated by committee work. Many of her colleagues considered relief a palliative for giver as well as receiver (Vellacott 1993: 38), turning their attention to the 'more positive goal of securing peace' (Hannam 1989: 163). Maude Royden said Courtney was taking a 'holiday' from the problems, including those of forming WIL, even if 'not actually running away' (Haslam 1999: 97). But few had ever experienced relief abroad, especially under such conditions. It required linguistic and administrative expertise, practical skills, diplomacy and patience. Courtney said (IWM. Courtney Docs. 32. 28.2.1916) difficulties often arose when even the simplest tasks were put into Serbian hands. Getting the hospital rubbish removed became 'a fearful toil and burden'. Serbs had a reputation for being dirty, which workers found to be undeserved, except in relation to the 'Cabinet'. But they had no sense of urgency. 'The Serbs are a difficult people in many ways. They are very anxious to open their mouths and be fed with a spoon.' It was 'difficult to devise forms of relief which will not develop their national characteristic of idleness'. Wilson (1944: 6) described this as 'refugee mentality'. A Serb put in charge of transporting refugees would only do so when bribed. A Mayor added the names of friends and political supporters to a list intended to be of those in need; consequently supplies of cloth went to the rich instead of to the poor. But the women of the village ousted the Mayor and installed their own honest candidate for the post. Nevertheless, women were unwilling to work unless it benefited their families; domestic service as practised in occidental countries was not understood and attempts to introduce it were sometimes disastrous. Men who were freeholders at home would not hire out their services. In fact, as Sir Edward Boyle wrote, 'In Corsica, no less than elsewhere, one has to face the criticism that relief work demoralizes' (IWM. Serbia 6/87). Yet despite this, a speech by one of the Serbian refugees when Kathleen Courtney left Serbia to return to England in July 1916, showed the high esteem in which she was held; she was also decorated by the Serbian Government.

Serbian relief committees, including various national Red Cross societies and American and French organizations worked in ignorance of what the others were doing, resulting in chaos. National rivalry between relief agencies inhibited co-operation, with the French concerned for their status, Americans convinced of their infallibility and the British idea of social work too rooted in Victorian *noblesse oblige*. When Margery Fry and Florence Barrow left Corsica after three weeks for the quarantine station on the island of Frioul, off Marseilles, Margery Fry had established 'a *very* shaky scheme of cooperation ... which is at least not the disgrace of open rivalry'. However, (Wilson 1944: 3) the 'French had a poor opinion of most Anglo-Saxons' and Mrs Carrington-Wilde, responsible for clothing in London, considered that 'the French don't want the British ... at all. We may send boots, nothing else.' Lady Grogan explained to Ruth Fry that the main part of the work would fall on women and the French probably would not allow anything agricultural. This meant fewer men would be needed. However, in early 1916 the SRF were short-staffed and, work being allocated by gender, they needed male workers to do accounts, store-keeping, and general work; also three women with experience of hotel or boarding-house management. Another woman was wanted for the *ouvroir* and, because the centres were scattered, five more for general social work. The proliferation of uncoordinated relief agencies did nothing to enhance the reputation of relief but Kathleen Courtney's comment is salutary (IWM. KC3. Letter 42): 'Relief can't do much. The need is for normal economic conditions to be restored.'

In November 1916 the British Red Cross insisted that all workers sent by the SRF to Corsica should sign the form of service with, and obedience to, them. The responses of the SRF or, more significantly the Society of Friends are not recorded. On 21 March 1917, an Information Bureau for Serbian relief was organized in an attempt to avoid reduplication and waste. By 1917 there were only 1,700 refugees left on Corsica, the others having been gradually dispersed to North Africa and southern France. Nevertheless, among them were some sick Serbs, including neurasthenics. In May 1917 the SRF Executive discussed a joint arrangement between themselves and the SWH in Corsica relating to their subsequent cooperation in sending 'nerve cases' there.

Relief workers were awarded medals by the Serbian military authorities and some lost their lives in Serbia, beginning in 1915 from typhoid when they were weakened by overwork. These included Sister Fraser and Margaret Ryle, aged 23, who were killed at Nish. Any cause gains increased publicity from the deaths of their martyrs. Lord French's sister, Mrs Harley, was killed on 8 March 1917 at Monastir having been found shot in the head by her daughter who was also in Serbia. Her death and work with SWH were well covered by the press. The Serbian Legation and London Units of the SWH arranged a Memorial service at St Margaret's, Westminster, and a memorial was unveiled to her at the Allies Cemetery at Salonika. *The Times* noted the suffrage connection. She was decorated by General Sarrail with the *Croix de Guerre*.

Dr Inglis's death achieved even more publicity. The SWH Russian Unit she formed in 1916 had served with the Russian Serbian Army and was evacuated from Archangel to Newcastle in November 1917. The day after arrival, 27 November, Inglis died. *The Times* reported on 28 November, this 'splendidly brave woman' was 'one of the keenest supporters of all forms of women's work and her interest in the advancement of women was untiring'. The Serbian Chief of Medical Staff referred to her as 'the guardian angel of Serbia'. The Serbian Minister went to Edinburgh to attend her funeral which was 'one of the most impressive ever seen in Britain for anyone other than a monarch' (Krippner 1980: 164). It was significant that women predominated, suffragists being well represented. This hints at why she was 'seen' at the time, but now known by few. The Queen sent a message of condolence to Dr Inglis's sister, Mrs Shaw McLaren. The 'Last Post' and 'Reveille' were played and pall-bearers were women and men. On 6 December a service of remembrance was held in St Margaret's, Westminster. Among the congregation was Lord Robert Cecil from the Foreign Office.

Seton-Watson wrote that Elsie Inglis's name would be recorded by History as a reminder that Florence Nightingale was not without successors. However, symbolizing her current obscurity, she and SWH, FWVRC and SRF women who died are commemorated near the Five Sisters' Window in York Minster but in small panels hidden behind closed carved shutters. As Krippner (1980: 9) writes: 'for some unaccountable reason the spectacular service ... of women doctors and surgeons ... remains little known and barely acknowledged'.

Corfu and North Africa

In contrast to Corsica, civilians were not intended to land in Corfu where the Serb government in exile were located and where the Serbian Army were disinfected and re-clothed. The SRF clothed, fed and housed both the Serbian Army and civilian refugees because troopships brought non-combatants who slipped aboard on embarkation. Among them were a husband and heavily-pregnant wife who gave birth on 9 May to the first Serb child to be born on Corfu, giving cause for ceremony and celebration. Like Belgian refugees in other countries whose numbers soon diminished, by April 1916 there were 'only hundreds, as the majority had returned to their homes at the request of the Austrian authorities' (IWM. Serbia 5/9. Patterson to Grogan).

Professor Robert Carr Bosanquet undertook responsibility for the distribution of food and underclothes on Corfu. He and his family had experience of philanthropic and religious social work. His father, Charles Bosanquet had been Honorary Secretary to the Charity Organization Society, and in 1902 Robert married Ellen Sophia Hodgkin, daughter of Quaker Thomas Hodgkin, and cousin of Margery and Ruth Fry. Bosanquet was Chair of archaeology at Liverpool when war was declared. Receiving no response to his offer of service to the War Office, he became attached to the FWVRC and was with the Serbs in Albania. Later, he was an agent of the SRF in Salonika until he returned home in poor health, having been awarded the Serb order of St Sava. Yet despite his social status the British Consul at Messina failed to respond to Bosanquet's request to give 'our people all the help in his power'. He got the consul at Brindisi to back the request, but from the summary in *The Friend* gathered that he did not do much (IWM. Serbia 5/1).

Eighty students who were to be taken to Marseilles or England were housed in a camp at Potamos cared for by Miss Simmonds who also cooked for and nursed 50 sick people. Because damp had ruined the store, in 1917 Mrs Askew distributed clothes 'from her own funds to a number of women of the artisan and employee class' who had 'difficulty in making both ends meet' (IWM. Serbia 5/78). She also took a villa to get women out of the town and for a while a hut in the garden was home to a consumptive girl, fresh air being a vital part of the treatment. The girl, who had been a telephonist, died one Friday night in June. Her funeral was attended by representatives from the Ministry of the Interior and the Ministry of Posts and Telegraphs.

Maurice Wilson was lent to the SRF by the Friends and sent to Bizerta, Tunisia, which was like an armed camp. He helped set up workshops for soldiers in the refugee barracks at Caserne Lambert but some were so badly injured or shell-shocked they were unable to work and needed particular care. Wilson asked Lady Grogan for his sister Francesca to help and Margaret McFie, an experienced worker, who could train Francesca, also went out. Margaret McFie had helped Sir Arthur Pearson to start his blind school in London in 1914 and he sent out Braille typewriters and equipment. McFie and Wilson first went to Corsica to wait for the necessary permits because Bizerta officially did not allow civilians. Disabled Serbs, survivors from the Albanian retreat, were technically discharged and therefore civilians, but subject to the diet and discipline of the Army. Nurses were male, as French women thought it improper to go into men's hospitals. Francesca Wilson wanted to establish a Home for these men and sent long reports to the London office which voted the money in January 1918 and promised more staff, having already sent Miss Hill and Miss Brown.

When evacuation of Corfu began in October 1918 civilians were the last to leave for Skoplje, the old, infirm and child refugees being left behind when the Serb Government recalled many of its officials. This may have been beneficial since there were no relief workers in Skoplje. Many of the boats were hospital ships. On 18 March 1919 an Austrian cargo boat arrived. Most people would have to sleep on mattresses or straw in the unlighted holds; the Serbian Delegues were so indignant they demanded the Serbs' luggage be taken off. However, as there was no chance of a better boat, Sir Edward Boyle encouraged the Serbs to accept because 'four days of discomfort would soon be forgotten in the joy of getting home' (IWM. Serbia 6/100).

Occupied Serbia

Although the main focus of the SRF in London was on evacuated Serbs, those in occupied Serbia were not forgotten. Mme Christitch, who had been born an Irishwoman, and was a writer on political and social questions, stayed in occupied Belgrade together with her daughter Mlle Annie, obtaining money from the SRF via a neutral to organize soup kitchens and give funds to destitute people. This had to be done surreptitiously, because the Austrians prohibited relief among people who were officially well cared for.

Nevertheless, food and clothing were urgently needed in occupied Serbia. Throughout the war years conditions were so bad that in April 1916 the SRF arranged for a deputation to see Robert Cecil to urge that the same principles which had been applied to the revictualling of Belgium and Northern France should be applied to Serbia. In May 1917, permission was granted by the French Government for 500 bales of clothing to be despatched from Marseilles to Geneva to be distributed to women and children by the agents of the Swiss Red Cross. At last in July the British Government felt it had been relieved of the pressure of Belgium and that something might be done for Serbia. Urging this, the SRF sent a letter to the Prime Minister, Lord Robert Cecil and other members of the Government. In September 1917, two SRF representatives went to see Cecil who asked for a letter he could use to pressure the Government which still had no plans to feed the civil population. In the meantime with the approval of the Foreign Office and French authorities a few hundred Serbian children, mostly boys, were brought to England for professional or technical training. In October a predominantly female committee set up the Society for Training Serbian Women in England. It aimed to educate some to enter the higher professions and return to Serbia in order 'to carry on the life and civilization of their country and, as many of them must necessarily remain unmarried it is essential that they should be trained to earn their own living' (IWM. Serbia 1/15). Nine girls were sent over from Mme Grujić's orphanage at Nish but two had to return because of home ties. In January 1918 the National Union of Trained Nurses' Quarterly Magazine reported that Miss Violetta Thurstan had been appointed Matron of the Scottish Women's Field Hospital on the Macedonian Front. It gave a brief extract from Thurston's letter of 20 February describing wolves howling outside the tents at night. In April she was awarded the 1914 Star and the Ribbon of the Order of St Sava from the Crown Prince of Serbia. Such medals confirmed the value the Serbs placed on the British women's work and the respect felt for them.

In February 1918 Mrs Carrington-Wilde proposed a scheme to liberate Serb children who were in prison camps in Austria and Hungary without their parents. The Foreign Office, the International Red Cross and the Pope were all asked to intercede. In July the Austrian authorities had 'practically consented' to their removal to neutral countries. By now the third phase of the Serbian war had begun with the Serbs successfully advancing, driving the Bulgars back into Bulgaria and the Austrians and Germans across the Danube. It became clear to workers in North Africa that, as a civilian group with undefined status that disturbed Army discipline, they could be of greater assistance in Serbia itself and consequently moved behind the advancing Serbian Army. Dot Newhall said that the advance was worse than the Retreat because so many cattle and prisoners died. It was her responsibility to be ahead of the others and clean up and prepare the ground and buildings before the Units arrived, some of them tented. The enemy had left everything in a terrible state with bits of human bodies in buildings that had been turned into sewage pits.

In July 1918, the SRF joined a scheme with the International and American Red Cross through the medium of the Swiss Federal Government and the American Legation in Berne for restricted relief in occupied Serbia. However, it was necessary for the British Ministry of Blockade to withdraw its veto on certain articles of food before such relief could be undertaken. This was unlikely to happen as long as hostilities continued.

In all this work one group of refugees were neglected. These were the 'Cheehas', 2,000 men too old and disabled from wounds to be in the front line. They were therefore not considered part of the Army, neither were they helped by societies for the wounded or civilians. Evelina Haverfield and Flora Sandes created a Comforts Fund for Serbian Soldiers and Prisoners which specifically appealed for the Cheehas. When mobile canteens were sent out to Macedonia, the SRF worker Anne McGlade, who spoke Serbian, went with the first Unit, with instructions that the Cheehas were to be helped. In late 1918 McGlade was still helping civilians, handing out 500 mugs of tea and soup each day to refugees, and after the Armistice opened an orphanage at Nish with her friend Sister Jean Rankin, maintaining it until overrun by the Germans in 1941.

The Armistice

The Armistice between the Allies and Bulgaria was declared on 30 September 1918, with Austro-Hungary on 3 November, and Germany on 11 November. Renewed suffering followed as thousands of people including civilian internees returned to shattered homes and decimated families. Miss A. Frances Parkinson from Tamworth had been in Nish when it was occupied by enemy armies. When released by the Armistice she travelled alone through Austria and Germany, including a fortnight in Berlin and subsequently gave talks about her experiences to continue to raise funds. There were 8,000 to 10,000 refugees expected to pass through Salonika from Bulgaria. Women and children were sent to one Serbian refugee camp, and men without luggage to another. One camp was full. The SRF supplied food for this vast number, some of whom had dysentery or other intestinal problems. In October 1918 an international scheme of control was planned, with all authority invested in a Council in Salonika. However, this meant that 'the affairs of the SRF have taken a suddenly unfortunate turn' because 'the Government plans taking over civil relief in Serbia' and therefore 'the SRF cannot continue its appeal to the British public for money' (FWVRC Box 9.5.1).

There were several reasons why this was 'unfortunate'. There was recognition of continuing need, sadness at an abrupt end to the work and relationships with Serbian people built up over the four years of war. Margaret McFie undertook a two months' tour of all English and American centres doing child welfare in Serbia, where her enthusiastic welcome from families reinstated in their homes made her realize that 'We meant *so much* to these people in Corsica.' Now back in sacked, burned houses, they were trying to rebuild and to educate children on:

> pathetic pre-war incomes which Serbia still metes out to her officials ... Even some of our worst characters would turn up and confess their provoking ways and say they were sorry. One woman said 'Yes, we behaved very badly and told lies to try to take advantage of you – and we used to be angry because you were very strict, but it was good for us and we liked you for it.' (FWVRC Box 9.5.2)

The Government's decision meant loss of independence of action but the main reason for concern was that Americans were now responsible for all relief; although generous, their plans were often inappropriately grand. As the war drew to a close on 30 October 1918, the SRF Vice-Chair reported that the *Commission Internationale de Ravitaillement* had prepared a scheme for the revictualling of Serbia which had been submitted to the French and American Governments. Until their assent was received the question of making use of the SRF organization was in abeyance. The SRF would be wholly dependent upon them for permits for all the materials they sent to Serbia. Ruth Fry was advised that (FWVRC Box 9.5.1) 'It might be wiser to stop our relief in Serbia at once ... What is happening is a natural evolution. We have played a very big and useful part when no one else was there to play it.'

After the war relief workers aided the return of refugees, established hospitals, orphanages and schools. Francesca Wilson, now an experienced 30-year-old, arrived at Nish on 25 February 1919 where the SRF was still running a hospital of 200 beds. She found many of the veterans from the first SRF units still working there. Those who had been on the Retreat were regarded as special beings, with raised status. Some of the women, like Anne McGlade, stayed in Serbia, their establishments surviving up to the 1940s. Cooperation between the societies meant that it was necessary to pay the staff similar wages and in June and July 1920, when the Montenegrin Red Cross asked the SRF to send a Unit, they needed to establish why two SWH nurses were being paid more than the SRF nurses. The reason being the length of service, it was decided this was satisfactory. As their war service drew to a close, SWH equipment was offered to other organizations. They offered orthopaedic equipment to SRF at a price of £4,000, but the SRF, who opened an orthopaedic hospital in May 1920, needed to haggle. The dropping exchange rate meant plans had to be curtailed. Nonetheless, the SWH endowed a chair for a medical faculty.

On 18 February 1920 Mrs Carrington-Wilde and Algernon Maudslay had an interview with Lord Weardale of SCF who had questioned them on Serbia. They had received £2,500 with promises of more. Further statistics were given to SCF and plans made for having 1,000 Serb children in England under canvas during the summer (FWVRC Box 9.5.2). Such close work with SCF enabled undertaking all aspects of child welfare but meant adhering to the contracts that accepting SCF grants entailed. During the three years' occupation the SRF had given unobtrusive relief to children, helping to maintain four orphanages and maintaining one completely at Nish near the SRF's HQ. In September 1920 this orphanage needed moving to a healthier situation because there had been epidemics of eye and throat trouble. It was built below the level of, and close to the cemetery, and entirely on one floor. Unsurprisingly, the water supply was unfit, so had to be brought in by ox kola.

Like many countries after the war, Serbia's boundaries were to change and its fate decided by the major powers of France, America and England. Modern Yugoslavia was created uniting Serbia with Slovenia, Croatia, Bosnia and Herzegovina. In February 1920 there was an International Conference of SCF at Geneva. A *Commission Serbe* was constituted, with Mme Vlajitch, delegate of the Mothers Association, Belgrade, and Miss Cristitch for the SRF. Indicating the complex network, Mrs Campbell represented Miss McFie's Child Welfare in Belgrade and also the American Serbian Relief Committee; Miss Bankart represented the Exeter Branch of SCF and her own Sanatorium at Koviljoca. However the SRF was concerned because their child welfare work was not mentioned in the SCF report and its unobtrusiveness over plans and actions meant it risked being sidelined.

That month there was a political upheaval in Serbia causing an entire change of Ministers in Belgrade. This involved making new contacts, an irritant because new Ministers wanted to know why Nish Hospital supported so many British Staff. Major Hardwick repeatedly explained that about half the staff there belonged to SRF administration and were not essential to the Nish Hospital itself. They therefore decided to move to Serbian Red Cross offices in the town.

Two years after the Armistice children were still homeless, and in the Hertzegovina-Montenegrin mountain villages conditions were worse than in Serbia itself. Evelina Haverfield opened a hospital for TB children and gave her life working there. Margaret McFie opened the first Yugoslav Blind School while her fellow Scot, Dr Katharine MacPhail continued relief work in and for Serbia, sometimes denigrated at home for working for foreigners. On graduation from Glasgow she had joined the SWH Serbian Unit, but caught typhus. While convalescing in France she worked at Sermaize and in Hilda Clark's convalescent home for French refugee women and children in Haute Savoie, where Miss Barnett wrote of her 'Dr MacPhail looks a dear – very Scotch' (IWM. DD. Miss C.U. Barnett). On returning to Serbia, Katharine MacPhail was interned by the Austrians and subsequently repatriated with Dr Inglis. After the Great Retreat she enrolled to serve in Corsica, where she nursed tubercular patients. She was one of the last to leave Bastia, and then went to Salonika to make enquiries about taking boys to Haute Savoie. Towards the end of the war she was in Macedonia, tending refugee women and children. After the Armistice she went to Belgrade to fight typhus and discovered a host of abandoned sick children. Using £25 of her own money she opened a hospital in a disused Army hut which was at first the only children's hospital in Yugoslavia. She told Mrs Seton-Watson (FWVRC Box 9.5.2): 'they bring the children to me when it's hopeless'.

Katharine MacPhail was helped by several voluntary societies, especially SCF, which continued to aid it until the country was invaded early in the Second World War. She died in 1947 still working for children with TB. Her work and that of all relief workers in Serbia was made more difficult by the superstitious culture. At Medvedja Banja the priest wrote charms on bits of paper which were swallowed or rubbed on the body to cure illness and Isabel Wicks (FWVRC Box 9.5.2) reported that children's sufferings increased during the Lenten fast. At the Child Welfare Centre at Zhitni-Potok her 1,143 patients included gastric cases, anaemia, scurvy, rickets and infantile paralysis. Those of age 7 and 8 born in the Turkish war also had spinal curvature. There were few children between ages 2 and 6. Babies born in peace showed a marked improvement, especially where mother's health was watched. Isabel Wicks said 'the history of the war is recorded on the physique of the children'.

PART THREE

Between War and Peace: The Armistice and Peace Treaties

It has been suggested that the British government went into the Great War as an escape from apparently unsolvable problems including unemployment, Ireland, and women's 'dangerous feminist aspirations'. According to Offen, (2000: 251) so-called 'social' questions, including women's liberation, have always been erased when something more important, such as a war, demands men's attention. Out of altruistic humanitarianism and as a continuing protest against their subordination by militarist hegemony which transformed people into refugees, many women continued their care of war victims during the inter-war period. There was a clear recognition that women and children suffered most and that they were vulnerable not only from their national enemies, but also from their own men, who pushed them aside, or abandoned them to save themselves, or raped them (Cahill 1999: 90). Eglantyne Jebb said that every war is a war against children and evidently war is also against women, both being increasingly vulnerable as refugees. As Wilson said (1944: 261), 'refugees have no rights: there is no Geneva convention for them as there is for prisoners of war', but this principle did not help thousands of civilian and military personnel who were trapped for years by vast distances and for whom no arrangements were made to return them to their home countries. Ethel Snowden helped prisoners in Italy to return home. Many refugees trudged back half-starved and diseased to where their homes had been and where there was little or no medical aid, but for others going home was impossible.

National boundary changes arising directly from the peace settlements altered existing nation states and formed new ones. Boundary changes sometimes led to statelessness; for example, Polish workers in Belgium failed to acquire Polish nationality according to the terms of the 1921 Treaty of Riga. There were 'large numbers of people who simply did not fit into the legal and political categories negotiated after the war. At any moment these stateless persons could become refugees, and many defined themselves as such from the moment the war ended, given the reluctance of any state to accept them' (Marrus 1985: 71). Although the peacemakers tried to draw lines around people rather than move people to fit the map, they nonetheless created minority groups within nations. Samuel and Thompson state that (1990: 18, 19): 'the collective memories of minorities need continual active expression if they are to survive being absorbed or smothered by the historical traditions of the majority', threatening the minority's sense of identity.

> For minorities, for the less powerful, and most of all for the excluded, collective memory and myth are often still more salient ... In this context it is often persecution and common grievance which define belonging.

This is typified by the Jews, Armenians, and other similar groups, and there are parallels for women.

Boundary changes meant that the defeated countries were stripped of much of their former territory, limiting their resources. Under the Treaty of St Germain, Austria was cut off from her raw material sources, and resultant financial conditions led to bankruptcy. Hungary's boundaries were disrupted by the Treaty of Trianon; consequently she had barely a third of her former land. The Treaty with Germany was signed, after German remonstrances, on 28 June in the Palace of Versailles. The US Senate refused to ratify it. Reactionary forces reinforced America's isolationism, preventing membership of the League which thereby weakened it, although the USA nonetheless exerted a powerful influence. As part of the settlement, Germany lost 27,000 square miles, between 6,500,000 and 7,000,000 people, and 10–13 per cent of pre-war resources. Alsace-Lorraine went to France, Schleswig to Denmark, and Eupen and Malmédy to Belgium. The Sudetenland, an area of German-speaking people, whose culture and traditions were German, wanted to become part of Germany; this was not allowed. Consequently, the Weimar Republic received close to 1,000,000 refugees. Fighting between Poland, Lithuania, and Soviet Russia continued after the Armistice, because boundaries between these countries were unsettled.

It cannot be assumed, therefore, that the Armistice brought a return to peaceful normality. The psychological effects of war meant that hatred for the foe and conditions of war continued after 11 November 1918. Problems in the Balkans, and Turks' repression of Armenians created more refugees. In the Near East, where Quakers and other missionaries concerned with women's rights had been undertaking relief from the late 1880s, workers became caught up in wars, pogroms, skirmishes, and forced evacuations.

They witnessed massacres of Armenians over many years and did what they could to aid survivors. In reality the war had not ended, since some 18 wars were still in progress. Some were civil wars, but others were manifestations of Britain's war against Bolshevism. Having crossed the divide between friend and foe because of its advocacy of the overturn of capitalism, Russia was also subjected to a blockade, as was Hungary. After the October 1917 Revolution the British authorities became gripped by fears of Bolshevism, and when the League of Nations was founded Russia was excluded from membership for this reason. Armenia was denied membership because of the insecurity of its boundaries.

The League of Nations and refugees

The Peace Treaties and the League of Nations were being constructed simultaneously with on-going relief in various parts of Europe. Holborn (1931: 124–35) states that the League of Nations' work for refugees was undertaken in response to appeals, the first being in 1920 from governments and voluntary organizations unable to cope. The main organizations at this time were the American Near East Relief; British and American Quakers, Save the Children and the American Relief Administration run by Herbert Hoover. On 20 February 1921, on behalf of a large number of voluntary, charitable organizations, the President of the International Red Cross approached the League Council, arguing that war and post-war experience with refugees had proved that co-ordinated efforts were more effective and seeking League intervention. Now refugee care became of international concern but women remained involved. In August the League appointed Dr Fridtjof Nansen, delegate for Norway, as High Commissioner for Russian and Armenian Refugees whose existence was central to the League's attempt to define 'refugee' and to begin to provide aid.

Nansen was charged with three strategies: to co-ordinate relief undertaken by other organizations, to which he gave priority; secondly, to organize refugees' resettlement in their original homelands, or if that was not possible, somewhere else. Finally, people needed legal status and therefore Nansen created a refugee passport which gave back some lost identity and encouraged nations to accept these otherwise stateless people. It was thought that these measures would achieve a quick settlement of the refugee problem. There is ongoing argument about why Russians and Armenians were selected. They were, of course, numerous and in particularly dire straits: there were more than 1,500,000 Russians throughout Europe at the Armistice, driven from their homes by the war, revolutions and famines. White Russians could not return to Red Russia and the Armenians lacked a secure homeland. According to Burgess (2001), the League of Nations rejected the proposition that the lack of diplomatic protection was sufficient to define a refugee, or any general definition that could be applied to all refugees. He says 'Hannah Arendt argues that these Arrangements suited the needs of states in helping to solve their refugee problems by making the refugees deportable, leaving open the accusation that the League's member states only sought to protect their self-interest.' It is difficult to rebut this conclusion.

Lord Robert Cecil was on the committee which drafted the League of Nations Covenant in 1918 and 1919, during the Peace Conference in Paris. Philip Noel-Baker, his principal assistant, later acted as an adviser to Nansen in his prisoner-of-war and refugee work. Elizabeth Rotten helped Nansen repatriate some of the millions of people from Poland and the Baltic who had been forcibly evacuated to Russia and Siberia. Nansen wanted and needed the voluntary organizations to act as a complement to the League. They played a vital role in establishing the League Commission for the Deportation of Women and Children in Asia Minor, which was primarily concerned with Armenians, creating precedents for future financial League support for similar work.

WILPF and most Quakers had deep reservations about the League because of the exclusion of the vanquished Powers and inclusion of provision for waging a League war; this, together with American self-exclusion, meant that it was half-aborted at birth (Swanwick 1935: 266). WILPF continued to call for a League of Nations structure more closely aligned to that planned by the talking centres, one that would be responsible to citizens, not to national regimes. At the All Friends Conference held in London, in August 1920, Elizabeth Cadbury reminded her listeners that 'As a Society we have stood aloof from the League of Nations because we did not wholly approve all its articles and all its intentions. But surely it is an enormous advance.' Arnold Rowntree thought there was nothing more important than getting America into the League but another Quaker, Christie Burn, considered the Press equally important. The effect of Press bias and propaganda had been to make truth a casualty of war. Quaker supporters of the League founded a Friends' League of Nations Society to win over their co-religionists; in 1938 the Friends had a pavilion at the League exhibition in New York, implying considerable Quaker support for the League by then as the best hope for peace.

The League of Nations was the biggest political change ever, but its success depended on men thinking internationally rather than nationally and the automatic, equal inclusion and acceptance of women who would bring to the League not only a wider awareness of humanity's needs, including those of children, but be educationally equipped for their work. Since the League was a league of victors, it was more a defence pact against previous enemies than a body designed to promote peace. Further, since it could not solve the problem of how to deal with belligerent, patriarchal member nations, it therefore could not prevent the conditions that created refugees. Nonetheless, as Andrews argues (1997), certain kinds of female position 'allowed' them by male-dominated societies held potential for irrevocably changing women's position in it. Women were now able to raise concerns for other women not only in their national contexts, but on the international stage at Geneva.

However, before examining League work further, it is necessary to consider wartime and post-war relief in Russia.

CHAPTER 8

An End to the War to End all Wars? Wars, Famines, Revolutions and Blockades

The War in Russia and Poland

Suffragists' aid to Russia

Just after the outbreak of War, refugees from Galicia and East Poland poured into Russia. The Imperial Duma decided that local committees should be formed for refugee aid and women were allowed on these government bodies for the first time. Russian feminists also started relief independently, informing their international colleagues of their activities through *Jus Suffragii*. Dr Schischkina Yavein, President of the Russian League for Women's Rights, described in January 1917 how they founded a lazaret with feminist doctors and nurses. They also established a home for about 20 girl refugees without family, finding them work, offering training in the League's courses or elsewhere, to assure them a future 'honest livelihood'. Dr Yavein feared prostitution. The refugee problem enabled the white slave traffic in Russia because there was no adequate legislation to protect homeless girls from being 'sold to houses of ill fame and large numbers were enticed away from their families'. Also, 'Young refugee girls were driven into the streets through pity for their starving parents, brothers and sisters, selling themselves to obtain bread.'

It was estimated 3,000,000 refugees fled along the route north-east from Poland to Moscow during the second half of 1915. In July there was famine in some areas, mainly due to the scorched earth policy of the retreating Russian soldiers. At the Siberian frontier feminists registered 20,435 families from Poland and Western Russia consisting of 79,648 adults and

29,875 children. In Orlov, southern Poland, the authorities notified workers that 10,000 refugees were being sent.

> A body of men and women volunteers formed themselves into a corps of guides and accompanied these helpless creatures on their long journeys, arranging accommodation and food for them which they would otherwise be unable to obtain. (*Jus Suffragii*, 1.4.1916)

Separate organizations received thousands of lost children and tried to trace their families. Children's sufferings were unabated by March 1917, when *Jus Suffragii* reported that 'One of the most piteous effects of the war has been the sufferings of children in invaded districts. In Poland the deaths from starvation of millions make a story of unparalleled horror.'

Immediately news of refugees' plight reached Britain the NUWSS offered to provide doctors and nurses for a maternity hospital under construction by the Tatiana Committee in Petrograd. In December the nursing organizer, Violetta Thurstan, went out, followed by the full complement: 12 female staff, and doctors Mabel May and Beatrice Coxon, who had been on the Serbian Great Retreat. The Red Cross Commissioner and the Tatiana Committee promised 1,000 roubles a month towards the upkeep. The British Women's Maternity Hospital opened on 13 March; it had 116 beds and planned to open an outpatients' clinic for minor ailments and a centre for refugee children. At the London Mansion House meeting in May, the Red Cross Commissioner, Ian Malcolm, MP, an anti-suffragist, said he was proud to be working with the NUWSS in refugee relief. Miss Thurstan described the refugees' suffering and the university students' relief work which she had visited in Kazan in Poland, then part of Russia. When the long vacation ended the students appealed to the British women for help. Dr May investigated conditions and was offered buildings for a children's infectious diseases hospital, staffed entirely by NUWSS. In June, emphasizing the suffrage foundation, the Russian Units were renamed the Millicent Fawcett Hospital Units for Refugees and that month their Kazan hospital was opened with Dr Stepney in charge; she was also appointed visiting doctor to two Polish Refuges. The National Allied Relief Committee of New York donated £400 towards a motor ambulance; packed with clothing for refugees, it was sent out on 4 August, the Russian Government providing free transport to Archangel.

During the winter, typhus, cholera, smallpox, and dysentery became rife. Medical work included delousing inhabitants in typhus stricken districts, a preventative work dangerous to workers. Richard Reynolds Ball, who had served with the Friends in France for two years before volunteering to go to Samara, died in December 1920 from typhus, the hunger and dirt disease. Three days later Gertrude Powicke, who had been a member of staff at the Manchester Girls High School, died aged 31. Violet Tillard, a Quaker by convincement Oldfield described as an unrecognized 'committed subversive', and Mary Pattison also gave their lives in the service of the Russian people, dying from typhus in 1922 (FWVRC Box 10.1.9.).

Four other hospitals dealing mainly with infectious diseases, including two general hospitals in the Kazan province, were then jointly supplied by the NUWSS, the Great Britain to Poland Fund and the Russian authorities. The Home Committee serving these hospitals was all female and included Lady Selborne, Mrs Fawcett and Alys Russell with Eleanor Rathbone for some of the time. Rathbone's later concern for refugees stems from this period. The NUWSS hospital at Zaleschiki in Galicia for civilian refugees, where Dr Helena Hall and Dr King Atkinson were in charge, switched to military work in 1916 and they were attached to the Russian Army. Alexander Kerensky, who became Prime Minister of the Russian Provisional Government on 2 July 1917, and General Brousiloff visited their surgical hospital. When the situation became unstable, the medical unit staff at Podgaetz in Galicia was evacuated by Commander Locker Lampson of the British Armoured Car Division, another voluntary set-up. Inglis's Russian SWH Unit, attached to 14,000 Southern Slavs of the First Serbian Division, survivors of the Great Retreat, had been sent to the Russian front and were also in danger. As Angela Smith and Viv Newman explained (Bristol, 2001), Inglis struck a bargain with the War Office, pointing out if they were not withdrawn they would be drawn into the Russian conflict and killed, but that they would only go if the Serb soldiers were pulled out as well. This event and its consequences were of such magnitude and significance they were hidden behind the 50 year rule. What followed challenges the conventional histories of war because the Serbs formed a new army which went to Salonika and instigated the Bulgarian collapse. It was as a result of this the Germans sued for peace. This also profoundly contradicts the idea that women, and relief work, could not influence foreign policy.

Quaker help

Also in 1916, Quakers offered help to Russia and four workers were sent to investigate. Scott (1964) believes Friends' concern with Russia dates considerably earlier than William Allen's time there in 1819 but through helping in the 1891 famine they became a household name, especially in St Petersburg where their periodical *The Friend* was discussed in Russian newspapers. The letter of introduction from the Foreign Office, Petrograd, to Count Vladimir Michaellovitch Volkonsky indicates the importance of Quaker reputation, saying 'these gentlemen are Quakers, a sect whose trustworthiness is beyond question. Perhaps you remember how helpful this society was to our people during the late famine.' Official estimates put the number of refugees at 2,768,395, of which 2,562,000 were in European Russia.

William Cadbury, Joseph Burtt and Theodore Rigg were taken to Buzuluk, a province as large as Belgium, with its capital of the same name. Robert Tatlock, who had worked in France and then spearheaded the work in Serbia, joined them later. Red Cross co-operation was vital. Burtt wrote (FWVRC Boxes 7.2.1, 7.2.2.): 'We have after some difficulty induced the Russian Red Cross people to recognize us and to give us their certificates and, it is stated, free use of Russian railways.'

By June 1916 the first Friends had arrived, some moving from France or Serbia to spend periods in Russia or Poland. The environment was completely different from anything so far experienced. The steppes were vast; dust, heat and flies in summer; mud or deep snow at other times of the year, each creating particular health problems. The roads were unpaved; there were no drains and no running water. There were also communication difficulties. In Samara, a medium sized town on the Volga, 28,168 refugees had to be provided for up to November 1915; the lack of accommodation and food was particularly serious during the cold winter months. The area served a population of at least 130,000 that included:

> Tartar and other similar races, also various branches of Finnish people, local Russians, Cossacks, Little Russians, Polish and other refugees and PoWs including Turks. Imagine the language difficulties. (FWVRC Box 7.2.2)

It was a mark of confidence when Tartar women were willing and permitted to enter the Friends' hospitals, such reluctance being attributed to their Muslim faith. At first there was only Florence Barrow, a trained social worker, and Annie Wells, both members of the FLWS, living in an abandoned peasant hut, to visit hundreds of refugees scattered in the villages. Later, two English doctors and four women worked at a small hospital of 24 beds in Lubimovka, which served an area of 700 square miles. A children's home, which also took elderly people, was opened at Mogotovo, 40 miles north of Buzuluk, with two male and six female workers. By the autumn of 1916, 30 workers were based in Buzuluk, mostly working in groups of three or four, but sometimes a single woman worked alone at an outpost. Despite Buzuluk being on the railway, workers were isolated and cut off from most news of the outside world including Moscow, where Jack Catchpool remained alone, registering refugees and where, according to the Russian Supplement of *The Times* (26.8.1916), 75 per cent of children died from measles; this disease was usually accompanied by whooping cough, lowering resistance. Another FLWS member, Elsie Fox, had an area covering about 1,000 square miles. Her Unit opened three hospitals, one of which was 100 miles away in the far side of the Buzuluk district. The peasants did not associate hygiene or diet with disease. Workers taught these things, including how to prevent and cure diarrhoea. Peasants' attitude towards child patients was contradictory. The child's wish was the ruling factor, yet medicine prescribed for the three-months-old baby might be given to the rest of the family. Unquestioning religious belief became superstitious fatalism. John Rickman (FWVRC Box 7.2.2) reported that prescribed medicine might not be administered because the sick person's improvement or deterioration was God's will, so it was pointless giving it. When food was short children might not be fed because there were so many of them and all life was 'in the keeping of God … the people who count are the bread-winners'. Friends gave no preference to the rich or to a particular race – everyone was seen in order, a factor emphasizing equality that impressed the local people.

As Russia struggled to determine whether some form of democracy would be created following the February 1917 Revolution, people became restless and crime increased. Consequently, some edgy youths at Mogotovo were taught woodwork, gardening and how to care for seedlings in a frame and during drought. They gained a sense of pride in their ability to contribute to the community's well-being. People fled before the Bolshevist armies and in July 1917 the majority of refugees in Buzuluk were women and children. That month Quakers recorded caring for 2,602 refugees in six centres and another 2,662 in outlying districts but this was acknowledged as 'a drop in the ocean'. There was bad housing, a lack of nourishing food, psychological depression, and a lack of means of self-support. Refugees came from a different area where life was not so hard; consequently their clothes were inadequate for the harsher conditions, and they were not used to working the more difficult soil. Government allowances were given to children under 15 and people over 50, but when these were reduced from six roubles to slightly under four, it made survival in the winter precarious. The harsh moral code meant that no separation allowances were given for illegitimate children of soldiers, who had to declare their intentions quickly to save their child and its mother from considerable suffering. Friends therefore opened soup kitchens and provided employment for the women, spinning wool, and knitting stockings, using the same methods of payment and sale as in France and Corsica.

When some Unit members returned home, those remaining operated with fewer personnel. However, six American women Friends arrived in Buzuluk on 26 August 1917, all except one were social workers without appropriate skills. As in France, where the first American workers arrived earlier that month, the difference in American and British culture was evident in the ways the two nationalities wanted to work. The English met individual needs personally, which the Americans thought wasteful, their statistical approach sometimes being more efficient; for example, their business-like card-index system enabled the reuniting of separated family members. Nonetheless, on arrival the Americans were allocated to different outposts to have individual help from an English worker in learning the language. Amelia Farbiszewski who spoke Russian, having trained as a nurse went to Lubimovka. This facilitated a much-needed tactical change in the hospital. Amelia taught two peasant girls to care for typhus patients; after initial distaste and refusal, they became sufficiently skilled to teach others. Reinforcing this, following another of Dr Rickman's plans, patients were only admitted if, instead of the usual elderly relative, a young female accompanied them to be taught proper care. John Rickman's Hospital Report indicates their workload. From 2 August 1916 to July 1917 there were 57,680 consultations and 253 operations, and they had travelled 5,573 versts. A verst was slightly more than a kilometre.

Field workers' reports gave the Home committee no indication of future plans. Home's sometimes unrealistic expectations, how much money was sent, the suitability of workers, the uncertainty of workers' position in a foreign country affected by war, famine and changing politics, and a different cultural environment all made commitment to forward planning unrealistic, as workers in France found in relation to hut building when Home complained of lack of progress. The Bolshevik rising in November created food shortages and further refugee movement, necessitating changes in workers' arrangements. Margaret Barber transferred to Lubimovka where she was able to put her plans for a hospital into effect and Amelia Farbiszewski went to Mogotovo. Communications became impossible and Quaker funds were trapped. The assistance of the American Red Cross was sought and eventually the money came through. By 31 December 1917 the situation was so critical that Friends in Russia were warned of the dangers, although not recalled home. This was the period of Lenin's successful second *coup*, the mutiny of sailors off Petrograd, the storming of the Winter Palace and the Kerensky Government being overthrown.

In the early months of 1918 the threat of famine in the Buzuluk region became a reality, creating more refugees. It was a time of uncertainty and confusion. Russian doctors and nurses returned from the Front; the work was wound up and some workers, including Florence Barrow, returned to England. Margaret Barber left to help Armenian refugees but was unable to do so. Transport was disorganized and the workers set up soup kitchens, trade schools, workshops and an orphanage. On 26 June 1918 Buzuluk fell to the Czechoslovaks and on 6 August Kazan fell. Workers struggled home through the autumn and winter, some being arrested as spies, and arriving bedraggled, emaciated and exhausted. A small number remained behind. The Great War was officially over; the need for relief was not.

Post-war relief in Russia and Poland

Poland received large numbers of refugees not only from the war and the Russian civil war, but also the Russo-Polish war. These complicated the relief effort. In December 1919 the Friends wrote to the Under Secretary of State at the Foreign Office, expressing their concern at distress among the women and children in Petrograd and elsewhere, wanting to send out another party of relief workers, because the ones who went out in 1916 were gradually returning. They were allowed to send stores including dried milk, soap, rice and medicines to Helsingfors, to be forwarded to Petrograd for use in children's hospitals. Three or four workers could go but His Majesty's Government could take no responsibility for their safety or return. Friends co-operated with SCF and two funds started by Emily Hobhouse in July 1919 – the Swiss Relief Fund for starving children from Vienna, Germany, Czechoslovakia and Hungary and the Russian Babies Fund. They sent over 50 tons of supplies in February 1920.

Due to severe food shortages, by late 1919 the Russian authorities had divided people into three classes for their food ration. Categories reflected socialist principles and the physical effort demanded of the body. Manual workers, housewives, all hospital and sanitary workers were first class; they got most food. Housekeepers with no family, and light clerical workers were allocated half the first class amount. Third class were those who:

> prefer to live without doing any work. And the amount allowed is a mere nothing, and holders of such cards must live by purchasing in the open market at prices from 20 to 30 times that of the food card prices. (FWVRC Box 7.2.1)

The Red Guards had three times the bread and twice the sugar of Class One. They also received meat, food and oil the others did not get. It is not clear where the elderly or the sick fitted into these categories.

Russia's plight deepened with a poor harvest in 1920, followed by lack of rain in 1921. Between November 1920 and March 1921 Catherine Marshall served as League of Nations Representative on an International Commission convened by the Red Cross in Geneva to tackle the Russian famine. It was a famine not only of food, but of everything including clothes and soap, exacerbated by a shortage of water. According to Wilson (1944: 149), 3,000,000 people in Russia died of typhus between 1919 and 1922 and Nansen appealed to the international community for help. Lady Muriel Paget's Mission, partly funded by money from New Zealand and the SCF, organized child welfare and relief work in Estonia, Latvia, and Lithuania, where there were many Russian refugee children as well as local children needing help. A problem that relief organizations had to grapple with was whether to provide short term relief or look to the future in their aid. In 1922 when SCF withdrew financial support from the Paget Missions, Nansen agreed with Lady Muriel's complaint that they favoured short-term feeding instead of long-term constructive work, affecting aid to Russia where she had been invited to help train child welfare workers. Hilda Clark made the same complaint concerning other SCF work.

Politics now directly affected by whom and to whom relief could be given, partly according to which side they supported in the civil war. Scott writes that (1964: 229) the Save the Children League of Moscow attempted to save children irrespective of the political affiliations of their relatives. However, Mennonites on the Volga wanted to undertake relief in conjunction with the Friends for their co-religionists in the Ukraine and Crimea. In February 1921 William Albright confirmed that they had not aided anti-Soviet forces but had complied with requisitions of horses, waggons and grain and organized a police force for self protection against a bandit army of 100,000 men; only about 10 per cent of the younger men had joined forces with General Denekin and General Wrangel who became commanding General of the pro-monarchist White Army in Southern Russia in the later stages of the civil war. In August, Ruth Fry gave a further reference stressing the historical connection between Mennonites and

Friends, referring to their work together in France and giving an assurance that they would undertake relief according to 'the Quaker spirit' (FWVRC Box 7.5.5). The relief work was allowed.

The inclusion of Jews into Friends relief work was more problematic. During 1921 a conference created a scheme for moving large numbers of Jewish children in the Ukraine to Canada, South Africa, and England. Mrs Leggatt was present, representing the SCF. Probably because of prevalent anti-semitism across the world it was considered that the:

> present inclusion of Jewish workers would menace their influence and lead to misunderstanding their work and thus defeat our purposes as well as theirs. We suggest prompt turning over of supplies available without publicity anywhere. (FWVRC Box 7.5.5)

Arthur Watts, secretary of the Friends Service Committee, whose suffragist mother Agatha helped establish the Manchester branch of WIL, went to Russia as a relief worker and remained there for the rest of his life. Under his leadership, with Buzuluk as the Centre, the Friends set up 900 feeding points in 280 villages where there had been a population of 450,000 before the famine. The Eastern part of the district was under the American Friends and Herbert Hoover's Administration, working as separate Unit, though cooperating with the British. However, Hoover insisted all American funds should be distributed under the Administration flag, whereas American and British Quakers wanted to work together; British Quakers held aloof from Hoover's machinery. Eventually Arthur Watts arranged that Friends should be responsible for administering relief in Buzuluk since they knew the area well and this was agreed to subsequently by Nansen's Refugee Commission with which the Quakers worked.

On 1 March 1922, the Friends joined with the Russian Famine Relief Fund and SCF to form the All-British Appeal, with Sir Benjamin Robertson of the British Legation directing operations. Polish refugees were returning to destroyed homes in Eastern Poland and about 500,000 Russians were trying to go in the opposite direction, aggravating distress. The main aim was to help people to survive until they could become self-supporting; it was reconstructive relief which looked to the future by assisting agriculture, a method adopted by Nansen. Villagers were allocated a forest timber ration for house-building so the Friends bought 1,000 horses from the Polish Army to bring it into the villages. About 1,600 acres was ploughed by tractor but this was abandoned in favour of ploughing by horses let in rotation to different villages enabling peasants to cultivate 24,000 acres rendered derelict by war. In addition, 5,000 spades were bought from the Reparations Commission and vegetable garden seeds and potato and grain seeds were distributed. By experimenting with cottonseed meal as a cattle-fodder Quakers discovered the milk yield increased by two and a half litres per day per cow. This was a vital food-stuff to a starving population, and was relevant everywhere. Quakers helped hospitals, renovated water systems, provided equipment for training colleges, and helped housing reconstruction west of Warsaw, supplementing the work with necessaries such as nails, bricks, and glass.

In March and April 1922 a Conference was held at Riga between Sir Benjamin Robertson, Mr Golden of SCF, and representatives of various organizations including the International Committee for Russian Relief and the Nansen Commission. Harrison Barrow, a suffragist Quaker, represented the Friends. As a result of the famine, relief work was now carried on as an immense business. Most of the executive work and organization of distribution fell upon the Nansen organization in Moscow and the field workers of the Relief Societies. Conference representatives had seen corpses of starved people lying in the streets of Buzuluk and dying children being carried to homes. They confirmed (FWVRC Box 7.5.6) 'In places, cannibalism is an undoubted fact.' The numbers of horses and cattle available for local transport had diminished and this was affecting the issue of relief stores. Camels were becoming the main beasts of burden, but camel meat was to be found on sale in most markets. Thatched roofs of cottages were eaten. Spotted typhus and relapsing fever were raging and no district or class of inhabitant was unaffected. Bubonic and pneumonic plagues were reported from the Novouzensk district. However, practically nothing had been done 'to alleviate the lot of the unfortunate adult, on whom depends the sowing and harvesting of the crop. It was estimated that at least half the adults were in need of relief.' In some areas 'practically the whole adult population was starving en masse'. The American programme supplied

Plate 6. Ruth Fry, Dr Craig and William Fogg in Poland. (Photograph courtesy of The Religious Society of Friends in Britain)

317,000 adult rations within the limits of the SCF Child Feeding area, but this represented approximately a quarter of the adult population. 'What is really required ... is a cereal ration of 1 lb. per day in respect of 250,000 adults to 1 September.'

In August 1922 Kathleen Courtney and Hilda Clark visited Poland on a fact-finding tour. They met Florence Barrow, now head of Friends' Relief work, and several American Friends. The work consisted of ploughing, establishing industries, distributing emergency rations and medical aid. In September, Francesca Wilson joined the Quakers at Pasmorowka, north of Buzuluk, meeting *en route* in Warsaw Marjorie Rackstraw who was now in charge of an outpost at Alexeevka, 75 versts from Buzuluk, the hardest hit area not far from the foothills of the Urals.

William Albright, who visited Russia in 1922 and 1923 with Ruth Fry, organized the shared relief at Minsk, principally carried on by the American Friends Service Committee and financed by the American Jewish Joint Distribution Committee. The All Russian Central Executive Committee and Central Committee for Relief of Starving authorized the specially formed

Anglo-American Society of Friends, Dr Nansen's International Fund for Help to the Children, and Swedish, German and Czechoslovak Red Cross Societies to continue helping. Indeed, hundreds of thousands of refugees were kept alive by the Quakers and SCF during this period.

Saving the Children: Relief in Europe During and After the Armistice

Breaking the blockade

Despite censorship, during the war Dorothy Buxton, helped by her sister Eglantyne Jebb, had been allowed by the Board of Trade to purchase foreign newspapers, and print translated articles about European social conditions in *The Cambridge Magazine*. By November 1917, the year Dorothy and her husband joined the Society of Friends, they knew the Allied naval blockade was causing mortality among the women and children in Germany. During the Armistice results similar to those of the Thirty Years' War became evident. The political and economic situation in Europe was unstable, with inflation, unemployment and people's precarious health deteriorating. There was typhus in Berlin, Greece, and Poland. Hoover, who had organized the relief of Belgium, now had the task, as he told Lady Kate Courtney in December 1918, to ration the world. He expected 12,000,000 to 20,000,000 people to die of starvation in Russia before the harvest.

The allied blockade against the Central Powers was prolonged and intensified for six months; this broke the terms of the Armistice and ignored the interdependency of European economics. It arose from political ideologies that identified certain groups as 'Other,' preventing military necessaries from being imported into enemy countries, stopping food from reaching the civilian population, and starving them of clothing and fuel in order to force acceptance of the Peace Terms. Norman Angell (Gilbert 1995: 351), who was later to receive the Nobel Peace Prize, denounced the blockade as a weapon 'against the children, the weak, the sick, the old, the women, the mothers, the decrepit'. Its continuation intensified the famine in Europe and Russia and was rigorously condemned. People began campaigning to get it lifted. MPs were interviewed at the House of Commons by 300 Quakers.

In January 1919, the Jebb sisters formed the Fight the Famine Council (FTFC). Amongst its aims was the education of the public about the need for a European economic system that would abolish hunger, also the raising of funds to give to other agencies for relief. The first meeting was held on 16 January 1919 at Lady Courtney's London house with Quakers, economists and internationally minded people on the Executive and as members. Mary Sheepshanks of WIL became FTFC Honorary Secretary, joint membership being common between FTFC, WIL, and FEWVRC, the now amalgamated FWVRC and FEC. Elizabeth Rotten, writing from Berlin in June 1921, named FTFC as being 'of the FEWVRC' therefore seeing the new Council originating from relief. Their joint war work on behalf of PoWs had formed a bridge between the two countries and became the basis of FTFC and of its sub-committee, Save the Children.

Henry Nevinson and other journalists sent home accounts of the starvation of women and particularly of infants, informing readers of the fact that more children were lost in the war than men on the field. He had been shown round hospital wards where babies were dying for lack of milk. No rubber teats were available for babies' bottles 'in the extremely few fortunate cases where a little condensed milk might be obtained to substitute the non-existent cows', goats' or mothers' milk', so they were sucking on bone teats which created painfully sore gums. He asked for 1,000,000 teats to be sent immediately to provide one for each baby under six months. The German Babies' Teats Fund was set up by Mrs Pope Hennessy of WIL; Mary Sheepshanks, Mrs Ayrton Gould and Mrs George Innes, formerly Miss Royds, who had served with the SWH in Salonika, organized the appeal. WIL had made it a rule not to branch off from educative pacifist work to relief, since they considered other organizations performed that task. Not all members agreed with WILPF's decision. Dr Ethel Williams reduced her donation because she wanted it to help Viennese children and most members undertook relief individually or through other organizations.

However, as this exception to the rule showed, the division between practical relief and political work was thin.

It was necessary to obtain permission to send goods abroad and, having been allowed to meet Dr Rotten in Holland in December, Ruth Fry wrote to the Ministry of Blockade on 4 January 1919, requesting permission to forward one or two cases of teats to her. In mitigation of this apparently enemy contact, it was pointed out that Dr Rotten's organization in Berlin was similar to FEC and she had looked after 'our women and children of interned PoWs and the civilian prisoners at Ruhleben and other camps'. She attached a list of names of Ruhleben PoWs who would testify to Dr Rotten's help. WIL was given permission for three cases, the Friends for two. The required shape was not normally used in Britain and WIL was uncertain if it could raise the £6,200 needed for purchase and packing in time. WIL bought all that were available of the required design but did not fill their cases, so combined theirs with the Friends'. Dr Rotten, herself suffering from malnutrition, was told not to publicize the coming relief in the Press. She got a young German artist to draw a poster of a baby's head which was shown in many German shop-windows, announcing the sending of the teats and where to apply (Swanwick 1935: 315). The first consignments arrived in Frankfurt on 25 February 1919. Dr Rotten's organization was used for reception and distribution in areas that included occupied territories, and stress was laid on the gifts as signs of friendship. WIL's appeal closed on 8 March 1919 with money still coming in but that day Kathleen Royds wrote to Miss Fox asking if the Friends could make a grant towards their deficit of about £400. They sent £250 three days later.

Friends then sought permission from the Foreign Office to send milk, food and clothing for women and babies to Germany, Austria and Hungary. Organizers were not allowed to make a public appeal, and the complicated and interlocking machinery set up to enforce the blockade caused delays. Eventually the difficulties were cleared away and further consignments of goods and medical supplies were sent to General Sir Richard Ewart, representative of the Red Cross in Berlin, who handed them over to Dr Rotten.

To publicize the effects of the blockade, WIL announced a protest meeting in Trafalgar Square on 8 April 1919 and a banner was erected on the plinth: *Lift the Hunger Blockade*. Some days before the meeting, the police arrested women handing out leaflets entitled *A Starving Baby* and *Our Blockade has Caused This*, showing a photograph of severely emaciated Austrian children. Daily newspapers asked soldiers to break up the demonstration but in contrast to meetings held by WIL, UDC and similar organizations in the earlier years of the war, the men now felt differently from the majority of the civilian population. Nonetheless, over 20,000 people were recorded as being present at the protest. Soldiers helped support the banner as Emmeline Pethick-Lawrence and Barbara Ayrton Gould marched to 10 Downing Street to hand in a petition. However, although there was considerable public support for the cause it had little effect on the political process. The leaflets had not been approved under the censorship laws of the Defence of the Realm Act; Eglantyne Jebb and Barbara Ayrton Gould were arrested. Gould was unable to attend the Zurich Congress in May because she was in court. Jebb asked the prosecuting council for a donation. They were fined £5 each.

On 15 April 1919, at the FTFC Executive meeting Dorothy Buxton proposed that a special sub-committee be appointed to raise a relief fund for children (Wilson 1967: 174). Nonetheless, Eglantyne Jebb is always credited with founding SCF. Dorothy and Eglantyne had worked from 1913 with the Macedonian Relief Fund, founded in 1903 by her brothers-in-law Charles and Noel Buxton, when Eglantyne helped not only the victorious Serbs, but victims of the war: the defeated Albanians and Moslem refugees who fled into Monastir from their burning villages. She was interested in suffrage and walked in a Woman's Suffrage procession in Guildford. SCF was publicly launched on 19 May at the Royal Albert Hall with Dorothy Buxton its Honorary Secretary. She expected it to be a short-lived national movement but it quickly became international and by securing League support for Jebb's Declaration on the Rights of the Child, provided a global humanitarian standard. SCF started by raising money and allocating it to other organizations working with children in Europe to provide food and clothing. They helped Armenian refugees in Asia Minor, Assyrians in France, and Jews and Russians seemingly everywhere.

Relief workers faced hostility from governments, the press and people of their own nations because they helped 'enemies' such as the Austrians.

Such relief was seen as unpatriotic and public opinion had to be changed; the journalist Philip Gibbs and some newspapers helped. Governments knew about the situation but did not act until officers such as General Plumer exposed it and journalists felt it safe to tell the truth. Fearing the rise of Bolshevism among the working classes, they then allowed relief to be sent.

Public animosity was demonstrated at a FTFC Conference in November 1919; economics experts from many countries were invited, including three from Germany and two from Austria. The Conference, held in private, was attended by about 60 people, mostly women, but at a public meeting in Caxton Hall, Westminster, various women hecklers shouted 'We don't want Germans here' until ejected. Speakers included Sir William Beveridge, Professor Maynard Keynes, Leonard Woolf, Dorothy Buxton and Hector Munro. Dr Wenckebach noted that diseases were caused by lack of certain unknown but necessary substances and food containing these should be sent to the famine areas. Emphasis was placed on the work of the London Lister Institute in 'investigating the nature of the substance called vitamines [sic]'.

At last in July 1919 Quakers were among the first civilians allowed to enter Germany. Joan Fry, Marion Fox, Elizabeth Rotten, Aletta Jacobs and the Americans Jane Addams and Dr Alice Hamilton went to assess the long-term effects of underfeeding on the population, particularly children; Hamilton later became a member of the League of Nations Health Committee with which America cooperated. Problems for these women, and for later workers, included overcoming hostility and the difficulty of creating goodwill as effective as agencies of war had been. Their report to the FEC in London details people's appalling physical condition. For three to four months in 1917, there was nothing to eat except turnips. People were still experiencing the effects of the 'Turnip Winter' two years later. At the WIL Congress in Zurich, Frau Lehmann of Göttingen reported that:

> what had distressed her country people the most was the death rate amongst 15- to 20-year olds from the influenza epidemic in 1918. They were so weakened by lack of food that all their resistance had vanished. (FWVRC Box 10.3.1)

This connection of the flu epidemic with malnutrition was evident throughout Europe but it not usually considered by modern investigators. Jane Addams, leader of the peace movement in America and President of WILPF, noted in 1920 the continuing impact of the food shortage on the bodies of women and children. She realized that deaths due to malnutrition occurred because people also could not keep themselves or their houses clean; typhus was inevitable if the lice infecting 10,000 houses in Berlin were not eradicated. People suffered from skin diseases. Women having given birth were more prone to childbed fever and babies suffered terribly due to the lack of absorbent cotton or ointments such as Vaseline. As Ruth Fry said at the All Friends Conference of August 1920 (FWVRC MS Vol. 51): 'It is a difficult thing to realise the misery of Central Europe without seeing it.' Photographs show children's bodies undersized by several years' lack of growth, distorted by rickets and other diseases caused by undernourishment. In some places people collapsed in the streets because their bones were too soft to support them. Elsewhere the suffering was hidden, betrayed only by silent cities.

Austria and Germany; the milk supply

Early in 1919 Eglantyne Jebb visited Dr Hector Munro whom she had never met before, and asked him to investigate conditions. He immediately organized help for starving children brought into hospitals to die. In December he and Eglantyne Jebb went to an audience given by the Pope who agreed to support the work by donating collections on Holy Innocents' Day. Various journalists reported on the situation. One reporter concluded: 'I have encountered dozens of children two years of age who have never tasted milk.' To help mothers and babies, short-term schemes were started. The *corbeilles circulantes*, or circulating baby baskets, provided a cradle and layette which were passed on when outgrown to the next mother. From March 1919 to March 1920 'Liebesgaben' (Love-gifts) used the principle of 'adoption' to send food and clothing for distribution through hospitals and other institutions such as German Welfare Centres to specified German children and mothers mainly in the Berlin area. Dr Rotten helped by preparing a leaflet to accompany every gift sent out from the UK.

German recipients of this British charity deplored that they could not fully appreciate this generosity because the distribution occurred just at the time when the 'terrible peace terms' foreshadowed an overburdened future for them (FWVRC Box 10.2.3). The reparations clauses in the Treaties demanded, among other things, 140,000 milch cows – an absolute catastrophe for German youngsters. From 1914 the milk supply for Berlin of 1,000,000 litres had gradually reduced and in the winter of 1919 was reduced still further because Germany was not now allowed to import fodder. Berlin's 7,000 cows were fed on potato parings and vegetable trimmings.

Ilse Scheffer of Dusseldorf (FWVRC Box 10.2.4) compared the 'hard-heartedness of the military wall which has been erected on the left bank of the Rhine' to 'all the dumb misery of the South African concentration camp, of which we formerly hardly dared to think', for which the British had been responsible. Schaffer drew a poignant image of children standing 'by the barrier on the Rhine Bridge in hundreds, because the rumour was circulated that they might go across and drink on the other side, until the sentries drove them away'. This spoke loudly of those who suffer. But children were not the only ones. There was a separate public office in Berlin to care for the 210,000 people sick with such illnesses as TB and nephritis. 10 per cent of the population were ill, and the old were sacrificed to the young, the incurable to those who had a chance of recovery, a policy that risked breeding callousness and despair. Limited food supplies meant that Quakers also usually excluded the elderly from relief but this resulted in many early deaths, and a devaluation of the older generation in the minds of the younger. It also left children without adult support. In Vienna, which was suffering particularly severely, being 'old' could simply mean being over 40 (Wilson 1967: 111). Most men died in their late 40s or early to mid-50s, while most women died in their mid- to late 50s. The hunger blockade had a devastating effect on older people. A relief worker wrote: 'There is nothing for the old in Central Europe now.'

The Friends' relief in Austria was initiated in July 1919 by Dr Hilda Clark who was in charge in Vienna for three years. During this period the Austrian Government imposed a maximum price on wheat, milk and coal below production costs. Hilda Clark considered supplies could be doubled if a higher price was paid to the producers. The falling value of the krone made foreign currency needed for buying cows from other countries more expensive. In October she approached the Yugoslav Government who refused to sell cows to people who had treated them so badly; the new state of Yugoslavia included Serbia. She returned to England and obtained permission from Lloyd George to export milk cows; this brought the Agricultural Department of the Friends' Mission in Vienna into being. Hilda had then nearly concluded negotiations for 150 cows and for a supply of fodder from Croatia. The American Dairy Cattle Company sent 750 cows to Bremerhaven from Galveston, Texas, with 16 young men. On arrival the cows were put in quarantine, the young men were treated to tours and then went home. The cows developed Texas-fever, a highly infectious disease. German cities were forced to pay their upkeep because they were technically still owned by Americans so slaughtering them was impossible. Germany really only needed oilcake and cattle fodder to improve the output from their own cows but this could not be said for fear of upsetting the Americans. Eventually 1,409 cows and bulls were imported into Austria from Britain, Holland and Switzerland. The farmers paid for them by sending milk free to the infant welfare centres of the city, where it was sold at a low price for babies under 2 years. In July 1921 Friends were feeding some 10,000 children daily with Quaker milk.

Hilda Clark also attempted to do something about the coal shortage. On 17 September 1919 (Pye 1956: 48), she wrote to Edith Pye from Vienna: 'Next week I shall go to Prague and have a heart to heart talk with Mazaryk about the coal situation.' Thomas Mazaryk had been elected President of the new Czechoslovakian Republic in December 1918. Only in January 1920 was more extensive relief possible when, after 13 months, the blockade was raised. However, conditions were only slightly alleviated when food imports were allowed because these took the place of exhausted German supplies. In some places the situation had deteriorated, for example in children's hospitals in Berlin, but a letter in March 1920 from one of the Sisters at the Friedenshort Home at Miechewitz, Upper Silesia, said the children were looking better because they were now drinking 'Quaker milk'.

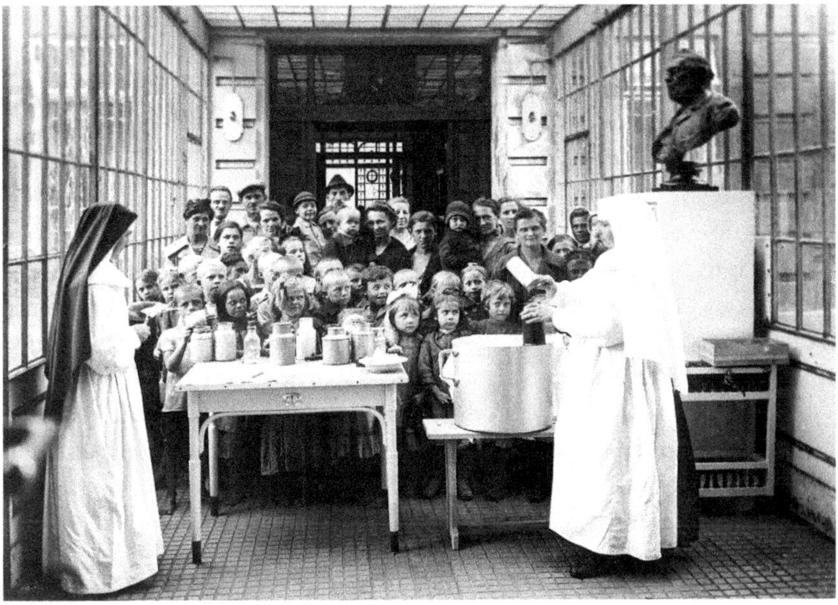

Plate 7. Milk distribution in Vienna. (Photograph courtesy of The Religious Society of Friends in Britain)

During May 1919, Mr Hoover started a scheme to give one good meal a day to school children between 3 and 17 in Vienna and other Austrian towns. However, this was alleviation not a cure, and did not help expectant and nursing mothers, infants up to three or sick children in TB homes. The SCR's first relief grant was given to Austria *via* the Friends after Hilda Clark began work. Alice Clark, Hilda's sister, a member of the FLWS, was Secretary of the Austria Committee in London and visited in February 1921. Edith Pye supervised infant welfare and Kathleen Courtney went out from time to time taking over from Hilda Clark in her absence which was sometimes for recuperation. A psychological difficulty for these workers was that to keep themselves fit they had to eat better than those they came to help. Hilda wrote that she would rather have shelling, because they shared this with the people. In November 1919, Francesca Wilson acted as Hilda Clark's interpreter when she visited Government and municipal authorities in Vienna and Lichtenstein. She admired Dr Clark and thought her a daring woman (Wilson 1967: 107).

Hilda Clark's full schedule required a wide range of skills. On a single day she conducted medical examinations, attended Committee meetings, visited the Embassy and had significant people to lunch. She then inspected barracks being transformed into wards for surgical TB cases, and visited workers. She dealt with correspondence to the USA; Kathleen Courtney with that to London. During 1922 Kathleen became seriously ill and was cared for by Hilda and an Australian doctor who was also helping with the babies. The work was exhausting and Lady Mary Murray, who in 1925 joined the Quakers, was among those who became over-tired from the work.

The Friends originally ran their relief on class lines from their Middle Class Bureau in the Hofburg where the Austrian Government allotted them several rooms. 'Mittelstand' were a wide group of professional Viennese deprived of food and everything needed for their intellectual lives by the falling exchange rate. They lived by selling their goods and using their capital. Some, like a bedridden woman, were dependent on hired help they could no longer afford. Margaret Whitelegge arranged distribution of clothing and weekly food rations. Although official records say Austrian women did the work, photographs show children, who went each day after school, weighing the food from sacks and boxes into smaller proportions. One 15-year-old girl created a large, colourful lithograph of this procedure, bringing the work and the young workers vividly to life.

Also distributed was cod liver oil for Dr Harriet Chick's patients suffering from malnutrition which resulted in softening of the bones, with consequent loss of teeth, sight and hearing. Dr Chick, Dr Dalyell and Margaret Hume of the Lister Institute worked at the University Kinderlinik. Their researches confirmed the importance of vitamins and the developing science of nutrition, revealing that starvation brought other diseases. On 17 May 1922 Hilda Clark visited them at Professor von Pirquet's clinic. They had discovered that cows should feed in sunlight; being fed greenstuffs in the stall was insufficient to provide milk of a quality to cure rickets.

In 1919 and 1920, middle-class Austrians realized that they could use suburban allotments to augment the diminishing food supply and built houses there to live as a community. Friends raised £12,000 and a member

Plate 8. Children doing the weighing of food for distribution in Vienna. John Fisher's Vienna Album. (Photograph courtesy of The Religious Society of Friends in Britain)

of the mission helped in the construction work. The first 'Land Settlement', the Baumgarten, was opened on 3 March 1921 by the President Dr Hainisch; Hilda Clark was present and the Society of Friends was specially thanked with 'nice things' being said about Edith Pye who was involved in fund raising. On 21 January 1922, President Hainisch opened another land settlement at Altmansdorf. The Belgian Minister, the Hungarian Minister, newspapermen and the cinematograph were there and Hilda gave an address (Pye 1956: 60–6). There was much interest in the settlements, and people were glad to do something other than emergency feeding; settlements supported Austrian enterprise and were more permanent. The LNU was involved in this endeavour and, indicating international awareness and support, members visited the settlements.

Relief in Hungary

The Peace Treaty with Hungary was especially severe. In 1919 SCF gave Hungary a grant through the Salvation Army and Theosophist Action Lodge. On 18 August 1919, following the *coup d'état* when the Bolshevist Government gave place to the Rumanian occupation, Noel Buxton sent a report to Sir William Goode about conditions in Budapest. Noel Buxton, MP, founder and Chair of the House of Commons Balkans Committee in 1903, was brother-in-law to Eglantyne Jebb and he, with others connected with SCF, worked in Hungary post-war. It is evident that there was a network of Europeans and Americans trying to alleviate the wretchedness endured by civilians throughout Europe. Hector Munro visited eleven towns occupied by the Rumanians and discovered that typhus, typhoid and cholera had been endemic for over two years. Hungary's enemies possessed her whole fuel supply of coal and wood; practically all the trees around Budapest had been cut down for fuel, and many wooded areas were in the hands of Czechoslovaks and Rumanians. Ruth Fry received a desperate plea for coal, without which all other aid was wasted because people died of hypothermia. On 30 October 1919 Rose Morgan French wrote to her friend Dr Ella Scarlett Synge describing her impressions of the situation and the confusion of relief work:

> I thought Wien was badly off, but Budapest is far worse ... [Relief] would be distributed justly and quickly without all the 'red tape' that seems to be necessary with all the Food Missions that are here now. English, Italian and two American, with dozens of men in khaki rolling round in Autos, but nothing being distributed ... children starving and freezing. Only *paper* clothing to be had. Do ... send out more cotton diaper cloth, nothing here but waste paper, which makes the poor babies' skin very sore. (FWVRC Box 5.6.3)

Babies' sufferings caused great concern and on 27 February 1920, Julie Eve Vajkai, who pioneered 'workschools' which were seen as models for SCF work in Asia and Africa, prepared a Report on Maternity and Infant Care showing that babies' average birth-weight was 1 to 3.5 kilos whereas pre-war it had been 3.5 to 5 kilos. Nursing mothers got one-third the amount of nourishment needed. Since 1916 Hungary had been entirely without children's boots and in 1920 it was calculated that 76,000 children in Budapest needed them, not counting the children of refugees and evicted people in the capital. Six months before the Armistice, the supply of lint for bandages gave out. People died from decubitis. In the State Lying-in Hospital in Budapest there was an entire absence of bed linen; when mothers delivered, others took their place on the same mattress, 'soiled with blood and effete matter – there was no alternative'. The reasons for this suffering were stated by M.W. Fodor of the *Manchester Guardian*, a Friend working in Budapest who wrote on 7 March 1920:

> The hatred of nations continues with unabated vigour; class hatred is intensified; social differences cross the path of national interests. Though the agony of mass-slaughter has ceased, the killing of the innocent still goes on. (FWVRC Box 5.6.3)

By January 1920 the Rumanian Army had plundered the occupied territory of everything it contained, including the meagre supplies of pharmaceutical material. Rumania was also in dire need: it lacked cattle, tools and seed, so there was no spring sowing; peoples' clothing was 'indescribable'. By February 1920, following the fall of Bela Kun's Communist regime, under which Rosika Schwimmer, leader of Hungarian feminists, nearly starved and had to be smuggled to Vienna, Budapest was nothing but 'waste spaces and dilapidated hovels'. The city was seething with revolutionist and militarist feeling; soldiers and gendarmes were everywhere, political posters on walls and in shop windows. Presaging the repressive regimes of the later twentieth century and the Holocaust, there were pogroms against the Galician Jews who were held responsible for the conditions; Jews were boycotted in business, schools, Universities and higher professions. Women were not allowed to return to the University, youths and women were flogged and people imprisoned without trial. There is no single term that adequately covers all these actions, which include anti-semitism and misogyny, but while akin to gender violence are broader and more deeply and widely rooted.

A plea was made for Friends to undertake relief work in Budapest with food and clothing distribution to be done through Vilma Glücklich, a friend of Schwimmer and member of WIL, whom Kathleen Courtney recommended as a 'pacifist and able, active woman, expert in administration', but warned she was unlikely to be liked by the authorities since she was 'of international views, believing in political freedom and in free speech'. In 1923 Vilma Glücklich submitted the WILPF Resolution, drafted by Emily Leaf, the Referent on Economic Questions, to appeal to the League of Nations to introduce Free Trade as a means of alleviating the bad effects of dividing the continent into more numerous separate units. It was carried unanimously and sent to the League. Free trade was impossible while the former Allies maintained severe restrictions against trade with their erstwhile enemies – a factor that facilitated the subsequent world-wide depression.

Quaker work in Hungary was connected with TB and its prevention. The Bureau of War Assistance's report published 30 September 1915, had put the number of war orphans in Hungary at 500,000 and so many were suffering from TB that Sanatoria with 5,000 beds were considered necessary. In October 1918, through the disaster of the Austro-Hungarian front, the number of war orphans had increased, but Hungary lost through foreign occupation not only all its institutions for tuberculosis invalids but also the bathing places where treatment was given. Prevention of TB included providing meals and creating clean buildings and bodies. At the Gomutiza School free dinners were distributed to about 50 children who arrived in the early morning and were fetched away in the evening. On arrival their dirty rags were removed and the vermin-bitten children washed and given a hot meal. Often barefoot, their feet were bandaged because of sores.

Adoptions

The idea of 'adopting' children originated in the English branch of the SCF in autumn 1920 and the Friends were given a grant to cover the adoption of 1,200 children of many nationalities. Francesca Wilson in January 1921 nominated Serbian and Macedonian children. From her Anglo-Serbian Children's Hospital in Belgrade Dr Katharine MacPhail made appeals; so did Flora Sandes, also in Serbia. Evelina Haverfield established a Fund for Serbian Children, the Honorary Secretary of which was Nina Boyle, later a member of the SCF council. Flora Sandes appealed on behalf of Haverfield's

SCF-linked work. Adopters asked for Russian, Ukrainian, Italian and Polish children but these were more difficult to arrange. In February 1919 Grace Vulliamy went to help relief work in Czechoslovakia and then to Poland, representing the British Committee for Relief. She liaised with the SCF about the dispatch of aid materials, grants and adopted children including some in refugee camps. During 1919 SCF sought Miss Vulliamy's advice on finding a suitable person in whose name an appeal might go out, because the writer and Miss Jebb were not well-known enough.

However, adoptions raised certain difficulties. Misunderstandings arose over the condition of children sent to the UK because they appeared quite as healthy as the average English child. In the Greycoat School the Mistress organising the scheme became unhappy about their adoptee, Ernst; having received his photo she considered he did not look starving. SCF wanted the Friends' help with suggestions in dealing with the increasing number of subscribers who had the same doubts. Archibald Jamieson, Press Secretary of the SCF, thought that SCF advertisements exaggerated the situation:

> the problem of food relief for the children is precisely the same as in our own Cities ... with the addition of the privation of the Middle Classes which is so pathetic in Vienna. (FWVRC Box 4.3.7)

This is partly true. Sylvia Pankhurst had advertised in *The Times* as early as 25 August 1914 for help for babies in danger of dying for lack of milk and in 1917 food shortages in Britain became so critical that children were dying from the effects of severe malnutrition (van Emden and Humphries 2003: 159, 189). At one point only four days' supply of sugar remained; wheat and flour would only last another two months. However, food shortages occurred in Austria, Germany and Hungary earlier in the war and generally, more people, especially women and babies, were suffering more acutely. It is also clear that Austrians and Hungarians were not distinguished as different nationalities from Germans and this may have increased the prejudice of British adopters. Repatriation of these children was not without some problems. For example in 1921 the return of 1,500 Austrian and Hungarian children, some of whom were orphans, was accompanied by rumours that they were not going back to proper homes and that in Hungary many of them might have to sleep in railway vans; the anonymous writer of this letter was, however, 'perfectly certain that the Friends will not allow this'.

However, most children were sponsored while remaining in their own homes. The SCF called for subscriptions of five guineas to cover the cost of food parcels that provided meals once a day for a year. Parcels consisted of small quantities of sweetened milk, flour, fat, sugar, cocoa, and one cake of soap. This supplemented the state-controlled rations of one 2½ lb. loaf, ¼ lb. sugar, 1 lb. flour per person per week. Children were visited and removed from the list when the need was no longer there. This also checked that ill or elderly family members did not receive the rations.

By February 1922, Friends thought their relief work in Vienna would close in May. This was partly because SCF was having problems with fund raising; the Friends' Home Committee thought too much was going to Austria in view of the fact that Russia's need was desperate and Austria was beginning to recover. Quaker by convincement Arthur Salter, Head of the Economic Section of the League Secretariat (Pedersen 2007: 32), 'hammered out the Austrian and Hungarian recovery plans'. However, as Brayshaw says (1921: 330), the main reason for the decision to close Austrian relief was a developing split in Quaker thinking. Some thought 'Imperative as might be the call for material relief and repair, far greater would be the outcome of spiritual healing.' Carl Heath, a Quaker member of UDC and Secretary of the National Peace Council who had been in relief from the first week of the war, referred at the All Friends Conference to the belief that although relief work would end, there remained the need for a 'ministry of reconciliation of profound international import'. The sense of despair in earlier documents is absent from Carl and Effice Heath's Report on their visit to Germany in March 1922. They were now concerned with the need for Quaker ideas to take root. There was still practical work in the TB hospital and Student Feeding relief, but production of Quaker literature, provision of speakers, and selection of students for Woodbrooke was to be the focus. He said in attempting to answer the question, why did Quakers 'do this thing', there was a call to permanent international service. He therefore proposed the establishment of Quaker Embassies; Ted Harvey was Chairman and co-founder (Greenwood 1975: 209). Nonetheless, as Mary

Ann Rawson, an independent evangelical, said (Van Drenthe 1999: 29): 'Prayer without action is mockery' and Hilda Clark wrote (Pye 1956: 52): 'Those who can justify it to their own consciences to eat the food and use the fuel needed by others without helping their material needs in such an emergency, must remember that if they are being maintained by the Committee, they must also justify it to the Committee.' In fact, during February, Hilda told Edith Pye that factories were likely to close and people were more despairing now than at any time she had known them. Despite this, on 1 February 1922, the Friends' Relief Committee handed over its remaining relief work in Germany to the care of the Friends' Council for International Service (CIS), which potentially fulfilled the need for more permanent service to disseminate Quaker beliefs and ideals, but also continued with some relief work. The SCF forwarded £900 for the Vienna Mittelstand adoption scheme and in June 1923 SCF was waiting for the results of the latest appeal for funds for Austria. But the scheme finally closed in April 1924 although relief continued in other forms until 1927.

Brayshaw (1921: 338) states that the FWVRC, with about 1,070 English and 780 American workers, showed about £1,500,000 through the London books, far more funds administered abroad and probably millions of civilian victims relieved in nine countries of Europe from 1914 to 1924 with more people helped in Germany than elsewhere. American Friends organized food for 1,000,000 children with funds largely provided from other sources, and English Friends fed 30,000 in Cologne. The Salvation Army also helped. As Greenwood says (1978: 210), none of the great voluntary agencies except SCF and the Red Cross were yet in existence to share the burden.

Marrus (1985: 82) points out the paradoxical nature of their work's results: by keeping so many refugees alive in this critical period, private philanthropy helped to maintain the pressure of refugee crises and to 'elicit a response from governments and from the international agencies set in place after the First World War'. Although as Pedersen writes (2007: 34): 'voluntary organizations with strong records of practical work had easy access to key League officials who sometimes used their ties to wealthy private philanthropies to compensate for member states' parsimony', League frugality, and the supremacy of national interests perpetuated the crisis.

CHAPTER 9

And Now will the Refugees Please Go Home: Women and Children First?

The Peace Conference at Versailles

At the Armistice all hopes rested on President Wilson as the saviour of democracy and the bringer of permanent peace, which was not a new hypothesis invented by him, but the title of a book on the concept published by Immanuel Kant in 1795. Wilson had been presented with the first usable proposals for an arbitration body and the fundamentals of peace settlements by Rosika Schwimmer, a Hungarian suffragist, on the outbreak of war, and this was followed by Julia Grace Wales's Wisconsin Plan for *Continuous Mediation without Armistice*. Now, during the Armistice, the victorious nations gathered in Versailles to draw up the terms of the peace treaties to be enacted between themselves and the defeated nations to put the notion into effect. Maynard Keynes, the economist member of the Bloomsbury Group, was in Paris as representative of the Treasury, where he was joined at the Hotel Majestic by Francis Birrell. Birrell (Sussex: Birrell Papers. File 1.31) described Keynes as 'almost a corpse, having contracted violent gastric influenza from the German financiers at Trèves' following the discussions there in January and February. In *Economic Consequences of the Peace*, Keynes (1919: IV.1) articulated what feminists and Quakers expressed at their Conferences: the Peacemakers were not concerned with the future well-being of Europe but looked 'to the future enfeeblement of a strong and dangerous enemy, to revenge, and to the shifting by the victors of their unbearable financial burdens on to the shoulders of the defeated'. Sir Eric Geddes said at Cambridge on 9 December 1918, Germany should be squeezed like a lemon until the 'pips squeaked' (Sharp 1991: 205; Swanwick 1924: 58). However, a special Commission, with Woodrow Wilson its

President, was established to determine the Articles of the League Covenant which formed the first part of each Treaty. Not complying with it implied breaking the relevant Treaty; in this way Wilson hoped peace was ensured. As Manson confirms (Manson 2007: 8): 'British study groups with which Leonard Woolf had closely worked influenced the League Covenant as it took shape'. Although facts in Part I of the Covenant were taken from his *International Government*, as Glendinning notes (2006: 484), Woolf acknowledged its influence was peripheral on the League's establishment and 'on the political novices of the Labour Party'.

Nonetheless, although significantly altered, much of the final Covenant text was British in origin but without Lord Phillimore, General Smuts and Lord Robert Cecil it would not have emerged. Cecil, a founder of LNU, campaigned tirelessly on behalf of the League; he had appointed Phillimore to head a Commission examining a League proposal in 1917. Phillimore served on the Friends Emergency Committee but apparently had not adopted their attitude towards enemies; the Commission turned the League into one that excluded Germany. Jan Smuts (Riddell 1935: 17–18), whose plan for a League of Nations was given to Lloyd George who passed it to President Wilson, argued for magnanimity at Versailles because like his friend Emily Hobhouse, he thought the peace terms too stringent.

Since the refugee crisis was an international problem, various concerned people went to Paris to try to obtain assistance from peace conference delegates and others. Robert Seton-Watson was joined on 15 February 1919 by his wife May as official SRF representative, to discuss further relief with the French, Americans and the Serbs who were also at the Conference. Lady Muriel Paget, a SRF Committee member, was also at Versailles. She had organized the London Kitchens for Belgian refugees and also relief missions to Czechoslovakia, for which Grace Vulliamy later led the training of local paediatric nurses and social workers. Lady Paget was a dynamic woman who expressed her views without deference to gender expectations. From Versailles, Harold Nicolson (1973: 133) wrote to his wife Vita Sackville-West: 'her energy is terrifying. She sends Prime Ministers scuttling at her behests.' Lord Weardale, a member of the FTFC who became President of the SCF from the end of 1919 until 1925 when the Duke of Atholl took his place, complained: 'Lady Muriel Paget ... makes commitments about which she has never consulted anybody' (SCF.EJ73).

However, a major flaw at Versailles was that women were excluded from negotiations and not included the draft Covenant; children and refugees were also ignored. The Central Committee of the French Suffrage Union arranged a conference in Paris from 10 to 16 February 1919 to which Allied delegates were invited, to attempt to rectify the situation. Rupp (1997: 211) concisely explains how on this occasion French patriotism and need to be close to the apparent seat of international power over-rode women's solidarity; calling a conference in Paris automatically excluded delegates from defeated countries. In addition, the League ignored the refugee crisis and the effects of the blockade. The majority of refugees were always women and children, so they were doubly omitted from consideration by the 'peacemakers'. According to a Channel 4 website in Britain, official German statistics attributed nearly 763,000 wartime deaths in Germany to starvation caused by the blockade.

As we have seen, women were the first to suffer in the war supposedly being fought for their defence and for democracy, which should provide equal access to power, representation and freedom for all persons. However, Swanwick (1935: 138) had learned as a young girl that the ineradicable root of the gender differences was that 'A boy might be a person, but not a girl' and during the 1920s, feminists in England and Canada had to fight for women's legal inclusion in the term. At Versailles, women's first task was to remind the peacemakers that pre-war values had begun to shift and some countries had moved towards a different definition of democracy by enfranchising them. They sent deputations to Wilson. One, led by Lady Aberdeen, who knew Wilson, was made up of feminists well known internationally and included Jane Brigode, Margery Fry and Avril de Sainte-Croix. Their resolutions covered (Whittick 1979: 71) 'the moral, political and educational aspects of women's life' and included references to children. This extended the boundaries of women's concern for women and children onto the new international platform of the League. Wilson promised action. However, he was struggling against the secret intrigues of Clemenceau and Lloyd George and the emerging antagonism of his own Senate over many important matters, and was strongly opposed in his wish to see women represented. Together with Vittorio Emanuele Orlando of Italy, these men formed the Council of Four.

The deputations were successful in that Article 7 (3) of the Covenant promised all League positions would be open equally to men and women but this apparently democratic guarantee was as illusory as most official assurances of equality (Brittain 1928: 115), partly because it depended on individual nations' adherence to the proposal. The number of women in an international body such as the League (and also the United Nations) therefore acts as a marker of women's position in such nations. However, the deputations' request that the League should suppress the traffic in women and children and licensed prostitution resulted in Article 23 which stated that:

> Members of the League will entrust the League with the general supervision over the execution of agreements with regard to the traffic in women and children, and the traffic in opium and other dangerous drugs.

This was the first charter ever framed for the regulation of social questions of common interest to every nation although connecting drugs and women in the same sentence indicates men's commodification of women and implies links between the trades. Nonetheless, Article 23 gave activists opportunity to raise matters accepted as part of their concern for other women, such as prostitution.

The League of Nations at Geneva

Catherine Marshall was concerned with the political processes of the League as a means of ensuring permanent peace. She had personal experience of Belgian refugees living in her Cumberland home, and as Alberti says (1989: 194), she also understood the refugee problem in its political context. After visiting Germany and Switzerland, she arrived in Paris while the Peace Conference and Treaty Commissions were still operating. The League operated through a complex Commission and Committee System which functioned during the Talks as did the Secretariat, which, together with the Council and the Assembly, carried out League functions. Sir Eric Drummond, the first Secretary-General of the League, had as his principal assistant Philip Noel-Baker, who from 1922 to 1924 was private secretary to the British representative on the Council and Assembly, thereby forming an important contact for Quakers and other internationalists. The League was not only concerned with matters directly relating to peace, such as disarmament, but broader social issues on which international agreement was necessary. It was in these areas that women could apply pressure more successfully. In September 1920, after the Secretariat's move from London to Geneva, Catherine Marshall joined Emily Greene Balch in Geneva and asked the Secretariat to show her the procedure rules, the first person to do so; she pointed out that they were undemocratic and changes were made.

The First Assembly at last took place in November 1920, and the issue of the white slave trade had been prepared in advance ready for discussion. Catherine Marshall undertook formal and informal talks with delegates, the Secretariat and the press and after seeing the League operate she told WILPF members 'The Assembly is where our hope lies. Get the small nations to assert themselves.' Lloyd George invited her to Chequers as a result of her League work in the 1920s. She tried to persuade WILPF to work closely with the League and in 1923 was an envoy of WIL to interview statesmen and get them to modify the reparations; France refused and sent troops to the Ruhr, thereby creating more refugees.

On 11 November 1920 Mary Sheepshanks went to Geneva as FTFC representative to try to secure the reception of a deputation by an Assembly representative. The following day she saw M. Layton and Mr Ibbotson James, the two secretaries of the Economic Section; as a result of her discussions with them she became convinced that more influential FTFC representatives should canvass delegates and urged that they should come out during the second and third weeks of the Assembly, or that she should be recalled. FTFC was urging investigation of economic and financial needs of the world as a whole and she pointed out that delegates were willing to see people and could be swayed, citing as an example that the Anti-slavery Society had influenced the Mandates Commission. Mary Sheepshanks spent several days in preliminary inquiries, seeing officials in charge of the press and publicity departments, securing documents and lists of delegates.

By this time, action by the Assembly on matters in which FTFC was interested had been decided. She then sent copies of the FTFC resolutions in French and English to all the delegates except some of the English and French as it had been said in London that it would be useless to approach them; neither of these Powers was a strong supporter of the League. Even Labour governments did not fully support the League, a failure of the Left in Britain which further elucidates the League's weakness. Vellacott says (1993: 41), it would become clear later that the participating governments saw the reality of international relations and power as located elsewhere, but the smaller nations, particularly the Scandinavians, fully supported the League. Mary Sheepshanks did, however, send a copy of the FTFC resolutions to Léon Bourgeois whom Birrell had referred to as the 'dear sponsor' of the FWVRC in France. She stayed for nearly six weeks, keeping records of speeches and discussions on the economic and financial duties of the League according to Article 23. These revealed that language handicaps and fears of Bolshevism were dampening international co-operation. She also discovered that the British Government was opposed to the formation of an international economic council.

Nevertheless, being in Geneva enabled Mary Sheepshanks to network. She saw the Swedish delegate Jonas Lofgren and his wife several times. He told her that FTFC's task was to convert British public opinion to an awareness of the continuing suffering and the realities of the economic situation. Mrs Lofgren, who was working with Swedish Liberal Women to start a Fight the Famine campaign in Sweden, later came to England and saw Emily Leaf, a prominent British suffragist, who had been immersed in relief work during the war. Mary also met Mrs Anna Bugge Wicksell, the Norwegian feminist, now a substitute-delegate. Mrs Wicksell told Mary that the economic situation was incessantly discussed in private, but everyone was afraid of a contentious debate if it were raised in public; therefore public debate could not help matters whereas action by commission or groups could. Anna Wicksell had been elected onto the Board of IWSA at their Geneva Congress in June, when Gulielma Crosfield, Helena Swanwick, Viscountess Astor MP, Edith Lyttelton and Kathleen Courtney were all present. Alberti (1989: 213) describes Courtney as 'the most skilful, persistent practitioner in group working towards political goals'. She focused on international affairs through WILPF and the IWSA. Confirming early association between IWSA and the League, its Librarian, Florence Wilson, was present at the IWSA Congress as Secretariat representative. Although a relative of Woodrow Wilson, this did not subsequently save her from losing her job to a man. Congress discussed the needs of the world's starving children and expressed concern about the forced deportation of Armenian women and children from Turkey (Whittick 1979: 76). Their resolutions on these issues ultimately bore fruit in that the Fifth Committee dealt with child welfare and the League Commission on Deported Women and Children in Asia Minor ('the Commission') was formed in 1921 to rescue the Armenians.

Women delegates and the Fifth Committee

Some countries, but not Britain, set up permanent delegations. A very few British women were briefly positioned in potentially powerful positions as government appointed substitute-delegates. No British woman was ever selected as a full delegate, although Swanwick was promoted to full delegate for two days during the 1929 Assembly when four delegates had left. Nonetheless, women delegates of most nations were closely connected with the women's movement and concerned with the effects of war on women and children. Most subscribed to the view of women's 'natural' caring qualities which they, and clearly men also, felt should be used for the benefit of others, even if, like Swanwick, they preferred to be involved in matters of arbitration and disarmament.

A constant concern was that female refugees turned to prostitution as a survival strategy, therefore this was one of the ways that refugees were brought to the attention of the international community. Prostitution, the white slave trade, subsequently renamed the traffic in women and children, and refugees were seen as closely linked and were dealt with by the Fifth Committee which Swanwick described as a low status 'hotch-potch' Committee. In Geneva it was known as the 'Sentimental Commission' because its resolutions were not backed by sufficient practical and financial understandings, confirming Swanwick's opinion that women needed the type of formal and informal education men acquired in order to raise their status. In addition, as Rachel Crowdy said (Bristol: Crowdy papers: DM941/105), women needed to have raised status in national diplomatic services in order to prevent relegation to social reform or intellectual cooperation.

Such patriarchal valuations of humanitarian work, which women internalized, were based on a circular process making them hard to break: the status was low because the issues were seen as women's matters, therefore women were allocated to it, perpetuating the low status. Vera Brittain was among those trying to convince men that the status of women was an international question, using the traffic in women as one example (Miller 1994: 222). Changing attitudes was therefore vital. According to contemporary thinking, women acted through instinct and emotion, not rational thought. However, it was beginning to be recognized that altruistic regard for others as a principle of action was a basic human instinct and therefore an inevitable practice for men as well as women. This meant that, as Hamilton explained (1953: 63–5), being part of a caring community is 'man's prime instrument of advance within the confines of the given tribe or nation and *in the relation between nations*' [my italics]. By attempting to confine humanitarianism to women's 'sphere' and thereby restrict them to undervalued social issues, the League founders were limiting their own possibilities of advance towards democratic and humanitarian internationalism, and to peace. The difference is exemplified through the experience of Kathleen Courtney, who, in the 1920s, sat in Geneva (Fletcher 1989: 129), month after month, following the 'stultifying convolutions' of the Preparatory Disarmament Commission, listening as men got bogged down in comparing sizes of different warships. Courtney recognized that security in Europe was vital to avoid war and was concerned with war's effects on individuals, refugees in particular. As Crowdy (1927: 53) had pointed out: 'you may disarm the world ... but unless you introduce better economic conditions, better social conditions and better health conditions into the world, you will not be able to maintain peace even if you obtain it'. Better social conditions included abolition of the regulation of prostitution and elimination of the traffic in women and children.

Ironically, the Fifth Committee, to which women were generally allocated, was the area in which the League had most success. It dealt with social and humanitarian questions such as illegitimacy and the rights of the child; refugee related matters were first raised there. Rachel Eleanor Crowdy, appointed DBE in 1919, who had a particular interest in regulated prostitution, was appointed head of two administrative sections of the League Secretariat, the Social Questions Section, which dealt with the white slave trade, and the Opium Traffic Section; these supported the Fifth Committee's work. She was a member of a League team sent to Poland to investigate the typhus epidemic and was given responsibility on opium because she had taken an apothecaries' diploma and run two dispensaries. Edith Pye also worked on drugs, her WILPF report in 1927 arousing considerable interest in the press and the League whose decisions were influenced by WILPF resolutions. Crowdy's friend Dame Katharine Furze served as an Assessor for Child Welfare on this Committee, as did Eleanor Rathbone and Eglantyne Jebb.

In the early 1920s British women substitute-delegates were constitutional suffragists; the exception was the anti-suffragist Katharine Stewart-Ramsay, Duchess of Atholl, appointed in 1925 when the Duke was President of SCF and Stanley Baldwin was Prime Minister. Swanwick (1935: 453) said Geneva called her 'la Duchesse de Not at all', and that she obstructed the work of the League in the name of the British Empire. Dame Edith Lyttelton was appointed in 1923, 1926–8 and 1931, also under Baldwin. She received the Grand Cross of the Order of the British Empire for her work which promoted education about the League as a means to future peace (Storr in Spence et al. 2009: 173). Women served on some of the Temporary and Permanent Advisory Commissions, including the League's Advisory Commission on Traffic in Women and Children but normally much in the minority compared to men. The Council for Representation of Women in the League of Nations put forward names of suitable women for various posts, but the international political scene was heavily defended against women's presence, not by a glass ceiling, but a concrete bunker of male prejudice and their idea that it was more important to be equitable with the men of other nations than with women; the position of 'token' woman, when granted, was shared between the nations. The Covenant provided for an international commission of medical experts but feminists had to persuade the Council to provide for the appointment of at least one woman.

The first British woman to be selected as a substitute-delegate to the League was appointed by Lloyd George to the Third Assembly in 1922. Winifred Coombe Tennant, an NUWSS executive member, President of Neath Women's Suffrage Society, had been a leading campaigner for Lloyd George's Coalition Liberals at the general election of 1918. She was appointed to the Fifth Committee and then selected as Rapporteur on the Traffic in Women at the Third Assembly. The Rapporteurs' reports were presented to the Assembly for its discussion; copies, including that of Avril de Ste Croix, delegate of the principal international women's associations to the Advisory Committee on Traffic in 1923, were sent to Alison Neilans at the Association for Moral and Social Hygiene, the British body concerned with prostitution, about which Rachel Crowdy was particularly concerned. Regulated prostitution was seen as encouraging the traffic in women. During the war the French government had opened two brothels just behind her flat in Boulogne, one for British Officers, the other for 'Tommies', Indians and Chinese. One night she counted between 700 and 800 men going into the three houses for 50 girls. Her initial reaction was to move, but she decided to stay, learn what she could and do whatever possible to end the intolerable state of affairs. At the League, male delegates were unwilling to accept that the regulation of prostitution, which they saw as necessary for men's satisfaction and well-being, encouraged the traffic in women, which was deplored. According to the *Bulletin Abolitionniste* (March–April 1925: 14–15), in July 1921 the League of Nations was exhibiting 'the old resistance in refusal to study the causes of traffic'. They wanted to protect the legalized system but suppress abuses.

The white slave trade and prostitution were already accepted as women's concerns, and they were now *expected* to know about refugees and political matters such as minorities and mandates. Members of the Mandates Commission included Marquis Theodoli, M. Rappard, and M. Orts, a Belgian – all believers in the League. Sir Frederick Lugard was a member of the League's Permanent Slavery Committee and of the International Labour Office's committee of experts on native labour (Bell 1947: 292–303). At the end of July 1923, he and Flora went to Geneva for the Mandates

Commission. Sessions lasted from 10 a.m. to 1 p.m., and 3.30 p.m. to 7 or 8 p.m., and between sessions she talked with delegates. She saw the League as 'a great educational force' and thought it was important to keep it alive and develop it. Sir Frederick went to Geneva each year, but Flora did not go again until 1925. In September the following year she had a serious heart attack and on 25 January 1929, she died aged 76.

Mandates were established under Article 22. Under them, the United Kingdom became responsible for Iraq, Palestine and other territories; France and Belgium were among the other administrating countries. For British women this meant that their imperial concerns had widened to international ones, a situation tacitly acknowledged by, and which applied to, all League member countries since it gave all delegates the right to raise matters concerning two nations other than their own – the mandatory power, and the mandated country. Feminists requested the League to require of members that abolition of regulated brothels should be a condition before they were granted the mandate of any 'undeveloped' nation. The Mandates Commission, the League's conventions on slavery and the traffic in women were based on the principles of fundamental human rights for the individual. However, mandates perpetuated racial hierarchy and power. They therefore doubled women's gender subordination, and raised spectres of prostitution, war and more refugees. The Fifth Committee required the Assembly to recognize that special attention should be given to women's situation in these circumstances.

Working through the Fifth Committee, WILPF drew the First Assembly's attention to the treatment of minorities such as the Armenians; this drew into the issue the majority ethnic group of Turks; Turkey was not a League member. In connection with this, two of WILPF's Memoranda, one on economic sanctions and another on violence and terror were printed in the League of Nations Official Journal and issued during the Assembly. America was offered but refused the mandate of Armenia, which would have given Armenians some protection.

Armenia and the Commission on Deported Women and Children in Asia Minor

The League (Toynbee 1925: 35) was 'primarily designed as an organization for dealing with certain permanent international problems which would not cease to exist if and when the problems of the peace settlement received their final solution'. The Armenian problem fitted into this category, but it was necessary to get the League to acknowledge this, however tacitly. As a result of various wars from the thirteenth century onwards, Armenia had lost most of its territory. Between 1894 and 1897 it is estimated that between 80,000 and 300,000 Armenians were killed in Ottoman pogroms and massacres. The Friends Rendel and Helen Harris had cared for Armenian orphans since the 1890s. Alice Stone Blackwell, the American suffragist, founded the Friends of Armenia in 1893 and this was central to launching the Americans' international human rights movement. Ann Mary Burgess, a trained nurse of Wisbech, Cambridgeshire, left England in August 1888 for the Mission hospital in Constantinople, then a Turkish city, and the London Meeting for Sufferings somewhat tardily established an Armenian Relief Committee in 1893 which began aid to the Armenians in 1899. Miss Burgess, who became a Quaker by convincement in 1901, over many years witnessed the sufferings of the Armenians. On 24 April 1915, in a chilling forerunner to the Nazi Night of the Long Knives, approximately 250 of the Armenian intelligentsia were rounded up and never seen again. Those who might have been able to make effective protest were thereby permanently silenced and this was to have serious consequences in the 1920s when the League of Nations discussed the Armenian crisis. From 29 May 1915, having conscripted, disarmed and removed the men (Reid in Hovannisian 1992: 42), Turkish soldiers and bands of Kurdish brigands robbed, raped and killed convoys of starving Armenian women and children and drove them at gunpoint through the hot, barren deserts of Syria and Arabia or into the marsh near the river Euphrates to extermination. Following these massacres, the American Near East Fund and the Armenian Refugees (Lord Mayor's) Fund were founded; Quakers were involved with the latter. Until America entered the war in June 1917, the American Embassy gave help to Allied nationals such as Miss Burgess. The Minutes of the Fifth Committee at the Eighth Assembly (Macartney 1930: 123–4) recorded that some of the younger Armenian children had been placed in Moslem homes as a means of saving them from starvation during the death marches of 1915 and 1916, although it was recognized that girls might be sold in marriage or boys used as slaves. At the Armistice, the Allied troops who occupied parts of Turkey released a huge number of Armenian women and children from harems; approximately 90,819 orphans were reclaimed from about six other countries.

Armenians were a religious minority, Christians in the Muslim world of Turkey. The Armenian problem was thought to be one of minorities, not religion but according to Sir Willoughby Dickinson at the 1929 WIL Conference in London, religious and racial minorities in Eastern Europe were synonymous. Certainly, each fuelled the other.

Assuming that Turkey wanted to become a League member, and recognizing that in the longer term the refugee problem needed political solutions, WILPF suggested good behaviour towards minorities should be a pre-requisite of League membership (Bussey & Tims 1980: 36–7). A clause was inserted in the first peace treaty with Turkey binding it to give all assistance to the League Commission to liberate the remaining victims. The Treaty was never ratified. Armenia applied for League membership in 1920, but this was refused. Undoubtedly due to oil at Baku, President Wilson vacillated over where its boundaries should be drawn so, as Innes says (1931: 32), its security was too precarious to be under-written by the League. According to Clara Zetkin (1922), oil was a source of antagonism between America and England. America controlled about 70 per cent of the oil production but England wanted the Baku and Mesopotamian oil wells. This, together with Wilson's ill health and political problems in America, over-complicated the drawing of new Armenian boundaries.

Henni Forchhammer, Vice-President of ICW and a member of WILPF, was largely responsible for the establishment of the League Commission (Bussey & Tims 1980: 37). Lous (2003: 8–9) records that Forchhammer used her connections with politically minded women and politicians to find out about the Armenian women before she attended the First Assembly in 1920 and discovered there were still at least 30,000 Armenians in Turkish harems or with Arab nomads. Forchhammer, who was acting as technical adviser for the Danish Government, and was appointed to the Second (Health) Committee, spoke on the traffic in women and children and asked the Assembly, through the Fifth Committee, for a committee of inquiry into the wholesale deportation of women and children from Asia Minor by the Turks during the war, and now held in Turkey; their possible ill treatment and present condition should also be investigated. Turkey, through its supporters expressed strong opposition to the establishment of the Commission which was nonetheless constituted by the Assembly in February 1921.

The Rumanian suffragist Mlle Hélène Vacaresco, who became interested in the League during the War through Lord Robert Cecil, according to Northcroft (1923: 2, 9) was deeply interested 'in the question of the deported women and children from Asia Minor' and campaigned on their behalf. Vacaresco, a poet and member of the Rumanian National Council of Women was secretary to the Rumanian delegation in 1920 and delegate to the Second Assembly from 1921. Her speech in the Assembly was 'a memorable affair' and made such an impact on the Turks that they effectively blacklisted her. An internet article refuting the massacres accuses her of 'Arabian Night stories' influenced by the Armenian and Greek 'exaggeration of violence' (Holdwater Tall Armenian Tale: n.d).

The first appointee of the League of Nations as Commissioner for the rescue of women and girls from Moslem harems was Dr Kennedy, the Near East Administrator of the Lord Mayor's Armenian Fund, a Canadian man living in Constantinople. Women Commissioners were Emma Cushman of Constantinople, an American who had lived in Turkey since 1899 and Karen Jeppe, a Danish woman who lived in Aleppo, a Syrian town under French Protectorate. She also had long experience of Armenia and the Near East, having gone out to Urfa in Mesopotamia to help the 'hapless Armenians' at the turn of the century. During the War Jeppe worked in an Armenian orphanage and like Ann Burgess and other missionaries in the area, became ill after witnessing the terrible sufferings of the Armenians from 1915 onwards. She began rescuing Armenians on her own responsibility and was not originally intended as a Commission member; instead a French woman, in favour of the Turks, was appointed. However, friends of Armenians world-wide protested strongly, as a result of which Jeppe was appointed in 1922.

Minorities and population exchange

The Peace Conference had drawn up a series of treaties to protect minorities; refugees as such were not considered; the Covenant was not changed to include refugees, as it had been to include women. The League's international obligations to protect the rights of minorities were the responsibility of the Minorities Commission, served by the Minorities Section of the Secretariat, the head of which was the Norwegian Erik Colban (Pedersen 2007: 20), who stated that their pre-eminent goals were political, not humanitarian.

An attempt to solve part of the minority problem was through the compulsory exchange of populations which was agreed by the Grand National Assembly of Turkey and the Greek Government at the Convention of Lausanne on 30 January 1923. The idea is sometimes attributed to Nansen but he told Hilda Clark his sole reason for supporting the proposal was to persuade the Turks to send back the 100,000 male Armenian men kept as hostages by the Turks, but this proved unsuccessful. He thought they were probably all dead. Starting from 1 May 1923, 1,000,000 Greek and 500,000 Bulgarians were forced to leave Turkish territory to go to mainland Greece; these numbers included other nationalities, such as Armenians. Poverty-stricken Greece could not cope with them. An international loan was raised and administered by the League Refugee Settlement Committee – England gave £1,000,000. Voluntary societies like SCF, the Red Cross and the Quakers came to the rescue. The exchange took approximately eight years to complete. Gibbs described it as (1930: 112–14) 'a dreadful episode in modern history, adding one more chapter of human agony to the long martyrdom of helpless peoples who get caught in the wheels of war's destroying chariot'. 80 per cent were destitute women and children.

An Armenian homeland?

The exchange of populations was undertaken because of the concept that there was a native soil to which people belonged. Where could Armenians go? Those who survived the massacres needed a permanent homeland and in May 1918 the Democratic Republic of Armenia was established in the Caucasus, with Yervan (Erivan) its capital. However, as early as 1919, possibly provoked by Armenian paramilitaries, the Turkish nationalists cooperated with the Bolshevik government in attacking the newly proclaimed Armenian republic. In the spring of 1921, more Armenians were driven toward the Mesopotamian desert and down to the Middle East. Armenian resistance was broken by the summer of 1921; the Kars region was occupied by the Turks so reducing the size of Armenia yet again. The number of orphans these conflicts produced is unmatched elsewhere. American missionaries and Near East Relief were allowed to take 110,000 orphans out of Turkey to Greece, Erivan, Syria and Lebanon. In 1922 the Turkish nationalists recognized the Soviet absorption of what remained of Erivan. The Armenians' persecution came to a head that year when hundreds of thousands became refugees, many of whom died after torturous suffering. Armenians were also among those who fled from Smyrna after it was burned in 1922. Immediate aid was needed and it was important to use all available networks. In November 1922, Rachel Crowdy contacted several women with whom she had served during the war. They included Lady Londonderry, an ardent constitutional suffragist, of the Women's Volunteer Reserve until 1915 when she formed the Women's Legion; Helen Charlotte Isabella Gwynne-Vaughan, of the University of London Suffrage Society and Louisa Garrett Anderson. They jointly appealed in *The Times* on 10 November to all women who had served with the forces to send warm clothes to the All British Appeal for the refugees from Asia Minor and Eastern Thrace. There were 600,000 refugees, 80 per cent of whom were women, children and old men, who had fled at night from the burning of Smyrna. Nearly 100 babies were born during the following morning at one of the centres, but neither milk nor clothing was available.

In addition, there was the constant threat of war in these areas. Nansen (1923: 16) warned that with 'the approaching cessation of the American relief work at Constantinople and the passing of that city under Turkish rule', the refugees' position would be rendered 'particularly difficult'. Further, he alarmingly stated there were 40,000 prostitutes in Constantinople. What he meant by 'prostitute' is open to conjecture and might, in this instance, mean any unmarried woman, or those whose clothes were particularly dilapidated. An appeal, in which SCF was concerned, was sent to 'our great and powerful women's organizations [which] are the right channel through which this desperate need could be made known to our countrywomen'.

In June 1923 Catherine Marshall learned that France and Great Britain had consented at the Lausanne Conference to give way to the Turks and stop the Commission's work. The British Section of WILPF charged Miss Rinder to enquire into this with a view to taking 'strong action with the Assembly'. This may have contributed in getting the League to change its collective mind since the work continued, but its vulnerability is indicated.

Quaker aid

In late 1922 Hilda Clark and Kathleen Courtney went to Greece to see if Friends could help. They decided it was possible, but there was too much for voluntary societies to handle. In December Courtney went to Constantinople to see for herself the condition of Armenian refugees. Alice Clark showed her around the infectious disease part of the hospital, empty because it would not admit them. Courtney (IWM. DD. KC4.72) discovered 'a refugee hospital for ordinary illnesses and confinements run entirely by three capable Armenian girls who have been trained in a hospital in Constantinople' but it had 'hardly got the bare necessities'. On her journey from Athens to Patras on New Year's Eve, Courtney thought the Turks were:

> determined to exterminate the Christians in Asia Minor and inflict a blow on the Greeks at one and the same time. So they have kept the able bodied men in Anatolia and will do them to death quickly or slowly … and have sent the aged, the women and young children to Greece in the hope that they will starve themselves and bring starvation to the Greek population.

This was a form of genocide. Lang (1970: 236) asks whether the use of the term is applicable, since it was not invented by Lemkin until 1944. However, if regarded as a translation of the Swedish word 'folkmord', used by the Swedish Social Democrat Prime Minister Hjalmar Branting, Nobel Peace Prize winner in 1921, then there is no anachronism. It is the only way of describing the enormity of the crimes perpetrated upon these people and even then does not grasp at the cruelty inflicted on women and children, some of which was recorded in evidence presented to Viscount Grey of Fallodon in 1916.

In February 1923, Dr Haigh and Dr Gauthier, Commissioners for League of Nations Epidemics Commission, advised Courtney and Clark to try to get a few suitable people to go out for personal work in Macedonia under the Friends' auspices, with a view to offering to administer the credits the League was trying to obtain for that district. Credit for reconstruction purposes in Greece would probably be granted but not likely to be in time for the spring sowing. Kathleen Courtney thought if something could be done immediately it would prepare the way for a League effort and be an opening for the Quakers' international service rather than relief in the ordinary sense of the word. She said the British Committee, probably meaning the Athens committee, had refused the help offered at the start. She wrote (Pye 1956: 94): 'Everyone is so callous about the refugees. I don't think anyone cares if the money is used well or badly.'

In 1923 and 1924 Clark and Courtney travelled through the Balkans getting an idea of the terrible extent of the need by seeing it repeated, and increasing their knowledge of other countries' politics. Caris Mills, an American formerly of Near East Relief and now of the League Commission, told them how Turkish refugees who had been in the exchange had been dumped in a field and left. They learned that the Peasant Government of Bulgaria had admitted 20,000 Armenian refugees, and more were pouring in but the current Coalition Government now had their own refugees from Yugoslavia and Macedonia to cater for. Hilda Clark learned that what the Bulgarians professed to feel the hardest was that while they were carrying out the Treaty, Greece and Serbia would not do their part regarding the treatment of the Bulgarian minorities and the League did nothing about it. She thought the League should get Serbia and Greece to carry out their obligations to the Bulgars who remained in their countries and not force them to flee. They met Colonel Corfe, Head of the Commission for the Exchange of Populations between Greece and Bulgaria and M. Charron in charge of the settlement loan. They saw camps of refugees from Thrace and Macedonia all along the border and wondered how they were coping. Hilda Clark wanted to organize settlements for these 'repatriated' people. She thought that a committee of Turkish women, formed for their emancipation, would be a good one to work with. On their journey to Salonika from Constantinople, they travelled with population exchange people on the boat *Propontis*. In Constantinople, they met the Quaker suffragist Maud Rowntree and her husband Maurice who were working there. Hilda Clark thought there was 'more of an opening here for the quiet and indirect influence of Friends than in any other country I've been through'. She wrote (Pye 1956: 107): 'All this refugee business done in cold blood makes us just sick with the cruelty of it.' It had caused economic waste and prolonged human suffering.

A joint conference of relief societies was held at the Society of Friends' London HQ, Devonshire House, on 21 October 1924. Present were representatives from the Committee of the Friends of Armenia, the Armenia Association of London, the Lord Mayor's Fund and the SOF, all working with Armenians. Quaker speakers included Rendel Harris, Ann Mary Burgess and Marshall Fox who was associated with re-housing Armenians in Syria. That year he had laid his concern before the Meeting for Sufferings for the 115,000 refugees from Cilicia herded together in large camps, as a result of which *The People of Ararat* was published in 1926. Two resolutions had been forwarded to the League and the United British Committee was formed. Conference delegates spoke of the thousands of Armenians in Cyprus, Palestine, Mesopotamia, Syria, Greece, Bulgaria, and elsewhere. They might also have mentioned Russia, since Plate 9, a photograph from Ruth Fry's album, shows one Armenian man with ten women and children sheltering in Moscow.

A ray of hope, showing the politicians ahead of the Christian churches, was the proposal of a grant for the 'final liquidation' of the Armenian Question, signed by Asquith and Baldwin and presented to Ramsay MacDonald in September. This was to be a grant-in-aid to the Armenian people

Plate 9. Armenian refugees in Moscow. (Photograph courtesy of The Religious Society of Friends in Britain)

towards a settlement proposed by the League which, in 1923, had approved gathering the scattered remnants of Turkish Armenia and settling them in Erivan. France, Italy and Belgium had contributed, but not Britain. Edith Pye suggested a deputation should go to the Government to urge Asquith's proposal be put into effect but Miss Coe of the Lord Mayor's Fund said many of the Armenian refugees did not want to go to Russian Armenia. Was that the right place? Two Armenians present said Armenia was the right place, but Erivan was all right, clearly distinguishing between Armenia and the small province it had become. Dr Harris wanted Britain to make up for her broken promises. Armenians were the brains of Asia. He spoke of two boy refugees at Byblos who immediately built dwellings and then set up an archaeological society. Ann Burgess closed the Conference by speaking on the religious implications of her work.

Fifth Committee work for refugees from 1924

In 1924 the first Labour Government was elected under Ramsay MacDonald and Helena Swanwick was selected that year to be a substitute-delegate. Under Labour, women stood a slightly greater chance of serving elsewhere than the Fifth Committee. The delegation to Geneva's Fifth Assembly that year consisted of Gilbert Murray, Lord Parmoor, Ramsay MacDonald, and Arthur Henderson. Substitute delegates included Lady Murray, Sir Hubert Llewellyn Smith, Sir Cecil Hurst, Charles Roden Buxton, all people with whom Helena Swanwick had worked over the previous ten years. Despite her experience with IWSA and WILPF, she was 'intimidated by the notion of having to find her feet among diplomats and officials', but knew she 'had enough experience of public speaking, committee work and the European situation, together with the constitution and technique of League of Nations' to feel that she should accept.

> I knew that as a woman, I was predestined for the Fifth Committee, a sort of rag-bag of miseries and forlorn hopes ... A woman, it appeared, was assumed to be well-informed about Opium, Refugees, Protection of Children, Relief after Earthquakes, Prison Reform, Municipal Co-operation, Alcoholism, Traffic in Women. I did know something about this last, but not the rest; nor did the delegation. (Swanwick 1935: 383, 385)

Most of these matters can be traced back to women's caring role in the previous century. However, earthquake relief and the opium trade were extensions from their relief work during war. These areas were, as Pedersen (2007: 33) says, 'more genuinely global' than the security and political sections of the League, mitigating its Eurocentrism. America cooperated with the work of the Health, Opium and Social sections. In the early years,

American women at the League included Dr Josephine Baker, Dr Alice Hamilton, Annie Baker, Grace Abbott and Florence Wilson.

Swanwick's preparation consisted of reading 'bulky reports' sent to her prior to going to Geneva. On arrival, Henderson appointed her Rapporteur for Refugees. This horrified her as she knew nothing of the duties, nor did anyone tell her. Rachel Crowdy was imprecise, saying 'It's just what you make it'. Swanwick was invited to meet Nansen and thought it an opportunity to learn from him, which she did, but not about refugees because he was focussing on getting Germany into the League that year. However, amongst other things, the Rapporteur needed to know the past history of the subject, keep track of the discussion, and answer questions. She had to collect amendments and preside over sub-committees which agreed the final resolution to be presented at the next committee. She was to 'reconcile disputants' and present the resolution to the Assembly. Usually Rapporteurs read the reports, which were circulated beforehand, but she took hers as read and made a speech as well. She was not impressed by the behaviour of the male delegates. They were ill-mannered, walked in and out and talked loudly. Swanwick tried to open committees to more women but the hierarchical, essentialist view of the sexes remained entrenched. Nevertheless, this highlights the significance of women's 'caring power' as necessary to their acceptance and role as international citizens.

That year (1924) the Fifth Committee dealt with the inter-related subjects of the repatriation of prisoners of war, Russian and Armenian refugees, and affairs in Asia Minor. Nansen and Albert Thomas, Director of the International Labour Organization (ILO), wanted the work on behalf of Russian and Armenian refugees transferred there. This League agency was closer to the ideals of the talking centres, being based on a foundation created by Sophy Sanger who was in another node of the discussion network. She became a pacifist after hearing Hilda Clark give a lecture at Newnham decrying the Boer War. Sophy's Draft on Labour Affairs was carried by the Second International Labour and Socialist Conference at Berne and was then presented to the Peace Commission, becoming the basis of the ILO which was founded under Part XIII of the Treaty. Women's presence at the League and the ILO as a result of their concern for other women represented a further important political step into the world of high international politics. As Innes said (1931: 130), the technical questions of employment, emigration and settlement were the means by which the refugee problem had to be solved and these were dealt with by the ILO which aimed to improve labour conditions nationally through international action. It had responsibility for social justice, mandates, and minority protection. It also became responsible for refugees, and had a watching brief over attempts to control drug trafficking and the slave trade, and authority to coordinate internationally the control and prevention of disease. It was more democratic than the League itself, having Workers', Employers' and Governments' representatives. Mabel Grujić was Government representative for the Serbs, Croats and Slovenes at the first ILO conference at Washington in 1919; Margaret Bondfield, the first woman Cabinet Minister, was a Workers' representative that year and in 1924 was a Government Delegate; Constance Smith represented the Government at ILO Conferences throughout the 1920s. However, Swanwick's ability to act on the issue of the transfer was constrained by Government instructions. Although she agreed with Nansen and Thomas, she was instructed to oppose them. Later this instruction was modified; so she re-persuaded delegates to abstain instead of opposing. The plan was that Nansen would retain responsibility for political and legal aspects of the problem and expenses be met through a revolving fund of $500,000 set up by the governments. This was agreed to by the Governing Body of the ILO, but their commitment was only to Russians and Armenians on a temporary basis. Swanwick's experiences reveal problems arising from the fact that delegates were appointed by governments whose international policy changed during the Assembly, or as the party in power changed. As ministers, they depended heavily on their departments; but she thought experts would be even less suitable. These difficulties had been discussed by the various talking centres. Swanwick thought the characteristics required as delegates meant that women were better fitted for a common-sense, courageous diplomacy, but they needed to be trained for the task and have equal access to information.

Rescuing Armenians: Karen Jeppe

In 1925 the Assembly attempted to end Karen Jeppe's activities although she had recently started the first Armenian agricultural settlement. Crowdy (Bristol: Crowdy papers: DM941/105) said that Jeppe and her agents constantly ran the risk of death, rescuing the 'Armenian slave children when they went down to the wells at night to get water for their households'. However, she managed to reunite the families of more than 70 per cent of those she rescued. Northcroft (1923: 16–17) wrote: 'As a result of the work of this Commission on Deported Women and Children some thousands of these unfortunate people have been rescued.' *The Friend of Armenia* (1928: 1) reported that the Society of Friends of Armenia also operated in Aleppo and Mrs Altounyan, Chair of the Girls' Hostel, of which she and her family were 'chief founders', also rescued Armenian girls.

Jeppe was warned that the funds to be granted by the League were in jeopardy and the Duchess of Atholl struggled to secure the continuance of her work. The French feared political difficulties with the Turks in Syria because, according to Crowdy, 'Miss Jeppe's energy was not always tempered with diplomacy. No taboo was too sacrosanct for her to break down, no official too high for her to speak her whole mind.' The French Delegate damned Miss Jeppe with lavish praise. He said she was the outstanding woman of her generation; what she had accomplished was formidable. But she should now move on to some greater sphere. Crowdy described how the British delegate had been given strict instructions that the League's budget must be reduced that year; here was a chance of effecting a saving.

> He supported all that had been said of Miss Jeppe's vision and courage, but added that as only between two and three thousand women and children had been rescued … the job was hardly big enough for a League enterprise. Miss Jeppe's answer as she stood before the representatives of fifty odd (and some of them very odd) countries was probably the shortest statement obtaining its end, ever made in an international governmental gathering.

Her response was, however, a deeply spiritual image and had a profound impact. '"It is a little candle, but the night is dark" she said and sat down, and the Fifth Committee of the Assembly voted unanimously that her budget should go on.'

Karen Jeppe was assisted by Edith Roberts, a member of the Friends Armenian Committee who became a Quaker by convincement in 1926 and whose work continued after the Commission was closed. In 1920, aged 31, she sought to go out to Syria to help the Armenians, but arriving in Geneva found that her unspecified qualifications were insufficient. She spent some time in Corfu, possibly with Ann Burgess who had fled there from Constantinople in November 1922 with a group of her Armenian refugees. Child refugees were taken there and the Lord Mayor's Fund moved there on 19 November. For a while Edith Roberts remained in Switzerland; she was strongly influenced by Eglantyne Jebb whom she heard preach in the Geneva cathedral. Edith became involved with the Armenian Home and child welfare; she wrote letters to the delegates at the Lausanne Conference in support of Armenia.

Karen Jeppe asked Edith Roberts to become her part-time Secretary, her fare from Geneva to Syria being paid by League. She returned to England to care for her dying mother, and when she returned to Aleppo, she felt that personal friendship linked her to the League; Dr Nansen wished her good luck and offered his help through the High Commission at any time (Frances Roberts 1947: 9). She was met with new arrivals of refugees, following fresh expulsions of Armenians from Turkey, with which the League lacked official freedom to cope. She shared in refugees' journeys across the northern desert, or in mud coming up their legs and across trackless moorland where wolf roamed. Twice, after the peasants were given land on which to settle, had made their ploughs, and prepared the land with the oxen that the Commission gave them, they were ordered to leave and try again at a safer distance from the Turkish frontier. In the 1930s Edith Roberts went to Erivan, afterwards notifying the Nansen Office she wanted to have no more part in sending Armenians there, but advised awaiting sounder conditions, justifiably fearing for their safety. As long as the Armenians lacked a secure homeland, it was a constant struggle for survival without the possibility of laying foundations for the future. Finally, in Aleppo she started weaving and hand-spinning industries and founded a home for the aged and the incapacitated. In 1935 a brick building was bought in Aleppo and set up as a Home called 'Shenk Doctor Nansen' for very destitute and afflicted old people, but in 1940, after her death in Beirut on 22 March 1939, this was enlarged as a memorial to Edith Roberts herself. She was disgusted by the Allies' betrayal of the Armenian people. During and after the war they kept promising the Armenians they would be free and have a national home – a promise 'to the valiant little nation' that was never fulfilled. In July 1938 writing of the reports of handing over to Turkey of the Sanjac of Alexandretta, where since 1915 hundreds of Armenian deportees had settled, she said (Frances Roberts 1947: 14–16):

> We're making a £10,000,000 loan to Turkey, coupled with a £6,000,000 war loan. A war loan to Turkey, whose previous policy was barbarous annihilation of those we had undertaken to assist. I stand, as Fridtjof Nansen did before me, with a bleeding heart.

Jeppe worked on the Commission until the end of 1927, when she considered that better work could be done in settling Armenians rather than attempting to rescue more because 'all those who can be saved will be rescued by then' (Crowdy 1927: 153–69). Two centres were left to become responsible, with private individuals and charitable organizations doing the work, helped by subsidies from the League of Nations. Caris Mills worked in Constantinople and over a three year period nearly 9,000 were helped at the League of Nations House, the Constantinople refuge, to which Kennedy took the refugees. As Macartney said (1930: 127): 'The wretched fate of the women whom salvation could not reach is one part of the horror of war.'

Two League schemes: Erivan and Syria

In addition to the rescue work, the League had two complementary schemes for settlement of Armenian refugees: the Erivan scheme which was directly under the League, and the Syrian scheme which had been handed over to the Refugee Section of the ILO. Some thought it might be better if the Armenian problem could be handled by one authority. Critics pointed out shortcomings of the schemes, but had no alternative solution to offer. The only alternative was *laissez-faire* which would leave the people in misery and destitution until semi-starvation and discouragement rendered them a prey to epidemics and more of the remaining Armenians died. The process of genocide, which began with the massacres and which Courtney had recognized, would be completed.

Edith Pye (*Friend*, 5.8.1927), now a member of the special sub-committee set up by the ILO to deal with the settlement of Armenians in Syria, described their situation in Greece and Bulgaria, and those in Syria for whose benefit a colonisation scheme, mainly agricultural, was operating. There was an area between Alexandretta and Aleppo which could support about 1,000 families, but it needed drainage and Dr Duguet, of the Syrian High Commission, thought the cost would be about £60 per family over three years. People in Alexandretta lived in shanties over the swamps, and consequently had malaria, so the camp, and that in Beyrout [sic] had to be destroyed. Plans had been completed for houses in Beyrout for camp refugees and the Lebanon Government voted £25,000 to the Refugee Department of the ILO for this work but help was urgent. In 1925 (Innes 1931: 34), Nansen reported to the Sixth Assembly concerning the need for water, irrigation and drainage in Erivan. A Commission was appointed to inquire into draining part of the area that made up Erivan, of which only some could be cultivated currently. Its favourable report was accepted, but the League was unwilling to raise money for a country which was part of Soviet Russia, even by an international loan. The British Government refused to help the Syrian scheme, despite public opinion to the contrary. The Erivan Scheme had no success, for the same reason. This left voluntary societies to cope alone.

Defining 'refugee'

Resulting from the Resolution passed by the Sixth Assembly regarding Russian and Armenian refugees, in 1926 Nansen convened a Conference of representatives of Governments at Geneva. They defined the term 'refugee' as:

> Any person of (Russian or Armenian) origin (formerly a subject of the Ottoman Empire) who does not enjoy or who no longer enjoys the protection of the Government of the Turkish Republic (the Union of SSRs) and who has not acquired another nationality.

As Wilson indicated (1944: 274), a refugee was therefore defined as a person of a particular nationality having no protecting government. This opened the door to consideration of other nationalities, since after the War political, racial and religious conflicts had disrupted relationships between various groups and their governments. In 1926, the Belgian Foreign Minister, Louis de Brouckère asked the League Assembly why assistance should be restricted to Armenians and Russians, but as Burgess (2001) says, influential figures such as British Foreign Minister Sir Austen Chamberlain chose to set the limits of the League of Nations' refugee work as narrowly as possible, asking who these other refugees were. The League Council asked Nansen to report on their character, their numbers and where they were distributed. They stipulated that refugees who were to benefit from international assistance should require it 'as a consequence of the war and of events directly connected with the war, and [be] living under analogous conditions' to the Russian and Armenian refugees. This effectively confined refugee assistance to allies of the victorious powers and the Turks, and claiming, as if on their behalf, that the Armenian problem was due to the War which, arguably, it was not.

Nansen again raised the question of homeless refugees at the Council Meeting in June 1927. He had received several appeals from a number of different international organizations and from LNUs across Europe, all requesting that the measures adopted for the Russian and Armenian refugees be extended to other unprotected groups. He had also received pleas for assistance from the refugees themselves. In coming to its decision about which refugees to help, the Council stated that the question for it to consider was whether there was a need to give relief and protection, and to provide employment for any new refugee groups. For the Council, it 'was not the lack of diplomatic protection that distinguished refugees, but the conditions they endured after their alienation from their countries of origin'. Consequently the Council adopted measures for the assistance of the

Assyrian and Assyro-Chaldean refugees. However, Chamberlain expressed the hope that it would not be necessary to make any further extensions and that it might be possible to bring to a close the League's refugee services, which (Burgess 2001) 'had unfortunately lasted already longer than had been originally anticipated'. Chamberlain was not an internationalist. Swanwick accused him of killing the Geneva Protocol in 1924, an act which she described as abandoning every League principle (1935: 431) since its purpose was to amend the Covenant to make arbitration compulsory and decisions binding. As Haslam explained (1999: 177), 'pacifists felt this was the key to peace' which would solve the problem of war-created refugees but Alice Hamilton recognized (1985: 316) 'nationalism is deep-rooted and the ... first duty'. She accused Chamberlain of sabotaging the League in 1928 for this reason.

Post-suffragists, Quakers and refugees

In 1929 Swanwick (1935: 486) was again a substitute-delegate. This time she was appointed to the Political Commission and was asked by Hugh Dalton to attend the Fourth (Budget) Committee at the Secretariat in his place. She was 'able to save some £2,000 for Nansen' because he 'had been telling me that very day that he must have the money or pay it out of his own pocket. So I was able to testify and the credit passed.' That year Mary Agnes Hamilton, now an MP, was selected to be on the Economic Commission of the League. At Newnham College, Cambridge, Hamilton had read economics, an unusual subject for a woman, and attended meetings given by Maynard Keynes, also an undergraduate. After Newnham, Hamilton became interested in foreign affairs and joined the ILP where she found members more alive than most people to the dangers in Europe. At Geneva she particularly appreciated the work of Arthur Henderson and, since Swanwick was suffering ill health, Hamilton helped with her work. On 12 September 1929 Swanwick (1935: 476, 478) wrote to her husband: 'This morning was "Refugees" which Molly Hamilton has, and she has made a good impression. This afternoon is "Traffic in Women" which is one of my subjects.' This change of responsibility indicates lack of continuity, even though Hamilton was undoubtedly capable. Swanwick was supposed to deal with Minorities and Mandates, but there was little for her to do. In August there had been a clash between Arabs and Jews over the right to pray at the Western Wall in Jerusalem resulting in 133 Jewish and 116 Arabs killed. She had to undertake that the British would deal promptly with the massacre of Jews. The massacre of the Arabs was not mentioned.

Hamilton (1944: 185) wrote: 'Geneva in 1929 and 1930 was a genuine International clearing-house of ideas ... There was hard work, and there was goodwill', and when a major Power such as Britain 'is determined to use it to the full as an instrument of international co-operation, it can give results'. Arthur Henderson was central to this. Hamilton found it 'exciting', because it meant close association with Dr Nansen and she had talks on the whole refugee problem with the Russian, M. Gulkevitch, introduced to her by Swanwick.

Other minorities also continued to be of concern. In March 1927, Hilda Clark sent a letter from the CIS at Friends House to *The Friend* entitled 'Bulgarian Refugees' Urgent Need'. She reported that considerable help had been given by Friends' funds and administered by workers the previous year. In April two workers had toured refugee centres; a kitchen for 2,630 people in villages and towns ran for two months until harvest, reopening from December to the end of February for 1,180 children. Nurses were sent by Germany, Hungary, Belgium, France, Sweden, Italy and England and the American Red Cross sent money. Nancy Lauder Brunton, whom Hilda Clark had met at the Ark in Salonika, had gone out again for CIS, with Maud Slattery from Ireland who had worked with Friends in Vienna. The Ark was the Friends' Salonika HQ attached to the American Farm School, from which they worked to control malaria, helped new refugee villages, and from which two Friends were feeding children in remote villages in Bulgaria.

In March 1929 the British section of WILPF, which had branches in many of the countries concerned, convened a conference in London to discuss whether the Minorities Treaties were being observed. The proceedings, which Philip Noel-Baker summed up, were opened by Kathleen Courtney. This conference, she explained, was an appropriate one for women to call because the issue came into the home in terms of the language used to teach children in school, and the question of which religion was taught. Professor Loewenfeld of Berlin (Loewenfeld in WIL 1929: 20) stated that 48,000,000 people were living in countries to which they belonged 'neither with their tongue nor with their heart'. He told delegates that 'Most of the wars of the modern epoch have arisen through dissatisfied Minorities', many of which endured severe discrimination. Mme Bakker van Bosse of Holland pointed out the difficulty of defining a minority. A government might disagree as to whether a group actually formed a minority, giving as an example that in Yugoslavia the Macedonians felt themselves to be Bulgarians, but the Government said they were Serbs, so therefore were not a minority, and repressed the Macedonian identity. Pedersen (2007: 20–1) rightly notes the Minorities Commission of the League was concerned to protect the fragile peace in the region, and dismissed petitions involving Macedonia as 'not receivable', thereby preventing smouldering ethnic conflicts from escalating into war.

Why did the League not do more? Finance was a prime issue, since some League members did not pay their dues, and national interests were pre-eminent. Nevertheless, it helped by getting the people away – the voluntary organizations could only do this in very small numbers. As Nansen wrote (1923: 29–31): they should not abandon their efforts but needed the League to have a constructive policy, which it lacked. Nevertheless, the fact that Karen Jeppe's work was supported by the League created a useful precedent. It had not usually been in favour of granting money for direct relief, but had done so in Jeppe's case. On 15 September 1934, in discussions about Russian women refugees in China, Forchhammer and Countess Apponyi, Chair of the Sixth Committee, wondered if it might be possible for another woman to do similar work for Russian refugee women, whose conditions were in many ways similar to those of the Armenians. It was suggested that women's organizations should help to find a suitable woman. Relief apparently had potential for changing international policy.

Epilogue

The examination of civilian relief work reveals that women and children formed the majority of refugees and the majority of relief workers were women, although this is obscured by the fact that men usually held the highest positions on committees. This survey also sheds important new light on how women involved in humanitarian aid were engaging with political issues through their duty of care from the moment war was declared, right through the 1920s and beyond. Suffragism had been founded on women's care for other women and given them political experience valuable in Great War relief. The connection of Friends with suffragism meant that the suffrage campaign was infiltrated by Quaker desire for permanent peace as a means of preventing suffering while previous Quaker relief facilitated joint suffrage-Quaker work in other countries. There was, however, considerable disjuncture between pacifists' ostracism and the behind-the-scenes use of FWVRC by the British and other Governments, together with acceptance of their relief work, from which arose considerable social and economic effects and benefits to various states. The French acknowledged this when they requested the Friends' help at Verdun by saying their work saved Government money through helping civilians to survive. It also reduced the amount of reconstruction needed after the war, enabling people to return to their homes more quickly than would otherwise have been the case. This ambivalence towards relief workers came not only from Governments, but also from some of the people among whom they worked, indicating workers' physical and mental vulnerability.

In certain ways the Belgians typified all refugees in respect of their differing social status and needs and in the way individual women such as Mrs Henry or women's groups such as the LSWS immediately assisted them. They rarely arrived as whole families. Children were lost *en route*, adults became separated and men were removed by various authorities. Refugees therefore consisted largely of women, children and men above conscription age, all needing support. However, whereas Belgians were invited to Britain, this was not so elsewhere and refugees as a category are shown largely to be unwanted by national governments although the public might react differently. Britain's experience shows the importance of public perceptions and the power of the press in forming them. This was the first war where the press had been used by the government for 'patriotic' propaganda purposes: Lord Beaverbrook was appointed Minister of Information, and Lord Northcliffe, Director of Propaganda in Enemy Countries in February 1918. It behoved the press to acknowledge an important democratic principle – that it has responsibilities as well as rights.

During the Great War civilians held society together and formed the grounding for the armed services; this was tacitly acknowledged by use of the blockade as a weapon of war and its continuation after the Armistice. Swanwick rejected relief as a means by which policy could be changed; however, as we have seen, this was inaccurate. The presence of relief workers stirred the French government into voting money for their civilians. In Holland it enabled exchange of prisoners. It is argued that the need to repatriate SWH workers from Russia changed the course of the war. In addition, experience of relief fuelled new political work and gave important insights unavailable to those not involved in 'caring'. Karen Jeppe's rescue work as League Commissioner for Armenian refugees combined political work with rescue and affected the League's commitment to subsequent refugees. However, policy regarding going to war is hard to change as people discovered at Geneva and, as the Quakers realized at their London Yearly Meeting in 1915, pacifism needs constructive alternatives merely to saying 'no'. The network of discussion groups in which women took part centred round the establishment of a League of Nations which they hoped would bring about an end to war. After the war, it became a matter of using the League to achieve peace by including in its programme the raising women's status and dealing with despised 'social issues' which were, in fact, fundamental to social justice and humanitarianism and therefore to peace.

With the partial enfranchisement of British women in 1918 the NUWSS changed its focus and became NUSEC with Eleanor Rathbone as its President. The women's movement reverted to single-issue focus. The LSWS, now renamed the Fawcett Society, continues to campaign for equality for women. As the 1920s became the 1930s the refugee crisis was still unresolved and women's collaboration in relief continued through Save the Children, the Friends and LNU, and in the form of small groups of personal friendships such as that of Katharine MacPhail and Sister Catherine O'Rorke in Yugoslavia, or Edith Pye, Hilda Clark and Kathleen Courtney in the Balkans, working in relation to the issues and with the organization that best suited their concerns, as well as across national boundaries.

The power of America, as a neutral able to disseminate relief and potentially to arbitrate between belligerents, has been confirmed. America was involved in relief through various organizations including Quakers, its women's societies and the CRB, and after the war through the Hoover organization and again, Quakers. Although it failed to recognize the emergence of its new role as the most significant international power, it maintained potent influence on Britain and France at the League. Keynes said that the Council of Four in Paris in 1918 was uninterested in the fact that Europe was starving and disintegrating before their eyes. It is this lack of concern for others that meant the League failed to develop a policy that could resolve emergent conflicts between nations, or the problem of minorities that led to governments oppressing or expelling a proportion of their population. However, as Lenore Coltheart claimed (1995: 1), it was successful in that it gained a wealth of experience in refugee relief. It interrogated governments, gathered data about refugees and visited refugee sites. By 1939, it had developed standards, rules and practices on which the United Nations subsequently built, its work being taken over by UNRRA. Nevertheless, had relief work not been undertaken by Quakers and suffragists during and after the Great War, this 'wealth' would have been much impoverished.

Men wanted women at the League to continue their role as women concerned for other women. 'Caring' gained women's entry into the League, and indicating the success of this, the first conference on any subject held in the League at Geneva was the one on the Traffic in Women. However, the limitations are also evident and the problems tackled by the Fifth Committee remain unresolved. When Rachel Crowdy (Bristol: Crowdy papers: Part L) wrote her notes for 'Have Women Progressed Since the War?' she queried:

> Have we been thinking so much of ourselves as *women* that we have failed as citizens and as human beings? Have we been so anxious to perfect our instruments that we have neither time nor energy left to use them effectively?

She believed in the intuition and inspiration which women supplied, but thought wholehearted co-operation of women and men afforded the best guarantee of success. This was what the League lacked. She once told delegates not to be afraid that their country's misdemeanours would be found out, but instead make them reform. This was the best kind of patriotism and could have far-reaching, positive results.

Nansen died in 1930, but his work was continued through the Nansen International Office for Refugees which, in 1932, settled some 14,000 Armenian refugees and 59,000 people of other nationalities. The fate of the Armenians and Jews shows that the more they are harried from place to place, the more they become not only unwanted, but their fate is perceived as comparatively unimportant. As some areas began to settle in the 1930s, refugees from Germany increased. There were also some 20,000 Russian refugees in China, rendered destitute by floods. In 1932, when the Sixth Committee considered the report of the Nansen Office (PRO. HO 45/20528), the Twelfth Assembly resolved to reduce gradually the work of the Office and liquidate it entirely at the end of 1938. Confirming that refugees were not a priority, money allocated to the Office declined although the number of refugees increased.

On 13 October 1930, the New German Reichstag opened with 107 Nazi Members in uniform, making clear their intention towards Jews, and on 30 January 1933 Adolf Hitler was appointed chancellor of a coalition government. In October 1933, when a Draft League Convention concerning the international status of refugees was being considered by the League, the British Foreign Office declared (PRO FO.655194/27):

> This is not an opportune moment for the League of Nations to press for the opening of national doors to refugees, both for residence and for employment. The Convention is possibly being pressed by certain nations who, mainly for political reasons, have encumbered themselves with a large and unstable refugee population.

It ended arrogantly, 'We have always stood clear in these matters because we have no refugee problem of this kind.' In January 1934 their attitude was made even clearer (PRO FO.655194/36):

> The problem does not affect us as it affects certain others such as the French who so often open their arms with impetuous generosity to refugees and afterwards lament their decisions and complain that others should have shared their burden.

Furthermore, indicating anti-semitism and fear of Communism, it continued: 'The Russian refugee population in this country is a small and dwindling one, and the problem will soon die out.'

From 1936 there was civil war in Spain and refugees began to pour into neighbouring countries and beyond. In 1938, Quakers and feminists such as Edith Eckhard and Edith Pye started work in Spain. Miss Vulliamy set up a canteen for wounded and worn-out men with the National Joint Committee and Dr Audrey Russell Ellis worked for the International Commission for Assistance of Refugees. Eleanor Rathbone, who had represented Women's International Organizations on the League Committee for Child Welfare, travelled to Spain in the spring of 1937 braving the Valencia bombardment with the Duchess of Atholl, Ellen Wilkinson, and Dame Rachel Crowdy, to review the situation of refugees and political prisoners for herself. In 1938, she gave a speech on the Czech crisis at a meeting held at the Friends House.

As these events were occurring, Michael Hansson, President of the Governing Body of the Nansen International Office for Refugees (WL. 3AMS/B/13/01), said at a Conference given by the Association for Moral and Social Hygiene at the Nobel Institute, Oslo, on 7 January 1938 that countries which had welcomed refugees had now 'taken on the character of a contest as to who can most easily get rid of them'. He added: 'All of us may some day become refugees, homeless, or stateless.'

To-day the Society of Friends monitors matters of global importance such as climate change, and looks to the importance of people's faith in surviving under the Mugabe regime in Zimbabwe. WILPF, the oldest women's peace organization, continues to campaign for equality and the full enjoyment of human rights for all. Among their 2009 concerns is that people continue to be raped in all situations of armed conflict and their bodies are increasingly the battleground. Save the Children continues its work of rescue following earthquakes, wars and other disasters. It reports that the number of people driven from their homes but still living in their own country, those whom the Quakers would have recognized as a type of *émigrés*, reached about 26,000,000 at the end of 2008. In addition to these internally displaced people, those seeking refuge in another country, whom we recognize as 'refugees', number 16,000,000. The need for relief still persists.

Although woman suffrage has been attained in many countries, the struggle for equality continues and wars are still fought. Nonetheless, the expansion of women's place into international society could not be retracted as their presence in the UN and the European Parliament show. The connection between sexual inequality and relief was underlined by the head of the UNHCR on 7 March 2009:

> It is a UNHCR policy priority to ensure that refugee women and girls have equal access to protection, basic goods and services as they attempt to rebuild their lives. In situations of forced displacement, no one is spared from deprivation and the threat of violence but women and girls suffer disproportionately. Violence, and particularly sexual and gender-based violence, is one of the defining characteristics of contemporary conflict.

The deleterious effects of women's inequality could not be clearer. It is not the fault of these early twentieth-century women if more needs to be done. If, as some think is the case, we are condemned to re-live a history we do not know, then, as Joanna Bourke writes (1999: 225): 'the choice between forgetting and remembering is ours'.

APPENDIX

Chronology of Important Dates

October 1899–1902	Boer War.
1901	
21 May	First meeting of Victoria League.
July	Ladies Commission goes to South Africa to investigate camps.
1913	
April	Cat and Mouse Act, Prisoners (Temporary Discharge for Ill Health) Bill.
1914	
28 July	Austro-Hungary declared war on Serbia.
2 August	Germany's ultimatum to Belgium demanding free passage for its troops.
4 August	Germany invaded Belgium. War declared by Britain.
5 August	Aliens Restriction Act published as Order-in-Council.
6 August	Actresses' Franchise League formed the Women's Emergency Corps.
7 August	Germans take Liège, capturing its last forts on 17 August. Belgian Government removed to Antwerp, then Ostend, and Le Havre.
8 August	DORA instated, modified in 1915 and 1916.
12 August	Dr Elsie Inglis proposed Scottish Women's Hospital units.
13 August	Madame Grujić returned to Nish, Serbia.
17 August	Flora Lugard telegraphed Captain Craig, Ulster Unionist leader.
20 August	Germans take Brussels.
22 August	Lyttelton and Lugard hold conference with Ada Streeter.

22–24 August	War Refugees Committee formed.
25 August	Fall of Namur and British Expeditionary Force retreat from Mons.
4 September	Hilda Clark calls for help for Belgians. 33 volunteers.
4–10 September	Battle of Marne.
6 September	Poland Street, Edmonton, and Hackney Wick taken for refugees; Belgian Legation moves to the Aldwych.
8 September	Maubeuge fell. Alexandra Palace taken for refugees.
8 September	Daily boats from Antwerp started, 1,000 refugees per day.
8 September	Circulars sent by LGB to Mayors' Committees seeking more hospitality.
9 September	Statement in Parliament; HM Government offered hospitality to Belgians.
9 September	Aliens Restriction Order.
9 September	Division of labour between WRC and LGB.
9 September	Endell Street taken for refugees.
26 September	Siege of Antwerp.
4 October	British Naval Division reached Antwerp.
9 October	Fall of Antwerp.
12 October	Bulgaria invaded Serbia.
12 October–11 November	First Battle of Ypres.
13 October	Suffragists organise relief of Flushng
15 October	Germans reached Zeebrugge and Ostend.
15 October	Earl's Court taken for refugees.
16 October	Ostend closed.
20 October	Exclusion of refugees from East Coast to Humber.
21 October	Exclusion of refugees from Norfolk.
26 October	*Amiral Ganteaume* torpedoed by German submarine U-24; 40 refugees drowned.
3 November	Allied Ambassadors leave Turkey.
5 November	First FWVRC group leave for France.
17 November	The first SRF Unit at Skoplje under Lady Paget.
28 November	Aliens Restriction (Belgian Refugees) Order.
10 December	Order in Council – compulsory registration of refugees.
12 December	West Hartlepool, Scarborough attacked.

1915

January	First SWH unit reaches Kraguievatz under Dr Eleanor Soltau.
February	Second SRF unit of 47 persons under Cornelia Lady Wimborne, to Skoplje.
March	Government Register of Women.
2 April	Second battle of Ypres including gas that day and again 21 May.
24 April	Armenian men removed.
28 April–1 May	Women's International Congress at The Hague.
29 May	Armenian women and children massacred.
13 August	Robert Tatlock reported in Sermaize on need in Serbia.
23 September	King Ferdinand of Bulgaria's order for army mobilization.
30 September	The Serbian Army began Great Retreat.
October	Derby Scheme.
8 October	Austrians take Belgrade.
12 October	Bulgaria attacks Serbia.
November	Inglis and some of her staff at Kruševac captured.
17 November	Ruth Fry and William Albright of FWVRC join SRF Committee. Relief sent out to refugees in Montenegro.

1916

January	Ka Cox, Margery Fry and Maurice Wilson go to Corsica under SRF.
28 January	Conscription for unmarried men.
April	Bill in Parliament for Conscription for married men.
May	Dr Inglis and Percy Dearmer appointed to General SRF Committee.
30 May	Aliens Restriction (Consolidation) Order 1916.
June	Second Military Service Act.
1 July	Battle of the Somme begins.

1917

February	First Russian Revolution.
8 March	Mrs Harley killed at Monastir.
5 April	USA declared war.
31 July–September	Third battle of Ypres – Passchendaele (September, mustard gas).

October	Second Russian Revolution.
27 November	Dr Elsie Inglis died.
6 December	Roumanian Government obtains ceasefire.
15 December	Brest-Litovsk negations end fighting on Eastern Front.
Winter	Turnip Winter in Northern Europe.
1918	
January	President Wilson's Fourteen-point Peace Plan.
February	Mrs Carrington-Wilde proposed scheme to liberate Serb children not with their parents in prison camps in Austria and Hungary.
26 June	Buzuluk falls to Czechoslovaks.
6 August	Kazan falls to Czechoslovaks.
30 September	Serbia signs Armistice with Bulgaria.
23 October	Commons vote to allow women MPs.
3 November	Serbia signs Armistice with Austro-Hungary.
11 November	Allies sign Armistice with Germany.
22 November	Belgian Government reinstated in Brussels.
8 December	Herbert Hoover talks with Lady Kate Courtney about distress in Europe.
11 December	General election. Women over 30 with property can vote.
1919	
16 January	Fight the Famine Committee formed.
10–16 February	Inter-Allied Suffrage Conference, Paris.
10 February	Joint Inter-Allied, ICW delegation to Wilson.
25 February	First consignments under German Babies Teats Fund arrive in Frankfurt.
18 March	Joint ICW, Inter-Allied deputation to Gompers, ILO.
8 April	Trafalgar Square protest
10 April	Corbett-Ashby and Aberdeen head delegation to Wilson.
15 April	Proposal to form Save the Children Fund.
12–17 May	WILPF Conference in Zurich.
19 May	Save the Children Fund launched, Royal Albert Hall.
28 June	Versailles Treaty signed.

July	Emily Hobhouse started the Swiss Relief Fund; also the Russian Babies Fund. Quaker relief starts in Austria. Relief workers allowed into Germany.
July	Hilda Clark in Vienna.
November	Fight the Famine Conference, Central Hall, Westminster.
15 November	First League of Nations Assembly.
December	Dr Hector Monro and Eglantyne Jebb have audience with the Pope.
1920	
January	Food blockade raised.
September	Catherine Marshall to Geneva.
November	Mary Sheepshanks to Geneva.
November	First League of Nations Assembly
1921	
February	Alice Clark visits Hilda Clark in Vienna.
February	Commission on Deported Women and Children in Asia Minor formed.
3 March	Baumgarten opened by the Austrian President, Dr Hainisch.
1922	
21 January	President Hainisch opens settlement at Altsmansdorf.
February	Fight the Famine meeting at Central Hall with European Reconstruction Council.
1 March	All British Appeal formed.
March/April	Riga Conference.
March	Karen Jeppe appointed to the Commission on Deported Women and Children until 1927.
August	Kathleen Courtney and Hilda Clark tour Poland.
November	Winifred Coombe Tennant first British Woman Delegate to League of Nations.
November	Rachel Crowdy appeals to friends for help for Armenians.
1923	
30 January	Convention of Lausanne.

1923–4	Courtney and Clark tour Balkans.
1924	
21 October	Joint conference of relief societies at Devonshire House.
November	Helena Swanwick League of Nations delegate.
1929	
March	WILPF Conference on Minorities.
November	Helena Swanwick and Mary Agnes Hamilton League of Nations delegates.

Bibliography

Journals and newspapers

Jus Suffragii
Common Cause
The Friend
The Englishwoman
The Times
Liberal Women's Review
British Journal of Nursing

University of Sussex

M.G. Fawcett Papers

Special collections

Leonard Woolf Papers
Birrell Papers

Bristol University

Crowdy Papers

National Archive, London (Public Record Office)

Home Office Records
Foreign Office Records
Ministry of Health Records
Security Service Records
White Papers: Cd 7750, 1914; Cd 7763, 1914

Imperial War Museum

Department of Printed Books: Women's Work Collection
Department of Documents (IWM. DD)

Friends House Library

Friends War Victims Relief Committee Minutes and Correspondence
Friends Emergency Committee Minutes and Correspondence
Armenia records

Women's Library (WL)

Autograph Letter Collection: Women's Suffrage, 9/01
London Society of Women's Suffrage, LSWS 371.1 & 2
Association of Moral & Social Hygiene, 3AMS
Papers of Kathleen D'Olier Courtney, KDC
Millicent Fawcett Papers, 7/MGF

London School of Economics

WILPF Papers

Save the Children

Sneddon, Susan: Catalogue of materials; Archive Papers. Sent to me privately by e-mail.

Unpublished theses, conference papers and miscellaneous

Tucker, Leigh. 1972. *The English Quakers and World War I, 1914–1920*. Dissertation submitted to University of North Carolina, Chapel Hill, NC.

2004. 'Strangers in a Strange Land'. In Flanders Fields Museum Colloquia, Ypres, Belgium:

Amara, Michael. 'Belgian refugees in the First World War'.
Kraaijestein, Martin. 'Belgian refugees in the neutral Netherlands during the First World War'.
Nagtegaal, Kees. 'Housing of "Belgian vermin"'.
Vandenbilcke, Annick and Chielens, Piet. 'About Kotjesvolk (people living in sheds) and Coffee houses, refugees in unoccupied Belgium, 1914–18'.

2001. Women's History Network Conference, Bristol University:

Newman, Viv. 'Standing up to the War Office'.
Smith, Angela. 'Suffragists at war: the Scottish Women's Hospital and the Vote'.

Internet resources

Burgess, Greg. 2001. 'Into the Protecting Arms: The League of Nations and the Extension of International Assistance to Unprotected Persons in the Middle East and Europe, 1926–1928'. Melbourne University. <http://arts.monash.edu.au/publications/eras/edition-1/burgess.php> (accessed 30 March 2007).

Channel 4. <http://www.channel4.com/history/microsites/H/history/c-d/dirty-hands.html> (accessed 20 May 2009).

Clarke, Ida Clyde. 1918. *American Women and the World War*. <http://www.lib.byu.edu> (accessed 9 September 2002).

Gaines, Ruth. *A Village in Picardy*. <http://raven.cc.ukans.edu/~libsite/wwi-www/picardyvil/GainesVP.html> (accessed 19 October 2000).

Gay, George I. and Fisher, H. H. 1929. *The Commission for Relief in Belgium*. <http://www:lib.byu.edu> (accessed 9 September 2002).

Holdwater. Tall Armenian Tale. <http://www.tallarmeniantale.com/644900.htm> (accessed 16 March 2007).

Kellogg, Charlotte. 1917. *Women of Belgium, Turning Tragedy to Triumph*. <http://raven.cc.ukans.edu/~libsite/wwi-www/Ckellogg/Wbelg.2.htm> (accessed 14 November 2000).

Lous, Eva. 2003. *Karen Jeppe – Denmark's First Peace Philosopher*. <http://www.freds-akademiet.dk/library/ukjeppe.htm> (accessed 16 March 2007).

Manson, J.M. 2007. 'Leonard Woolf as an Architect of the League of Nations' *South Carolina Review*. <http://www.clemson.edu/caah/cedp/Woolf_League.pdf> (accessed 29 June 2007).

Matthew, H.C.G. 'Herbert Gladstone', *Dictionary of National Biography*. <http://www.oxforddnb.com/view/article/33417> (accessed 14 November 2000).

Mitchell, Percy. 1922. *The American Relief Clearing House. Chapters 1–3*. <www.lib.byu.edu/~rdh/wwi/memoir/Clearing/arch1.html> (accessed 16 December 2005).

Pedersen, Susan. 2007. 'Back to the League of Nations'. *American Historical Review* Vol. 112 (4). <http://www.historycooperative.org/journals/ahr/112.4/pedersen.html> (accessed 12 December 2007).

WILPF. <http://www.wilpf.int.ch/PDF/humanrights/HRC11/SCR1820.pdf> (accessed 19 June 2009).

Zetkin, Clara. 1922. 'The Struggle Against New Imperialistic Wars'. *The Communist Review*, July 1922, 3 (3). <http://www.marxists.org/archive/zetkin/index.htm> (accessed 7 April 2007).

Articles, reports and pamphlets

Burton, Antoinette. 1991. 'The Feminist Quest for Identity.' *Journal of Women's History*, Vol. 3: 46–81.

Bush, J. 2001a. 'British Women's Imperial Politics and the South African War (1899–1902)'. *Women's History Notebooks* 7 (2): 2–9.

——. 2001b. 'Ladylike Lives? Upper Class Women's Autobiographies and the Politics of Late Victorian and Edwardian Britain'. *Literature and History* 10 (2): 42–61.

Crowdy, Rachel. 1927. 'The Humanitarian Activities of the League of Nations'. *Journal of the Royal Institute of International Affairs* 6 (3): 153–69.

Day, Suzanne R. 1916. 'A Travers Bar-le-Duc'. *Englishwoman*, Vol. 30: 131–40.

de Schaepdrijver, Sophie. 2002. 'Death is Elsewhere: The Shifting Locus of Tragedy in Belgian Great War Literature'. *Yale French Studies* 102, Belgian Memories: 94–114.

Gerodetti, Natalia and Bieri, Sabin. 2006. '(Female hetero)Sexualities in transition. Train stations as gateways'. *Feminist Theory* 7: 69–85.

Holborn, Louise W. 1931. 'The League of Nations and the Refugee Problem'. *Annals of American Academy of Political and Social Science* Vol. 203 (Refugees): 124–35.

Holton, Sandra S. 1994. '"To Educate Women into Rebellion", Elizabeth Cady Stanton and the Creation of a Transatlantic Network of Radical Suffragists'. *The American Historical Review* 99 (4): 1112–36.

Kennedy, T.C. 1984. 'The Quaker Renaissance and the Origins of the Modern British Peace Movement. 1895–1920'. *Albion* 16 (3): 243–72.

Kushner, T. 1999. 'Local Heroes: Belgian Refugees in Britain during the First World War'. *Immigrants & Minorities* 18 (1): 1–28.

Lunn, Pam. 1997. '"You have lost your Opportunity". British Quakers and the militant phase of the women's suffrage campaign: 1906–1914'. *Quaker Studies* 2: 30–55.

Miller, Carol. 1994. 'Geneva, the Key to Equality: interwar feminists and the League of Nations'. *Women's History Review* 3 (2): 219–45.

Myers, Kevin. 2001. 'Belgian Refugee Children'. *History of Education* 30 (2): 153–62.

Nansen, Fridtjof. 1923. Report on the work of the High Commission for Refugees, presented to the Fourth Assembly. London: League of Nations.

Nyak, Meghana and Suchland, Jennifer. 2006. 'Gender Violence and Hegemonic Projects: Introduction'. *International Feminist Journal of Politics* 8 (4): 467–85.

Pye, Edith. 1915. 'Relief Work in the Devastated Department of the Marne'. London: FWVRC: 1–12.

Rempel, R.A. 'British Quakers and the South African War'. *Quaker History*, 1975, 64 (2): 75–95.

Riedi, Eliza. 2002. 'Women, Gender, and the Promotion of Empire: The Victoria League, 1901–1914'. *The Historical Journal* 45 (3): 569–99.

Storr, Katherine. 2002. 'Belgian Refugee Relief: an example of "Caring Power" in the Great War'. *Women's History Network Magazine*, June: 16–19.

——. 2003. 'Belgian Children's Education in Britain in The Great War: Language, Identity and Race Relations'. *History of Education Researcher* 72: 21–31.

Vellacott, Jo. 1993. 'A Place for Pacifism and Transnationalism in Feminist Theory: the early work of the Women's International League for Peace and Freedom'. *Women's History Review* 2 (1): 23–56.

Vellacott-Newbury, Jo. 1977. 'Anti-War Suffragists'. *History* 62 (206): 411–25.

Women's International League. 1929. 'Minorities and the League of Nations.' London: WIL.

Chapters in books

Callaway, Helen and Helly, Dorothy O. 1992. 'Crusader for Empire: Flora Shaw/Lady Lugard' in Nupur Chaudhuri and Margaret Strobel (eds), *Western Women and Imperialism: Complicity and Resistance*. Bloomington, IN: Indiana University Press.

Lerner, Gerda. 1992. 'The Majority Finds its Past: Placing Women in History' in Maggie Humm (ed.), *Feminisms: A Reader*. Hemel Hempstead: Harvester Wheatsheaf (first published 1979 in Gerda Lerner, *The Majority Finds its Past: Placing Women in History*. New York, NY: Oxford University Press).

Porter, Roy. 1992. 'Introduction' in Roy Porter (ed.), *Myths of the English*. Cambridge: Polity Press.

Rathbone, Eleanor. 1936. 'Changes in Public Life' in Ray Strachey (ed.), *Our Freedom and Its Results*. London: Woolf.

Reid, James J. 1992. 'Total War, the Annihilation Ethic, and the Armenian Genocide, 1870–1918' in Richard G. Hovannisian (ed.), *The Armenian Genocide: History, Politics, Ethics*. Basingstoke: Macmillan.

Rooij, Piet de. 2006. 'Preface' in M.M. Abbenhuis, *The Art of Staying Neutral*. Amsterdam: Amsterdam University Press.

Storr, Katherine. 2009. 'Thinking Women: International Education for Peace and Equality, 1918–1930' in Jean Spence, Sarah Aiston and Maureen Meikle (eds), *Women, Education, and Agency, 1600–2000*. London: Routledge.

Vernon, B. 1998. 'Beatrice Webb and Margaret Cole: Fabian Politics and Pacifism' in W.K. Chapman and J.M. Manson (eds), *Women in the Milieu of Leonard and Virginia Woolf: Peace, Politics, and Education*. New York, NY: Pace University Press.

Winter, J. 1988. 'Some Paradoxes of the First World War' in R. Wall and J. Winter (eds), *The Upheaval of War*. Cambridge: Cambridge University Press.

Books

Abbenhuis, M.M. 2006. *The Art of Staying Neutral. The Netherlands in the First World War, 1914–1918*. Amsterdam: Amsterdam University Press.

Alberti, Johanna. 1989. *Beyond Suffrage: Feminists in War and Peace, 1914–1928*. Basingstoke: Macmillan.

Andrews, Maggie. 1997. *The Acceptable Face of Feminism*. London: Lawrence & Wishart.

Bell, E. Moberly. 1947. *Flora Shaw (Lady Lugard DBE)*. London: Constable.

Binyon, Laurence. 1918. *For Dauntless France*. London: Hodder & Stoughton.

Bourke, Joanna. 1999. *An Intimate History of Killing: Face-to-Face Killing in Twentieth-Century Warfare*. London: Granta Books.

Brayshaw, A. Neave. 1921. *The Quakers – their story and message*. London: Allen & Unwin.

Brittain, Vera. 1928. *Women's Work In Modern England*. London: Noel Douglas.

Brown, Heloise. 2003. *The Truest Form of Patriotism. Pacifist Feminism in Britain, 1870–1902*. Manchester: Manchester University Press.

Brownmiller, S. 1975. *Against our Will: Men, Women, Rape*. London: Penguin.

Burgess, Alan. 1963. *The Lovely Sergeant*. London: Companion Book Club.

Bussey, G. and Tims, M. 1980. *Pioneers for Peace: Women's International League for Peace and Freedom, 1915–1965*. London: WILPF (first published 1965, Allen & Unwin).

Cahalan, Peter. 1982. *Belgian Refugee Relief in England During The Great War*. New York: Garland Publishing, Inc.

Cahill, Audrey Fawcett. 1999. *Between the Lines: Letters and Diaries from Elsie Inglis's Russian Unit*. Bishop Auckland, Durham: Pentland Press.

Cesarani, D. and Kushner, T. (eds). 1993. *The Internment of Aliens in Twentieth Century Britain*. London: Frank Cass.

Coltheart, Lenore. 1995. *Laughing at Boundaries: the idea of Edith Campbell Berry*. London: Sir Robert Menzies Centre for Australian Studies.

Coote, W.A. 1910. *A Vision and Its Fulfilment. Being the History of the Origin of the Work of the National Vigilance Association for the Suppression of the White Slave Traffic.* London: National Vigilance Association.

Crofton, E. 1997. *The Women of Royaumont.* East Linton, Scotland: Tuckwell Press.

Dobbie, B.M. 1979. *Nest of Suffragettes in Somerset.* Bath: Batheaston Society.

van Drenthe, A. and de Haan, F. 1999. *The Rise of Caring Power.* Amsterdam: Amsterdam University Press.

van Emden, R. and Humphries, S. 2003. *All Quiet on the Home Front: An Oral History of Life in Britain during the First World War.* London: Headline.

Fawcett, M.G. 1924. *What I Remember.* London: Fisher Unwin.

Fisher, John. 1971. *That Miss Hobhouse.* London: Secker & Warburg.

Fletcher, Ian, Mayhall, Christopher, Nym, Laura E. and Levine, Philippa (eds). 2000. *Women's Suffrage in the British Empire, Citizenship, Nation and Race.* London: Routledge.

Fletcher, Sheila. 1989. *Maude Royden – A Life.* Oxford: Basil Blackwell.

Foucault, Michel. 1979. *History of Sexuality, Vol. 1.* London: Allen Lane.

Fry, A. Ruth. 1926. *A Quaker Adventure.* London: Nisbet & Co. Ltd.

Gann, L.H. and Duignan, Peter. 1979. *The Rulers of Belgian Africa, 1884–1914.* Princeton, NJ: Princeton University Press.

Garnett, David. 1955. *The Flowers of the Forest.* London: Chatto & Windus.

Gibbs, Philip. 1930. *Since Then.* London: Heinemann.

——. 1933. *The Soul of the War.* London: Hutchinson.

Gilbert, Martin. 1995. *First World War.* London: HarperCollins.

Glendinning, Victoria. 2006. *Leonard Woolf.* London: Pocket Books.

de la Grange, Baroness Ernest. 1916. *Open House in Flanders 1914–1918. Château de la Motte au Bois.* London: Smith, Elder & Co.

Greenwood, J.O. 1975. *Quaker Encounters: Vol. 1. Friends and Relief.* York: Wm Sessions Ltd.

——. 1978. *Quaker Encounters: Vol. 3. Whispers of Truth.* York: Wm Sessions Ltd.

Haig, Margaret, Viscountess Rhondda. 1933. *This was my World.* London: Macmillan.

Hamilton, Alice. 1985. *Exploring the Dangerous Trades.* Boston, MA: Northeastern University Press (first published 1943, Little Brown).

Hamilton, M.A. 1944. *Remembering my Good Friends.* London: Jonathan Cape.

——. 1953. *Uphill All the Way.* London: Jonathan Cape.

Hannam, June. 1989. *Isabella Ford.* Oxford: Basil Blackwell.

Haslam, Beryl. 1999. *From Suffrage to Internationalism: the Political Evolution of Three British Feminists, 1908–1939.* New York, NY: Peter Lang.

Hewison, H.H. 1989. *Hedge of Wild Almonds.* London: Currey.

Hirst, Margaret E. 1923. *The Quakers in Peace and War*. London: Swarthmore.
Holloway, Gerry. 2005. *Women and Work in Britain since 1840*. London: Routledge.
Holton, Sandra Stanley. 1996. *Suffrage Days. Stories from the Women's Suffrage Movement*. London: Routledge.
——. 2007. *Quaker Women: Personal Life, Memory and Radicalism in the Lives of Women Friends, 1780–1930*. London: Routledge.
Hoover, Herbert C. 1959. *An American Epic: The Relief of Belgium and Northern France, 1914–1930. Vol. 1*. Chicago, IL: Regnery.
Humphreys, Robert. 1995. *Sin, Organized Charity and the Poor Law in Victorian England*. Basingstoke: Palgrave.
Innes, Kathleen E. 1939. *The Story of Nansen and the League of Nations*. London: Friends Peace Committee.
Jones, Enid Huws. 1966. *Margery Fry, the Essential Amateur*. York: Wm Sessions Ltd.
Jordan, G. and Weedon, C. 1995. *Cultural Politics*. Oxford: Blackwell.
Keynes, John Maynard. 1919. *The Economic Consequences of the Peace*. Basingstoke: Macmillan.
Krippner, Monica. 1980. *The Quality of Mercy: Women at War, Serbia 1915–1918*. London: David & Charles.
Lang, D.M. 1970. *Armenia, Cradle of Civilisation*. London: Allen & Unwin.
Lewis, Jane. 1991. *Women and Social Action in Victorian and Edwardian England*. Aldershot: Edward Elgar Publishing Ltd.
Lyttelton, Edith. 1917. *Alfred Lyttelton, an Account of His Life*. London: Longmans, Green & Co.
Lyttelton, Oliver, Viscount Chandos. 1968. *From Peace to War: A Study in Contrasts, 1857–1918*. London: Bodley Head.
Macartney, C.A. 1931. *Refugees, the work of the League*. London: LNU.
McLaren, Barbara. 1917. *Women of the War*. London: Hodder & Stoughton.
MacNaughtan, Sarah. 1915. *A Woman's Diary of the War*. London: Nelson.
Marrus, M.R. 1985. *The Unwanted: European Refugees in the 20th Century*. New York, NY: Oxford University Press.
Mitchell, David. 1966. *Women on the Warpath, the Story of the Women of the First World War*. London: Cape.
Moorehead, Caroline. 1992. *Bertrand Russell: A Life*. London: Sinclair-Stevenson.
Nicolson, Nigel. 1973. *Portrait of a Marriage*. London: Weidenfeld & Nicolson.
Northcroft, D.M. 1923. *Women at Work in the League of Nations*. London: Page & Pratt.

Offen, Karen. 2000. *European Feminisms, 1700–1950: A Political History*. Stanford, CA: Stanford University Press.
Oldfield, Sybil. 2001. *Women Humanitarians*. London: Continuum.
Orwell, George. 1959. *The Road to Wigan Pier*. London: Secker.
Pankhurst, Sylvia. 1987. *The Home Front*. London: Cressett (first published 1932, Century Hutchinson).
Playne, Caroline. 1931. *Society at War*. London: Allen & Unwin.
Poincaré, Raymond. 1929. *Memoirs*. Translated from French by Sir George Arthur. London: Heinemann.
Prochaska, F. 1980. *Women and Philanthropy in 19th Century England*. Oxford: Clarendon.
Pye, Edith (ed.). 1956. *War and its Aftermath: Letters from Hilda Clark, from France, Austria and the Near East, 1914–1924*. Wells: Clare & Sons.
Rabinow, P. (ed.). 1984. *The Foucault Reader*. London: Penguin.
Riddell, Lord (ed.). 1935. *The Treaty of Versailles and After*. London: Allen & Unwin.
Roberts, Brian. 1991. *Those Bloody Women: Three Heroines of the Boer War*. London: John Murray.
Roberts, Frances. 1947. *Dreams and Deeds of a Radiant Peacemaker*. London: Society of Friends.
Rowbotham, Sheila. 1975. *Hidden from History*. London: Pluto.
Rupp, Leila J. 1997. *Worlds of Women: The Making of an International Women's Movement*. Princeton, NJ: Princeton University Press.
Samuel, R. and Thompson, P. 1990. *Myths We Live By*. London: Routledge.
Scott, Richenda. 1964. *Quakers in Russia*. London: Michael Joseph.
Sharp, Alan. 1991. *The Versailles Settlement: Peacemaking in Paris, 1919*. Basingstoke: Palgrave Macmillan.
Stephens, W. Owen. 1921. *With the Quakers in France*. London: C.W. Daniel Ltd.
Stewart, A.T.Q. 1967. *The Ulster Crisis*. London: Faber & Faber.
Swanwick, Helena. 1935. *I Have Been Young*. London: Gollancz.
Tatham, M. and Miles, James E. (eds). 1920. *The Friends' Ambulance Unit 1914–1919. A Record*. London: Swarthmore.
Thane, Pat. 1996. *Foundations of the Welfare State*. Harlow: Longman.
Thomas, Anna Braithwaite (ed.). 1933. *St Stephen's House: Friends' Emergency Work in England 1914 to 1920*. London: Society of Friends.
Toynbee, Arnold J. 1925. *Survey of International Affairs, 1920–1923*. Oxford: Humphrey Milford, Oxford University Press.
Trollope, Joanna. 1988. *Britannia's Daughters*. London: Century Hutchison (first published 1983).

Walby, S. 1986. *Patriarchy at Work: Patriarchal and Capitalist Relations in Employment*. Cambridge: Polity Press.

Wall, Richard and Winter, Jay (eds). 1988. *The Upheaval of War*. Cambridge: Cambridge University Press.

Webb, Beatrice. 1926. *My Apprenticeship*. London: Longmans, Green & Co.

Whitlock, B. 1919. *Belgium under the German Occupation: a personal narrative. Vols 1 and 2*. London: Heinemann.

Whittick, Arnold. 1979. *Women into Citizen*. London: Athenaeum.

Wilson, Francesca M. 1944. *In the Margins of Chaos, Recollections of Relief Work in and Between Three Wars*. London: John Murray.

——. 1967. *Rebel Daughter of a Country House: the Life of Eglantyne Jebb, Founder of Save the Children Fund*. London: Allen & Unwin.

Winter, J.M. 1986. *The Great War and the British People*. Basingstoke: Macmillan.

Index

www.ingramcontent.com/pod-product-compliance
Ingram Content Group UK Ltd.
Pitfield, Milton Keynes, MK11 3LW, UK
UKHW021852100926
8556IPUK00020B/1193

9 783039 118557